CW00552570

ANTHROPOCEN|

This ground-breaking book critically extends the psychological project, seeking to investigate the relations between human and more-than-human worlds against the backdrop of the Anthropocene by emphasising the significance of encounter, interaction and relationships.

Interdisciplinary environmental theorist Matthew Adams draws inspiration from a wealth of ideas emerging in human–animal studies, anthrozoology, multi-species ethnography and posthumanism, offering a framing of collective anthropogenic ecological crises to provocatively argue that the Anthropocene is also an invitation – to become conscious of the ways in which human and nonhuman are inextricably connected. Through a series of strange encounters between human and nonhuman worlds, Adams argues for the importance of cultivating attentiveness to the specific and situated ways in which the fates of multiple species are bound together in the Anthropocene. Throughout the book, this argument is put into practice, incorporating everything from Pavlov's dogs, broiler chickens, urban trees, grazing sheep and beached whales, to argue that the Anthropocene can be good to think with, conducive to seeing ourselves and our place in the world with a renewed sense of connection, responsibility and love.

Building on developments in feminist and social theory, anthropology, ecopsychology, environmental psychology, (post)humanities, psychoanalysis and phenomenology, this is fascinating reading for academics and students in the field of critical psychology, environmental psychology and human–animal studies.

Matthew Adams is based in the School of Applied Social Science at the University of Brighton, UK. His previous books include *Ecological Crisis, Sustainability & the Psychosocial Subject* (2016) and *Self & Social Change* (2007).

Concepts for Critical Psychology: Disciplinary Boundaries Re-thought
Series editor: *Ian Parker*

Developments inside psychology that question the history of the discipline and the way it functions in society have led many psychologists to look outside the discipline for new ideas. This series draws on cutting edge critiques from just outside psychology in order to complement and question critical arguments emerging inside. The authors provide new perspectives on subjectivity from disciplinary debates and cultural phenomena adjacent to traditional studies of the individual.

The books in the series are useful for advanced level undergraduate and postgraduate students, researchers and lecturers in psychology and other related disciplines such as cultural studies, geography, literary theory, philosophy, psychotherapy, social work and sociology.

Most recently published titles:

Madness and Subjectivity
A Cross-Cultural Examination of Psychosis in the West and India
Ayurdhi Dhar

Decolonial Psychoanalysis
Towards Critical Islamophobia Studies
Robert Beshara

Subjectivity and Critical Mental Health
Lessons from Brazil
Daniel Goulart

Psycurity
Colonialism, Paranoia, and the War on Imagination
Rachel Jane Liebert

Beyond Care
Boundaries to Science, Health and Subjectivity in Capitalism
Owen Dempsey

Queer Politics in India
Towards Sexual Subaltern Subjects
Shraddha Chatterjee

Subjectivity, Language and the Postcolonial
Beyond Bourdieu in South Africa
Hannah Botsis

ANTHROPOCENE PSYCHOLOGY

Being Human in a More-Than-Human World

Matthew Adams

Routledge
Taylor & Francis Group

LONDON AND NEW YORK

First published 2020
by Routledge
2 Park Square, Milton Park, Abingdon, Oxon OX14 4RN

and by Routledge
52 Vanderbilt Avenue, New York, NY 10017

Routledge is an imprint of the Taylor & Francis Group, an informa business

British Library Cataloguing-in-Publication Data
A catalogue record for this book is available from the British Library

Library of Congress Cataloging-in-Publication Data
A catalog record has been requested for this book

ISBN: 978-1-138-57024-5 (hbk)
ISBN: 978-1-138-57025-2 (pbk)
ISBN: 978-0-203-70369-4 (ebk)

Typeset in Bembo
by Nova Techset Private Limited, Bengaluru & Chennai, India

Printed in the United Kingdom
by Henry Ling Limited

Humans are always in composition with nonhumanity, never outside a sticky web of connections or an ecology of matter
—Sarah Whatmore

Beware o wanderer, the road is walking too
—Rainer Maria Rilke

In memory of my friend Martin Jordan (1967–2017)

For Clare, Dylan, Amelie & Leila

CONTENTS

FOREWORD

We humans cut up the world, cut out animals to make us what we are, and then cut ourselves up. This book shows how we do this at a material, ideological and psychological level, taking us to a novel, necessary and urgent analysis of what geologists have recently agreed is the 'Anthropocene'. In their specification of our times, our relatively short time on earth as sentient beings, the geologists have, of course, made an ethical-political choice, and critical psychologists now need to follow suit, taking up the challenge that has now been posed to us. We could quibble, of course, with this naming of these times – times which look like end times and which the global climate strikes have been responding to – and demand a little more precision, but this would risk skewing the analysis we need to something too partial.

We could say, for example, that the climate crisis is the product of the peculiarly exploitative political-economic system that turns human creativity and the natural world into commodities, and so a more accurate name for the geological age we find ourselves in now is 'Capitalocene', rather than Anthropocene. Or we could specify this condition in terms of a feminist analysis which attends to the stereotypically masculine patriarchal concern with 'prediction and control' so beloved of mainstream psychology, and so settle instead on the name 'Androcene' to insist on that. In both cases here, there is a focus on the organised nature of the cutting out and cutting up that is taking us all to the edge of destruction. However, we surely need to take responsibility for this state of things, and look deep, deep into ourselves and into the history that has made us who we are. However, this book does actually give us analysis that is critical of commodification and profoundly feminist.

Matthew Adams points, in this conceptually rich and passionately argued book, to something that goes beyond a partial view of the world – a partial view that we humans have been guilty of for so many years, and a view that psychology as a discipline has itself been symptomatic of – something that we might call 'intersectional'. Instead of separating out the different kinds of identity that psychology so often trades in, we need to weave them together, and we can do that by simultaneously stepping back and embedding ourselves in the problem at hand. We step back by treating 'human' as a property of those beings who have, with the aid of the discipline of psychology, pretended that those who are other are lesser; other beings in the world that we have cut out of our own worldview are, this book shows, not lesser at all, they are 'more-than-human'. We embed ourselves in the problem by always considering what we are doing when we turn the rats and dogs and other experimental subjects into objects, and how, in that process, we turn ourselves into instruments of destruction, of others, of other beings, of the world itself. Nature in the Anthropocene is indeed organised, and this book, *Anthropocene Psychology: Being Human in a More-Than-Human World*, gives us a critique and an alternative. By simultaneously stepping back and embedding ourselves, it operates 'outwith' the Anthropocene, with humility and steadfastness. Whatever else we do with psychology, we have at least to do this; this path-breaking book takes us beyond ourselves so that we can remake ourselves, and in the process, eventually leave self-destructive human-centred psychology behind.

Ian Parker
University of Manchester

ACKNOWLEDGEMENTS

Firstly, I would like to thank series editor Ian Parker for his enthusiastic support. So many encounters have been important in shaping the ideas in this book, conversations with lots of people, and much kindness and support, that have all been to key to me writing anything at all. I am especially indebted to the work of Donna Haraway, Eduardo Kohn, Vinciane Despret, Anna Tsing, Zoe Todd and Daniel Todes. Thanks to the University of Brighton for granting me the time and space to write a substantial chunk of this book, and to my colleagues in the School of Applied Science for fostering an environment of critical enquiry with geniality and a healthy dose of irreverence. Thanks to the critical and radical geographer's forum for helpful suggestions when I was researching human-whale entanglements; to my co-researchers James Ormrod and Sarah Smith who were integral to the voluntary shepherding project; to Kate Monson, for inspiring Anthropocene conversations and an introduction to Zoe Todd's work; and to Sam Jermy for unfailingly asking how the book was coming along, and always appearing interested in the response. I'm forever grateful for the support of my mum, dad, brother and sister, and my friends, a loving, funny and unruly bunch of fellow travellers. Finally, I would like to thank Dylan, Amelie and Leila, for the laughter, tears, loving, learning and so much more that they bring into our lives; and Clare, for being who she is and lovingly and patiently sharing that with me.

1

WELCOME TO THE ANTHROPOCENE

A parenthesis of infinitesimal brevity

Human nature is an interspecies relationship.

Anna Tsing

Introduction

The title of this book brings together two words rarely considered together – Anthropocene and psychology, so to begin, perhaps some explanation of that title is in order. For a number of years, I have been interested in how we respond to knowing about human-induced climate change and related environmental problems and how that knowledge gets translated into action – what we do, or do not do, individually and collectively, about 'environmental issues', depending on where and who we are. Fairly recently, the Anthropocene has come to the fore as a powerful way of framing our current era as one in which, for the first time in its history, the Earth is being deeply transformed by one species – the human (*Anthropos* is Greek for human; the *-cene* suffix refers to a substantial geological time period within the current 65 million year old *Ceno*zoic era). Although originally proposed by atmospheric scientists and then geologists advancing the idea that future proof of our planet-dominating existence will be evident in rock strata and biosphere, it has rapidly become shorthand for the 'overwhelming global evidence that atmospheric, geologic, hydrologic, biospheric and other earth system processes are now altered by humans'

(Ellis, 2013). As discussed below, the idea of the Anthropocene has rapidly become influential in shaping discussion of ecological crisis across academic disciplines and in wider public debate. It offers a great deal of material in making sense of our predicament, whilst even as it emerges and takes shape, is subject to criticism on many fronts. The Anthropocene has been effectively utilised as a point of coalescence for mounting evidence of anthropogenic ecological degradation. This book is not an attempt to add to that body of work. Introduced below, and explored in detail in the chapters to follow, the intention in this book is to take up the Anthropocene as an invitation.

Why psychology? Chakrabarty makes the point that as an idea, the Anthropocene represents 'the makers of geology inscribing themselves into their own rock record' (2009, p. 207). In this sense, the Anthropocene is also something intimately disconcerting, a reflexive turn, troubling in a 'deeply existential way... the environment is in us, and we humans are in the environment' (Åsberg, 2018, p. 186); the contemplation of human activity as now the single most decisive force shaping the planet 'a profound realisation' (Garavan, 2015). Descriptions such as this challenge or invite us to recognise the deep material, emotional and existential resonance of the Anthropocene. Whilst it might seem to consolidate the notion of human influence *on* ecological systems, the Anthropocene also amplifies the interrelationship that defines the co-constitution of human *with* other forms of life; and 'the multiple, interdependent relations within nature, within different forms of materiality, within technologies and within social systems' (Lidskog and Waterton, 2018, p. 39). Psychology, especially social psychology, has always been interested in the part encounters, interactions and relationships play in shaping our personal and social realities, though for the most part, this has been exclusively in human terms. The Anthropocene imaginary invites a radical extension of meaningful relationality, understanding and attending to human–animal and multispecies encounters as worthy of theoretical, methodological, ethical and political attention.

Accordingly, this book is about critically extending the psychological project to being human in a more-than-human world. The term 'human and more-than-human worlds' was coined by US philosopher David Abram to refer to all forms of earthly life – animals, plants, landforms – and to make salient the fact that the world exceeds the human in ways we are nonetheless a part of, the human *and* more-than-human world (Abram, 1997). So the book is titled *Anthropocene Psychology* and subtitled *Being Human in a More-Than-Human World*, to make explicit that the book is an attempt, however modest, to contextualise the human in the life forces and liveliness of what is other than human. It does so largely by attending to specific and situated places. Before summarising the chapters that follow, however, some reflections on time offer a further contextualisation of the way in which the Anthropocene is approached in this book.

Deep time

Deep time is the concept of geological time used 'to describe the timing and relationships between events that have occurred throughout Earth's history' (Warmold, 2017, p. 3) – an approximate 4.54 billion year history. We struggle to grasp the huge scale of a sense of time that is so, well, deep, especially in comparison to the shallow time of our everyday experience, our lifespan, the history of our nation, culture, even of human history in general.[1] Geologists work with stories of deep time, 'the immense arc of *non-human* history that shaped the world as we perceive it' (Farrier, 2016; emphasis added). Theirs is a story which takes in unimaginable stretches of life on Earth and its transformation, told through cycles of sedimentation and erosion. Geology divides deep time into segments, which makes it easier for us to digest, but these are also meaningful divisions, distinctions in rock strata that reflect shifts in global climate and biology. Earth's time is divided into large segments called eons, within which are eras, periods and epochs. We live in the Phanerozoic Eon, a 451-million-year history which marked the beginning of abundant plant and animal life on Earth. It incorporates numerous eras, the current being the Cenozoic, a mere 66 million years old. The Cenozoic is notable for the rise of mammals as dominant life forms, making the most of a sudden 'mass-extinction event' that wiped out almost all larger life forms. The Cenozoic is subdivided into shorter epochs, the six previous averaging 10 m years each. We are now into the seventh – the Holocene, which follows the end of a glacial period and at 11,700 years old is barely into its stride. Although in existence for perhaps as long as 300,000 years (Hublin et al., 2017), the Holocene marks the global spread of *homo sapiens* as the ice retreated and the climate warmed. So we have raced through deep time to the almost-present. However, something else of significance has been happening in the blink of an eye, and it concerns the impact of a single species, for, as far as we know, the first time in Earth's history – *homo sapiens*.

Remarkably, we are now talking about the impact of human activity as it has accumulated over the last 300 years, perhaps even the last 70, radically unsettling the Earth's biodiversity, carbon cycles, climate, ocean chemistry and so on, on a scale equivalent to deep-time processes – 'millions of years of slow evolution' (2016).[2] Welcome to the Anthropocene.

The cumulative effects of human activity are well known in relation to climate change – derived primarily from extracting and then burning or boiling fossil fuels such as coal and crude oil. Fossil fuels are essential to the manufacture of many materials such as plastic and many practises that require power – transportation, electricity and heat, manufacturing and construction and agriculture; whilst other activities like deforestation and waste systems also contribute. The impacts of such activities are also now familiar to many – air, water and land pollution; loss of biodiversity; desertification; mass extinctions; acidified oceans; extreme weather; drought; eroding coastlines. As a conceptual framework, the Anthropocene broadens this impact beyond climate. The proposed markers of the Anthropocene include carbon spheres emitted by power stations; radioactive elements from nuclear bomb tests; plastic pollution; nitrogen and phosphate in soils (from fertilisers) and domestic chicken bones; the growth of global cattle populations; species extinction rates; various types of habitat loss; the rise of industrial fisheries and, of course, greenhouse gas emissions (Crutzen and Stoermer, 2000; Steffen, Crutzen and McNeill, 2007). Human practises are embedded in these processes on a scale staggering in its variety and banality. The briefest browse of accounts of human practises considered responsible in one form or another for ecological degradation includes colonialism, the plantation system, the steam engine, radioactive isotopes, the mining of tar sands, the redistribution of fresh water, the cruise ship industry, data cloud storage, avocado production and drinking coffee. Clearly, the world's economy is far from dematerialising, and the Anthropocene is as much about stratification, inequality, injustice, power and politics as it is about extraction, production, distribution and consumption practises. But it is also about time.

Deep time is profoundly uncanny – it is disorientating to consider a human life span, or even the life span of humanity, against a non-human history stretching back over eons, the immediate reality of being as an embodied and temporal experience within a timescale of imponderable proportions. The Anthropocene is a kind of double-uncanny – human beings entering into deep time's register by disrupting it. The deep time of an ancient Earth and an indifferent universe is uncanny in its own right, that we humans might be disturbing this unknowable teleology, and how, more so. In other words, told straight, the Anthropocene is an outlandish tale of science fiction, but one that is really happening. The shock of the Anthropocene, then, is 'to reveal humans as planetary agents on a deep spatial and temporal scale. The corollary to that shock was of course to place humanity within long-running Earth processes' (Ginn et al., 2018, p. 214).

A parenthesis of infinitesimal brevity

It is remarkable how quickly the Anthropocene moniker has become culturally ubiquitous – the subject not just of academic texts and conferences but art, magazines, travelogues, poetry, even an opera. It has rapidly become what the anthropologist Elizabeth Reddy calls a 'sort of charismatic mega-category', establishing itself as the lens through which to make sense of our current predicament. There is already plenty of criticism of the idea of the Anthropocene. We have recently seen attempts to double down on the specifics of human history and aggregate activity responsible for environmental crises, rather than lumping all humans, and their responsibility, together as *Anthropos* – offering alternatives terms like Capitalocene and Plantationocene (Haraway, 2015; Moore, 2017). Whether rapid devastation or slow degradation, those who are the least responsible are already positioned to experience the brunt of ecological crises for now, and the least equipped to successfully mitigate against. Ignoring such enormous variation and positing a simplistic 'species-thinking' is a form of 'bourgeois mystification' (Malm and Hornborg, 2014: 67). It clouds a sense of specifics – of what is driving our predicament, of the power asymmetries involved, of where (in)action matters, who has access to the lifeboats and who is left to sink with the ship. In this book, I largely follow Haraway's lead, in accepting the usefulness of the Anthropocene ambivalently as a motif, as a story that matters, whilst committing to addressing its shortcomings and inconsistencies as we go along, in the working through of particulars (Haraway, 2016).

Other critics argue that the Anthropocene framing is inherently hubristic or triumphalist (e.g. Clarke, 2014; LeCain, 2015). Whilst particular framings can lend themselves to this kind of rhetoric, in the embraces of techno-salvation, or space colonisation, for example, I do not think it is inevitable. A more subtle problem is that if we accept that a deep time narrative offers a profound challenge to anthropocentrism, the dawning of the Anthropocene reinserts 'humanity' into that narrative, front and centre, in that 'we humans have become that sublime force, the agents of a fearful something that is greater than ourselves' (Farrier, 2016). Humanity as a 'fearful something' is hardly triumphalism, but a different kind of human exceptionalism persists, one which a final consideration of deep time, informed by John Michael Greer's analysis (2017), helps unsettle. Greer accepts the unprecedented influence of human activity, including the biospheric and geospheric and scale of that influence. However, he returns to geological markers of change to tell a different story.

As noted above, around 66 million years ago, a 'mass extinction event' took place, wiping out around three-quarters of all species. This was most likely the result of an enormous asteroid impact. Geologists are confident about this after discovering a thin but distinct layer of sediment in the geologic record from this time, found across the Earth, containing elements abundant in asteroids but rare on our planet. The dinosaurs being out of the way offered new ecological niches, an opportunity for the rise of mammals as dominant life forms – ushering in the Cenozoic ('new life' or 'new animal') era. This thin layer of comet dust in the rock record represents a brief but vital transition – in between much thicker preceding and subsequent layers. No one refers to what followed the mass extinction event as the 'Cometocene' (Greer, 2017). That just would not make sense – the comet's impact is significant in the context of deep time only in that it ushered in new foundations for life that then stretched out for millions of years into the far future.

What if the same could be said of *Anthropos*? Would whoever, or whatever, looking back from that far future consider the moment of industrial civilisation (or the emergence of capitalism, plantation system or other suggested harbinger of human inflected dominance), be drawn to declare the Anthropocene? A provocative argument is that however significant as a transition, the cumulative effects of the Anthropocene are better framed, to borrow historian Stephen Kern's evocative phrase, as 'a parenthesis of infinitesimal brevity'. Even with the well-documented impacts of the Anthropocene still accumulating, we are talking about a mere blip in the context of deep time. Industrialism's tendency, in particular, to aggressively and rapidly draw out a finite supply of resources to power its dominion is inseparably twinned with the precipitous planetary effects of doing so (again, in the context of deep time, this is no 'slow emergency'). The everyday perpetuation of (some forms of) collective human existence undermines the conditions of (multiple forms of) that existence. Caught in this configuration, human dominance, in the context of deep time, will be unremarkably short lived – a *transition* between eras. Thus, Greer considers *Holocene-Neocene transition*, H-N transition for short, as a more accurate term, with *Neocene* being a placeholder for whatever emerges next (2017). Our geological legacy is like the comet dust – 'a slightly odd transition layer a quarter of an inch thick'. As a remarkably adaptive species, humans may find ecological niches to survive and flourish in this far future, but we will not be dominant. We cannot, after all, have our Anthropocene and eat it.

Whilst Greer's *H-N transition* is a bit of a mouthful, it helps unsettle the emerging Anthropocene story, a challenge to both the hubris and the hand-wringing that might lean towards anthropocentrism or human exceptionalism. In the context of deep time, the Earth will continue to meander on without us, and it will hardly notice we are gone, just as it hardly knew we were here. However, this brief sojourn into temporal depths is not intended to be depressing or defeatist. It is to offer what the artist Rachel Sussman calls a 'jolt of recognition at the shallowness of human timekeeping and the blink that is a human lifespan'. In this introductory discussion, it is meant as a reminder of life itself as something to approach with reverence and awe: our species as interdependent and interconnected, not somehow apart, and to chip away at any residual hubris in the idea of the Anthropocene. This, for me, is a vital beginning point for the discussion to come, an important rejoinder to the tendency to adopt 'an all-too-human fantasy of control' (Clarke, 2014, p. 104), one that can help us orientate the vagaries of an Anthropocene psychology.

Summary of chapters

The chapters that follow are not a systematic response to the Anthropocene as invitation. They are loosely connected accounts that share a commitment to particularity – to engaging with specific and situated human and more-than-human entanglements rather than attempting to advance a relational ontology in the abstract. Each chapter is an attempt to broaden and deepen a fledgling Anthropocene psychology, focusing where appropriate on psychological theory and methods but more often than not reaching beyond the discipline to draw on developments elsewhere. The first half of the book focuses on human–animal relations, starting with an experimental encounter familiar to psychologists. The next two chapters take on human–animal interactions more deeply embedded in society and culture as defined in terms of the Anthropocene. More specifically, Chapter 2 takes its cue from the interdisciplinary 'animal turn' and the development of human–animal studies (HAS) to unsettle how psychology as a discipline understands its own entanglements with more-than-human worlds. In pursuing a commitment to particularity, the focus is a specific example of human–animal relations that features heavily in the canonical history of psychology, Pavlov's experiments with dogs. The apparently familiar figure of Pavlov and his dogs, and their subsequent representation, offers a situated, specific and accessible entry point for thinking about interactions between human and more-than human from a fresh perspective and what this reveals about how we understand human identity, otherness and the persistent issue of ethical responsibility in psychology. Also taking human-animal relations as its focus, Chapter 3 addresses how those relations embody and are embedded in intersecting social, political and psychological processes of the Anthropocene and what the possibilities are for imagining and enacting alternative practises collectively. Maintaining an emphasis on specific and situated cases, it does so by focusing in on an especially fraught and complex manifestation of those relations – animal agriculture and the problem of meat, embodied in the figure of the broiler chicken. This creature has become emblematic of the Anthropocene, the skeletal remains of the billions slaughtered annually offered as one of its key identifiable features. Whilst the broiler chicken is the starting point for this chapter, the discussion opens out to incorporate the psychological and social dimensions of 'meat culture' (Potts, 2016) and documents a new and resurgent willingness to lift the veil on that culture and our own intimate psychological investments in it. Chapter 4 continues a focus on human–animal encounters, taking sheep as its focal point. It describes the knots of reciprocating complexity that constitute human–sheep relations in the Anthropocene and their antecedents. It builds on ground-breaking scholarship in the psychology of human–animal relationships initiated by Kenneth Shapiro (e.g. 1990; 2010), in tandem with historical and ethnographic approaches of interdisciplinary human–animal studies (DeMello, 2012). It frames the human–sheep relational history within the Anthropocene, in which their processing as meat is foremost. However, in accepting the Anthropocene invitation, it asks what else is possible, exploring other opportunities there might be for crafting new attachments and connections. Continuing an emphasis on specific and situated cases, the chapter offers a reflection on a volunteer urban shepherding programme I have been involved in as a researcher.

The final two chapters of the book broaden its relational focus, moving beyond human–animal to incorporate other species and dynamics. Grounded in an account of street tree protests, Chapter 5 focuses on place as the situated and specific context through which Anthropocene realities are known and articulated. The discussion incorporates psychological and geographical analysis in which 'place' is a factor or variable in assessing health and well-being, centring on the concept of solastalgia, but goes further, taking in vital and animist perspectives on place, often informed by indigenous perspectives, which challenge straightforward distinctions between people as complex meaning processors and places as relatively inert. Resurgent scholarship and activism dedicated to granting natural entities legal personhood, and broader emphasis on the importance of love and care for place, here enters the configuration of an Anthropocene psychology. Following the explosion of multi-species, posthuman and transspecies theory and research, Chapter 6 explores what happens when we radically extend what we consider to be 'a meaningful encounter', whilst engaging with approaches that enrich and challenge established academic perspectives. To that end, the chapter traces numerous recent calls to 'indigenise' and 'decolonise' the Anthropocene, especially the work of Indigenous feminist scholar Zoe Todd (e.g. Todd, 2015; 2016). Via the particular figure of the whale, or more accurately human–whale encounters, Anthropocene psychology is advanced through an appreciation of *specific* indigenous ontologies, by focusing on locally informed responses to *in situ* challenges, and, finally, through reading and citing Indigenous scholarship.

Notes

1. As Darwin attested, 'What an infinite number of generations, which the mind cannot grasp, must have succeeded each other in the long roll of years!' (Darwin, 1859, p. 287).
2. There are numerous analogies out there for helping us comprehend this enormity, like the 24-hour clock. I like this one, as you can visualise it simply enough by holding out your arm: If the earth formed about 4.54 billion years ago at the shoulder, animals of any kind appear within the palm, more familiar (to us) life forms originate at the first knuckle. Movement along the fingers represent the periods that followed,

incorporating, for example, the Jurassic. If you want to fit this into the history of the cosmos, just imagine two more people behind you with their arms stretched out, hand on your shoulder – the shoulder of the one at the back is 13.82 billion years ago – the estimated age of the universe. Oh yes, and humans – the 11,700-year-old Holocene marks the start of a global spread of *homo sapiens* – 'a microscopic sliver at the tip of a fingernail'. What is more remarkable still is that a tiny shard within this microscopic sliver marks the beginning the proposed Anthropocene, whether we go with a starting point of 400 years, 70 or somewhere in between, radically unsettling the Earth's biodiversity, carbon cycles, climate, ocean chemistry and so on at a speed and scale equivalent to millions of years of slow evolution. Visual image accessed here: 21/08/19 http://nautil.us/issue/17/big-bangs/the-greatest-animal-war.

References

Abram, D. 1997. *The Spell of the Sensuous: Perception and Language in a More-Than-Human World*. New York: Vintage.

Åsberg, C. 2018. Feminist posthumanities in the Anthropocene: Forays into the postnatural. *Journal of Posthuman Studies*, 1(2), 185–204.

Chakrabarty, D. 2009. The climate of history: Four theses. *Critical Inquiry*, 35(2), 197–222.

Clarke, B. 2014. 'The Anthropocene,' or, Gaia shrugs. *Journal of Contemporary Archaeology*, 1(1), 101–104.

Crutzen, P. J. and Stoermer, E. F. 2000 The Anthropocene. *Global Change Newsletter*, 41, 17–18.

Darwin, C. 1859. *On the Origin of Species by Means of Natural Selection*. London: John Murray.

DeMello, M. 2012. *Animals and Society: An Introduction to Human–Animal Studies*. Columbia: Columbia University Press.

Ellis, E. 2013. Anthropocene. *The Encyclopaedia of Earth*. Accessed 29/08/19 http://www.eoearth.org/view/article/150125/

Farrier, D. 2016. Deep time's uncanny future is full of ghostly human traces. *Aeon*, 31 October, 2016 https://aeon.co/ideas/deep-time-s-uncanny-future-is-full-of-ghostly-human-traces

Garavan, M. 2015. *Living in the Anthropocene – A Frame for New Activism*. The Foundation for the Economics of Sustainability (Feasta). October 25 2015. Accessed 28/08/19 https://www.feasta.org/2015/10/26/living-in-the-anthropocene-a-frame-for-new-activism/

Ginn, F, Bastian, M, Farrier, D and Kidwell, J (eds) 2018. 'Unexpected encounters with deep time'. *Environmental Humanities*, 10(1), pp. 213–225.

Greer, J.M. 2017. Confronting the Cthulhucene. In Hine, D. and Wheeler, S. (Eds.), *Dark Mountain Issue 12: Sanctum*. Padstow: Dark Mountain Project, pp. 91–103.

Haraway, D. J. 2015. Anthropocene, Capitalocene, Plantationocene, Chthulucene: Making kin. *Environmental Humanities*, 6(1), 159–165.

Haraway, D. J. 2016. *Staying with the Trouble: Making Kin in the Chthulucene.* Durham, NC: Duke University Press.

Hublin, J. J., Ben-Ncer, A., Bailey, S. E., Freidline, S. E., Neubauer, S., Skinner, M. M., Bergmann, I. et al. 2017. New fossils from Jebel Irhoud, Morocco and the pan-African origin of *Homo sapiens*. *Nature*, 546(7657), 289–292.

LeCain, T. 2015. Against the Anthropocene. A neo-materialist perspective. *International Journal for History, Culture and Modernity*, 3(1), 1–28.

Lidskog, R. and Waterton, C. 2018. The Anthropocene: Its conceptual usage and sociological challenges. In Boström, M. and Davidson, D. (Eds.), *Environment and Society: Concepts and Challenges*. Basingstoke: Palgrave, pp. 25–46.

Malm, A. and Hornborg, A. 2014. The geology of mankind? A critique of the Anthropocene narrative. *The Anthropocene Review*, 1(1), 62–69.

Moore, J. W. 2017. The Capitalocene, Part I: On the nature and origins of our ecological crisis. *The Journal of Peasant Studies*, 44(3), 594–630.

Potts, A. 2016. *Meat Culture*. New York: Brill.

Shapiro, K. J. 1990. Understanding dogs through kinesthetic empathy, social construction, and history. *Anthrozoös*, 3(3), 184–195.

Shapiro, K. J. 2010. Psychology and human-animal studies. In DeMello M. (Ed.), *Teaching the Animal: Human–Animal Studies across the Disciplines*. Brooklyn, NY: Lantern Books.

Steffen, W., Crutzen, P. J. and McNeill, J. R. 2007. The Anthropocene: Are humans now overwhelming the great forces of nature? *AMBIO: A Journal of the Human Environment*, 36(8), 614–621.

Todd, Z. 2015. Indigenizing the Anthropocene. In Davis, H. and Turpin, E. (Eds.), *Art in the Anthropocene: Encounters among Aesthetics, Politics, Environments and Epistemologies*. London: Open Humanities Press, pp. 241–254.

Todd, Z. 2016. An Indigenous feminist's take on the ontological turn: 'Ontology' is just another word for colonialism. *Journal of Historical Sociology*, 29(1), 4–22.

Warmold, D. 2017. *Deep Time: A Public Engagement Literature Review*. London: Natural History Museum. Accessed 11/12/19 https://www.nhm.ac.uk/content/dam/nhmwww/about-us/visitor-research/Deep%20Time%20Lit%20review.pdf

2

WHY PAVLOV'S DOGS STILL MATTER

Animals, experimental psychology and the Anthropocene invitation

> *What happens if experimental animals are not mechanical substitutes but... significant others with whom we are in consequential relationship in an irreducible world of embodied and lived partial differences, rather than the Other across the gulf from the One?*
>
> *Donna Haraway*

Introduction

The argument offered in this book is one that accepts the Anthropocene as an invitation to address human and more-than-human worlds as essentially interrelated, realities wrought through countless points of intersection, mutual influence and co-becoming.[1] In doing so, it draws on developments well underway in sister disciplines and interdisciplinary movements. Of course, various strands of feminist, critical, social and developmental psychology have long recognised a profound sense of relatedness and interdependency as constitutional of the human, challenging the individualist ontologies and epistemologies of mainstream psychology as reflections of established political conventions and historical and cultural mores. Rarely, however, has psychology ventured beyond the human or sought to extend a relational ontology that might somehow further trouble notions of what it is to be human and, with it, a reframing of issues integral to psychology such as agency, ethics, prejudice and power. In considering potential points of entry, there are so many, it is difficult to know where to begin. To get us started, this chapter homes in on nonhuman animals, influenced specifically by the interdisciplinary 'animal turn' and the development of human–animal studies.[2] It takes an example of human–animal relations that features heavily in the canonical history of psychology, Pavlov's experiments with dogs. What have experiments carried out a century ago got to do with the Anthropocene? As we shall see, the apparently familiar figure of Pavlov and his dogs, and their subsequent representation, offers a situated, specific and accessible point from which to commence thinking about interactions between the human and more-than-human from a fresh perspective; one that reveals much about how we understand human identity, otherness and the persistent issue of ethical responsibility under the sign of the Anthropocene.

Haraway's list of 'human-animal worlds' where 'ordinary beings-in-encounter' take place is instructive as to the range of research being undertaken in the emerging field of human–animal studies, as well as many parallel developments, including posthumanities, multi-species ethnography and anthrozoology: 'in the house, lab, field, zoo, park, truck, office, prison, ranch, arena, village, human hospital, slaughter house, vet clinic, stadium, barn, wildlife preserve, farm, city streets, factory, and more' (Potts and Haraway, 2010, p. 322). Though psychology might readily take an interest in any of these domains, the lab is perhaps the most obvious. However, in psychology, little attention has yet been paid to human–animal relations in experimental laboratory studies, past or present. Where work exists, to date it has tended towards examples of biomedical experimentation (e.g. Giraud and Hollin, 2017; Holmberg, 2008; though see Davis and Balfour, 1992). Only a handful of essays and articles, mostly outside of the discipline, have extended multi-species scholarship to the psychology laboratory (Birke, 2010; Despret, 2004; Haraway, 1989; Pettit, 2012).[3] Yet the laboratory has served as a crucible for psychology's complex relationship with nonhuman animals since its inception. As DeMello points out, 'ironically, while built for and on animals, the laboratory is not considered a home for human–animal relationships and it remains the task of HAS [Human–Animal Studies] to undertake that study' (2010, p. 259). This chapter is an attempt to take up this task. Elsewhere, I have argued for the kind of more-than-human psychology that is needed to meaningfully contribute to an interdisciplinary and fast-developing human–animal studies – staking claims for the necessary theoretical and methodological tools (Adams, 2018). The aim of this chapter is different – to advance the 'animal turn' in psychology by going backwards. It engages in a revisionist analysis of a key figure in psychology, Ivan Pavlov (1849–1936), to make the case for a theory and ethics of human–nonhuman animal entanglement at the heart of an Anthropocene psychology. It will unsettle the familiar image of Pavlov and his dogs – especially his dogs – and encourage a rapprochement on different ground. Today, Pavlov is remembered for his experimental work on conditional reflexes in (salivating) dogs (Pavlov, 1941), but also for his anointment as one of the behaviourist movement's founding fathers, an association that continues to this day in both Western and post-Soviet science and culture.[4] As Jarius and Wildemann (2017, p. 322) attest, Pavlov's concept of classical conditioning is now considered 'the foundation of the modern science of learning and, in particular, of the influential theories of Watson and Skinner and the entire school of behaviourism'.

Pavlov is also the focal point because he remains one of the most visible figures of psychology's history, appearing in every undergraduate textbook and popular psychology treatise, and he remains to this day one of the most cited psychologists of all time (Diener et al., 2014; Griggs and Proctor, 2002). Yet, as will be argued in what follows, the received image of his life and work is largely unchanging. As an uncontested historical example, relatively fixed and unquestioned in the narrative trajectory of psychology, it will be claimed that an act of defamiliarisation is both necessary and significant. In doing so, this chapter might be seen as contributing to a wave of revisionist approaches to canonical experimental studies in psychology, often facilitated by new access to archival materials (e.g. Briggs, 2014; Gibson, 2013; Griggs, 2015; Reicher et al., 2018). Whilst it may have some similarities, it is distinctive, however, in following a human–animal studies tradition of moving 'beyond anthropocentric histories and social narratives by putting animal life in the spotlight' (Johnson, 2015, p. 299).

To place Pavlov's dogs in the spotlight, we must look beyond their moment on the experimenter stand, in which they are perpetually suspended in countless print and pixel representations like flies in amber. It entails paying close attention to the realities of life in the labs and the broader contexts in which they lived and were entwined with others. For this purpose, Daniel Todes's scholarship is especially germane (1997a; 1997b; 2000; 2002), not least his extensive and thorough biography of Pavlov (Todes, 2014), which delves deep into archival materials and the neglected research of his many co-workers. Whilst human–canine relations are by no means the central concern of this work, in attending to the minutiae of Pavlov's methods, alongside other passing references to dogs' involvement (e.g. London, 1949; Rüting, 2007; Smith, 1995; Windholz, 1990; 1997), his life, those around him and the wider social, cultural and political context, dogs repeatedly step into the picture. In this chapter, the canine experience, entangled in the lives of others, takes centre stage.

The first section offers a critical overview of contemporary representations of Pavlov's work. This is followed by a brief summary of the 'animal turn' and related developments, including posthuman and multi-species scholarship, as a foundation for exploring their relevance for an analysis of Pavlov and his dogs. Subsequent sections utilise the conceptual lens of the animal turn to examine the significance of Pavlov's adoption and development of 'chronic' experimental methods, and the vitally important shift from physiological research to the study of 'psychic secretions' and conditioned reflexes. These sections are followed by a focus on the significance of the interrelationship of dogs and co-workers, before considering how these relationships are manifest in Pavlov's later attempt to incorporate his results within a typology of canine character. Finally, the significance of a reading of key aspects of Pavlov's work through the animal turn for psychological theory is considered.

Contemporary retellings: 'hard-set laws' and a 'comfortable recovery'

Pavlov's work is continually re-presented and re-circulated in reassuring canonical narratives of psychology's historical timeline. In contemporary retellings, Pavlov's achievements carry all before them, and the dogs appear as 'matters of fact' – dispensable objects, empty experimental vessels, conduits for Nobel-prize winning knowledge development, discarded matter in the progressive teleology of psychology-as-science. The emphasis instead is on descriptions of 'classical conditioning', on Pavlov's terminology, on one of the most celebrated 'accidents' in the birth pangs of the behaviourist movement in particular and experimental psychology in general. To document just a few examples: in a relatively early comparative analysis of Pavlov's theory and methods, Kubie repeatedly emphasises how Pavlov's object of focus was the 'conditioned reflex under the constant conditions of the laboratory' (Kubie, 1959; p. 31), only mentioning 'dogs' once in passing; Çevik reiterates a mechanistic portrayal of Pavlovian conditioning, that is, a 'conditioned stimulus (CS) acquires the ability to trigger a new response by virtue of being paired with an unconditioned stimulus (US)' (2014, p.), whilst never mentioning dogs at all – common practice in many extensions, overviews and appraisals of Pavlov's work. The 700+ page *Handbook of Operant and Classical Conditioning* (McSweeney and Murphy, 2014) mentions only once that dogs were used as subjects in Pavlov's experiments. The role of dogs as *living* animals rarely features in accounts of Pavlov's contribution to psychology. They are subsumed in the clamour for scientific credibility:

> hard-set laws derive from Ivan Pavlov's studies of animals' higher nervous activity, which allows animal behavior to be broken down into predictable and modifiable reflexes... Pavlov's famous experiment of the drooling dog shows that there are two types of reflexes: innate reflexes that are evoked by the irritant itself and acquired reflexes that are evoked by subsequent associations
>
> *(Cherkaev and Tipikina, 2018, p. 29)*

Hard-set laws, predictability, modifiable reflexes – these experiments are offered as a formative example of the scientific method being used to remarkable effect in the early days of psychology; with Pavlov championed as an 'outstanding practitioner' in general and for devising 'a simple, elegant experimental paradigm with which to study learning' in particular (Tully, 2003, p. 117). This forgetting extends to the overwhelming majority of scholarship on Pavlov (e.g. Bitterman, 2006; Kubie, 1959; London, 1949; Rüting, 2007; Smith, 1995; Windholz, 1997; 2000), where dogs appear only in passing as interchangeable experimental objects (and are rarely, if ever, named).

In textbook coverage, where undergraduate students might first encounter Pavlov and his dogs, we find a similar state of affairs.[5] Here are two standard psychology textbook accounts of Pavlov's experiments with dogs:

> In Russia, Ivan Pavlov was investigating how involuntary responses – reflexes – could become conditioned to appear in response to new forms of stimulus... In a series of experiments with dogs reported in 1927, Pavlov showed that they could learn to produce the salivation response to the sound of a bell, if that sound was repeatedly paired with the presentation of food. This was significant, since salvation in response to food is an involuntary

response, and not the sort of thing which an animal can produce deliberately

(Hayes, 2000, p. 577–8)

Pavlov received a Nobel Prize for work which exploited the (delightful) fact that dogs salivate at the merest expectation of food. Pavlov demonstrated, by repeatedly pairing a particular stimulus (the food) with a sound (most famously a bell, but more probably a metronome), that his dogs would eventually salivate in response to the sound (or conditioned stimulus)

(Banyard et al., 2015, p. 32)

Factual errors aside (Pavlov did not use a bell; he was awarded the Nobel prize for his work on digestion, which was *prior* to his study of salivation and reflexes), textbook outlines such as this are often accompanied by a diagram, followed by some discussion of concepts relating to 'classical conditioning' such as discrimination and extinction (e.g. Banyard et al., 2015; Eysenck, 2004; Glassman and Hadad, 2013; Gross, 2015; Hayes, 2000, p. 577–8; Myers and DeWall, 2018). Dogs are routinely absent in tables and figures explaining 'classical conditioning' or are interchangeable illustrations of salivation, in amongst a focus on terminology and the steps involved in 'the establishment of a stimulus-response bond' (e.g. Nolen-Hoeksema et al., 2014, p. 228; Train, 2007, p. 228). Salivating dogs feature in the service of recounting Pavlov's experimental method as marking a 'ground-breaking step in the emergence of psychology as a truly scientific, rather than philosophical discipline' (Tomley, 2012, p. 37) and his collected studies on conditioned reflexes 'one of the classic texts of psychology' (Hayes, 2000, p. 577).

Despite the eminence granted to Pavlov and his experimental approach, here too little account is given of the canine involvement in experiments themselves. There is no description in any of these texts – academic, undergraduate, popular – of the conditions in which the dogs were kept, their lives, the detail of the procedures beyond evasively rudimentary descriptions such as 'his experiments used a machine that measured the amount of saliva a dog produced when given meat powder' (Train, 2007, p. 228). The most detailed description of the process in terms of canine involvement found in my (admittedly brief) survey was as follows: 'they isolated the dog in a small room, secured it in a harness, and attached a device to divert its salvia to a measuring instrument' (Myers and DeWall, 2018, p. 282).

Wholly absent is any critical discussion of Pavlov's methods in terms of ethics or epistemology, even when 'critical thinking' questions are offered (e.g. 'Do you think that Pavlov's theory of conditioning can account for human processes of learning?' Gross, 2015, p. 263), nor are there in more specialist textbooks dedicated to conceptual and historical issues and debates in psychology (e.g. Brysbaert and Rastle, 2009; Tyson et al., 2011). Tucker's brief survey of Pavlov's studies is unique in that his primary point *is* to frame them as amongst the most 'bizarre and distressing experiments being performed upon animals... in the twentieth century' (p. 13). Here I have summarised how Pavlov is represented today. In the discussion that follows, my intention is not to retrospectively damn Pavlov. Closer attention, adopting the conceptual lens of the 'animal turn', reveals a more complex portrait of human–canine interrelationship, one that I will claim has important lessons for a contemporary psychology of human–animal relations. First, the 'animal turn' is considered as a vitally important academic context for this discussion.

The 'animal turn', multi-species scholarship and psychology

Some time ago, Melson claimed that in psychology, 'the study of human-animal relationships historically has been ignored and continues to resist attention' (2002, p. 347), an accusation that has since been repeated on various occasions (e.g. Birke, 2010; Serpell, 2009; Shapiro, 2017). There have, of course, been exceptions across various psychological topics (e.g. Bruni et al., 2008; Clayton et al., 2011; Kazdin, 2009; Opotow, 1993; Sevillano and Fiske, 2016), most specifically in the study of the human health benefits of animal contact (e.g. Holcomb and Meacham, 1989) and the study of the apparent correlation between human abuse of nonhuman animals and other humans (e.g. Miller, 2001). However, since the beginning of the twenty-first century, the humanities and social sciences have witnessed a more thoroughgoing 'animal turn' – 'a shift from a major focus on the social construction of other animals to attempts to get at "animals as such", as they actually experience the world' (Shapiro, 2017, p. 3) and which recognises 'the fact that human and animal lives have always been entangled and that animals are omnipresent in human society on both metaphorical and practical, material levels' (Cederholm et al., 2014, p. 5).

Going further, this shift has been accompanied by the demand for a radical rethink of established ontologies, epistemologies and methodologies founded on human exceptionalism. New ontologies of relatedness are growing from a recognition of species interdependence in the biosciences, as Haraway evocatively asserts here: 'There has been an explosion within the biologies of multi-species becoming with; understanding that to be a one at all you have to be a one of many, and that is not a metaphor; it is about the tissues of being anything at all; and that those who are have been in relationality all the way down' (Haraway, 2014). Multiple logics are drawn upon to interpret and frame these encounters, including Latour's network theory (2005; e.g. Nimmo, 2011), Deleuze and Guattari's rhizome (1987; e.g. McLeod, 2014) and Haraway's conceptualisation of companion species (2003, 2008, 2016; e.g. Lorimer, 2010). These and other approaches are reflected in many developments – Anthropocene studies, human–animal studies, Indigenous knowledge, posthumanism and feminist posthumanism, multi-species ethnography and transspecies psychology – sharing a radical re-orientation of the human in a multi-species, more-than-human context.[6]

Such a challenge simultaneously encourages numerous disciplines to consider the ethical and political dimensions of our relationship with nonhuman animals, not least as they are inscribed in psychological, social, cultural and material conventions. It involves not just a focus on the subjective experiences of animals but an understanding of the ways in which human and animal experiences are interrelated. Describing what various perspectives share beyond a commitment to 'new ways of thinking about animals and about human-animal relationships' (Potts, 2010, p. 291) is a tricky venture, considering the variety of disciplines and traditions involved. On my reading, one might cautiously assert the following: epistemologically, it entails a readiness to 'engage with the alterworlds of other beings' (Kirksey and Helmreich, 2010), which in turn, methodologically, demands the cultivation of novel methods of observation and interpretation – an invitation to 'attend deeply' and develop 'arts of attentiveness' (Head, 2016; Tsing, 2015) – that attempt to 'become less hard of hearing in the context of a communicative and vibrant more-than-human world' (Country et al., 2015, p. 278).

Ethico-politically, it requires approaching animals as more than merely 'passive objects for humans to act upon or use as tools or resources' (Mullin, 2010, p. 148) and therefore incorporates an explicit recognition of speciesism as a form of psychologically embedded, socially structured inequality and injustice, and seeks to 'practice methodology that challenges human superiority' (Head, 2016, p. 69). Theoretically (especially in terms of ontology), it seeks to evidence a growing understanding of multi-species interrelatedness, including animals, but often extending to other nonhuman forms, beings, things, places and elements of the 'more-than-human world' (Anderson et al., 2010; Country et al., 2016; Ingold, 2005). It is effectively an attempt to develop a relational ontology within a theoretical framework that can incorporate human and nonhuman as distinct but mutually constitutive and interdependent.

Following these leads, in the remaining sections of this chapter, I attempt to selectively adopt the conceptual lens of the animal turn, multi-species and posthuman scholarship to attend more deeply to the canine experience and to human–dog encounters, as mutually constructing the reality of Pavlov's experimental regime. This is achieved by focusing in on a number of key motifs and moments in Pavlov's career: the treatment of dogs in his earlier 'chronic experiments', the shift to the study of 'psychic secretions', and the later focus on a typology of 'higher nervous activity'. In doing so, I hope to unsettle contemporary retellings of those studies but also to draw out some important lessons for a contemporary critical psychology of human animal-relations.

Chronic experiments in the kingdom of dogs

> The physiologist is no ordinary man. He is a learned man, a man possessed and absorbed by a scientific idea. He does not hear the animals' cries of pain. He is blind to the blood that flows. He sees nothing but his idea, and organisms which conceal from him the secrets he is resolved to discover.
>
> *Claude Bernard*[7]

Pavlov was first and foremost a physiologist and spent his early career studying digestion in dogs (for which he won the Nobel Prize). A visitor to Pavlov's laboratory named it the 'kingdom of dogs' (cited in Todes, 2014, p. 494) for good reason. The majority of dogs who found themselves on the experimenter stand were brought in from elsewhere – they had a prior existence (Cuny, 1965).[8] As strays, they may have lived in the company of dogs, scavenging and surviving day to day perhaps – we can only guess how well they lived, their attachments to humans and other dogs and the extent to which they were affected by their sudden removal and relocation.[9] The later use of dogs bred and raised on site is a different consideration – their existence was fundamentally imprinted by their experience of the laboratory space. For all the dogs in Pavlov's care, however, life on the experimenter stand and in the kennels of

St. Petersburg (then Leningrad) University, the Military-Medical Academy and later Koltushi, his 'science village', became a constant and permanently defined the rest of their lives.[10]

For over twenty-five years, up until the late 1890s, Pavlov's studies concentrated on the relationship between eating and variation in the secretion of gastric, pancreatic and salivary fluids in dogs as proxies for human physiological processes. Pavlov was interested in physically intact dogs – at all stages of his career, he wanted to keep the dogs alive and functioning 'normally' as much as possible (Smith, 1995). He consistently emphasised the superiority of 'chronic' over 'acute' experiments; the latter relied on live vivisection, during or immediately after which dogs died or were killed, often in extreme pain. For Pavlov, such methods, though he used them where he considered necessary, offered no parallel to 'chronic' methods where surgery was undertaken (e.g. to insert a pancreatic fistula), and the dog survived and had a chance to recover, *before* an experiment – or more commonly a series of experiments – began.

Whilst acute experiments resulted in immediate death, chronic experiments lengthened an experimental dog's life, for the sole purpose of extended observation of physiological processes following various surgical interventions. There are no precise numbers available, but hundreds, perhaps thousands, of dogs commandeered as experimental animals died throughout Pavlov's career, as they did in countless parallel physiology studies undertaken globally. Countless dogs died as Pavlov and his co-workers developed and refined surgical procedures (Cuny, 1965, pp. 22-3). Operating techniques routinely failed, whilst new developments and the promise of success often increased Pavlov's fervour 'I'm trying – and will now shred dogs without mercy. You know, I have not worked so hard for a long time' (cited in Todes, 2014, p. 106).

In refining another procedure, an attempt to partition the stomach and create a 'gastric pocket', a co-worker of Pavlov states that 'thirty dogs were sacrificed in vain' (cited in Harré, 2006, p. 153). Even when surgery was 'successful' and dogs were kept alive, their remaining life was curtailed and/or their subsequent health complicated. For example, to 'solve the problem' of observing and measuring digestion-related secretions accurately, Pavlov and his co-workers performed surgery on the dogs which made possible his 'sham feeding' system:

> Pavlov would remove a dog's [o]esophagus and create an opening, a fistula, in the animal's throat, so that, no matter how much the dog ate, the food would fall out and never make it to the stomach.

> By creating additional fistulas along the digestive system and collecting the various secretions, he could measure their quantity and chemical properties in great detail
>
> *(Specter, 2014, p. 3)*

All whilst the dog was still living, and went on to live, for a while at least, so that further experiments could be conducted or refined, and meaningful comparisons made. Pavlov spoke proudly of a dog living for two and a half years with an isolated stomach sac, and exultantly of one that lived for nine years but 'survivors usually developed fatal conditions long before their natural lifespan had expired' (Todes, 1997a, p. 226).[11]

None of this violence is especially surprising once we recognise that Pavlov's preference for chronic experiments was not primarily born of an ethical or animal welfare impulse (Dror, 1999; Rüting, 2007). For Pavlov, the side effects of vivisection obscured normal physiological processes, contaminated the data (though, to reiterate, vivisection did still have a role in Pavlov's experiments when he considered the method appropriate) and made studies over time impossible (Cuny, 1965). Deriving knowledge from studies of physically intact dogs over the 'long duration', he firmly believed, was simply the most effective way of understanding 'normal' physiological processes, and here he echoed the beliefs of many of his contemporaries (Dror, 1999, p. 220). The dogs' experiences were more 'normal', perhaps, than the horrors of live vivisection, but a disingenuous basis for comparison which masks the violence and suffering involved. Normal 'in so far as the nature of the procedure permits', as the science historian S.D. Tucker points out, 'was a bit like saying that someone would soon be back up on their feet again following a double leg amputation' (Tucker, 2016, p. 13).

In sum, the detail of Pavlov's earlier chronic experiments depict something darker and more complex than a Founding Father finding his way to greatness. They describe a messy human–canine interrelationship defined by suffering and violence, but legitimated, if also partially obscured, by the authority of science and Pavlov's own standing. Placing Pavlov's dogs in the spotlight during this stage in his career reveals elements routinely overlooked in standard accounts of his life and work. Being more transparent about this history is worthwhile in recognising the reality of the lives of creatures integral to the development of psychology, otherwise reduced to expendable experimental objects. As discussed later, the fact that contemporary retellings still do not grant Pavlov's dogs space as living beings is a reflection of a more widespread, and still ongoing, form of human exceptionalism in psychology. Before that, however, we consider how a shift in Pavlov's methods heralded a different staging of human–canine relations, which demands a more nuanced theoretical and ethical framing.

Psychic secretions and conditional reflexes

Whilst the experiments just discussed refer to Pavlov's early career, today he is much better known for his later studies of 'conditional reflexes' in dogs.[12] It is because of this work, and its subsequent impact on the psychology of learning and the development of the Behaviourist school of thought, that he looms large as an iconic figure in historical and popular accounts of psychological science today (Benson et al., 2015; Brysbaert and Rastle, 2009; Harré, 2006; Hart-Davies, 2018). In the course of studying the physiological mechanisms of salivation described above, dogs were regularly fed whilst on the experimenter stand and their saliva measured. At some point, Pavlov and his staff noticed the dogs salivating 'prematurely' in anticipation of food, often in response to environmental cues that normally momentarily pre-empted feeding. This was not especially surprising, but Pavlov was attempting to systematically control the variables contributing to salivation, and a dog's 'thoughts about food' were considered an intrusion. Unable to explain away what he termed 'psychic secretions', he and his staff became increasingly interested in them, eventually turning more or less the whole of his laboratory resources to their study (Windholz and Lamal, 1986). From this point onwards, Pavlov and hundreds of co-workers, human and nonhuman, now embarked on the systematic and almost exclusive study of saliva drops and what were now termed 'conditional reflexes' via thousands of chronic experimental trials.

The measurement of salivation depended upon a surgical procedure that was relatively unobtrusive (compared to pancreatic and stomach fistulas) – the insertion of one or more fistulas into a dog's cheek or neck to divert saliva from the three salivary glands into a measuring device. There is no suggestion in the literature that this surgical intervention, in itself, affected a dog's duration or quality of life. They were thus in keeping with Pavlov's commitment to chronic experiments; in fact, they likely extended the number of experiments any one dog could be involved in considerably. Considered as human–canine interrelationship, this state of affairs is intriguing from a multi-species perspective, as it suggests the possibility of more numerous and closer encounters between experimenters (and separately employed handlers) and dogs, and on ground less readily defined by experiences of violence and suffering and, therefore, a qualitatively different encounter. That said, Pavlov's new direction introduced novel complexities to the human–canine interrelationship, including physical and affective demands upon the dogs (and the researchers), discussed below. A consideration of the detail of these studies, even though they are now canonical components of the history of psychology, is rarely considered in psychology, especially in terms of the canine experience.

Once he settled on the systematic study of these secretions as 'conditioned reflexes', Pavlov sought to eliminate any further anomalies, fastidiously striving to remove all extraneous variables through cutting-edge laboratory technologies. When resources were available, he made great efforts to control the experimental environment – temperature, noise, distractions and so on. Within this set-up, the dogs were, of course, central figures. But in the image handed down to us, they are merely another component of Pavlov's experimental apparatus, an opaque vision of something akin to an assembly line of machine-like dogs producing saliva on demand, establishing 'conditioning' as mechanist learning process. It is surprising how little we stop to consider the circumstances of a dog's life in Pavlov's set-up, what it was like to *be* a dog or the details of the work carried out *with* them, during this prolific – thousands of experiments – period of Pavlov's career. Informed by the work of Donna Haraway in particular, these circumstances are now considered further.

A subject-transforming dance

Haraway approaches 'domestic' human–animal encounters, including laboratory work, as relational configurations, through which both human and animal mutually constitute, and transform, each other (Haraway, 1989; 2008; see also Birke, 2010; Despret, 2004). In describing the complexity and dynamism of human–canine interrelationships in the context of dog agility work, Haraway uses the evocative phrase 'subject-transforming dance' (Haraway, 2008, p.176) to capture how, over time, shared practices transform both dog and human, a point she extends and elaborates on in describing her own experiences. At first glance, we might hesitate to consider Pavlov's experiments in a similar light. Surely these dogs were rendered docile and passive, any residual expressiveness redundant, and similarly the experimenters, impersonally carrying out instructions, remain effectively immobile, intractably distant? Following Haraway, we can say that opportunities for transformation might be more curtailed, but in emphasising co-presence, interaction and interconnected understandings and practices, we must also acknowledge that such dynamics *always* operate from 'inside the complexities of instrumental relations and structures of power' (2007, p. 208). This is why Haraway calls for approaching human entanglements with experimental animals as 'face-to-face, in the company of significant others, companion species to one another' (2008, p. 93). Though our resources are limited by time elapsed, in what follows we approach Pavlov's dogs accordingly.

What must this have been like as an experience? Did dog and human worker make eye contact, greet each other enthusiastically, sympathise with each other, engage in a form of 'kinesthetic empathy' by which the experimenter 'attempts to directly sense the motor intention or attitude or project of the animal' which Shapiro considers a vital component of any attempt to study human–dog encounters meaningfully (Shapiro, 1990, p. 188) and, we might presume, vice versa? What also of the dogs' own 'relationship concerns'– soliciting and offering security, for example, (Shapiro, 1990)? Even a brief survey of what we know, or can try to guess, about what it is like to be a dog, and even acknowledging the ontological impossibility of doing so, suggests the experimenter stand was at best a profoundly strange situation for dogs, at least partially defined by regular encounters with human handlers and experimenters (with implications, as we shall see, for Pavlov's human co-workers too). Biomedical, humanities and social science canine research points to the vividness of a dog's experience (Safina, 2015); of emotions keenly felt (Albuquerque et al., 2016) and to dogs as receptive, expressive and empathic communicators (Martin, 2017), capable of complex forms of (inter)subjectivity (Irvine, 2004; Kirk, 2014). Work in an ethnographic tradition also highlights how human–canine interaction is always a 'spatially situated activity' (Laurier et al., 2006), and the role of space shared with others in which 'embodied relational meaning emerges' is an ongoing negotiation (Sanders and Arluke, 1993; Shapiro, 1990).

During a 'standard' conditioning study, dogs were routinely restrained on the stand for the duration of a single experiment, which often lasted for hours at a time, whilst being repeatedly subjected (by the human experimenter) to a range of stimuli, repeated or refined over many days (by the same human). Stimuli studied included those that fit the familiar portrait – exposure to a buzzer, metronome, bubbling water, cooling of the skin, a flashing light, rotating figure or particular shape – but also 'strong electrical stimuli', that is, electric shocks, the forced ingestion of acid and 'home-made mechanisms' – designed to intermittently inflict pain (Todes, 2014, p. 313). All of these and many more were used to stimulate a dog's senses before/during being presented with food in attempting to create, maintain or inhibit a conditioned response, that is, salivation in response to the stimuli alone.[13]

Does an emphasis on emergent properties of a relationship make any sense in the highly controlled, mechanistic environment of Pavlov's labs described here? Although it is routinely assumed that 'in Pavlovian conditioning the animal remains essentially passive' (Glickstein and Berlucchi, 2008, p. 117), in practice, this was not the case. At times, a dogs' resistance was literal and active – stubbornness in refusing food or other inducements, bridling at specific stimuli, expressing hostility towards an unfamiliar co-worker, refusing to enter particular spaces (Todes, 2014, p. 494). There were subtler, unintentional forms of resistance too. Whilst the dogs had little room for manoeuvre on the stand, closer scrutiny indicates how they consistently evaded Pavlov's meticulously coordinated expectations.

The discovery of 'psychic secretions' was initially an anomaly, one which shifted Pavlov's frame of reference and led him to design a different apparatus. Despite the subsequent discovery of (apparent) regularity in the production of saliva that the 'conditioned reflex' attests to, even the simplest and most 'basic' patterns in the way conditioned responses worked were subject to a great deal of variation and complexity – a fact well known by Pavlov and his co-workers, but actively erased from academic publications and public pronouncements and maintained as an 'industrial secret' (Todes, 2014). Initially at least, Pavlov was profoundly troubled by the simple fact that different dogs responded to the same conditioned stimuli in different ways, in terms of the amount and timing of salivation; some conditioned responses were reinforced much more quickly in some dogs compared to others, and so on, just as the same dogs responded differently on different days – however much Pavlov refined his experimental apparatus to control extraneous variables. As a result, Pavlov had to constantly revise and update the foundations of his theory of learning – a clear indication of just how much the unpredictable vitality of animals resisted experimental objectification and exhortations of machine-like docility, a point to which we return below.

Multi-species perspectives place not just the neglected animal in the spotlight, but human–animal encounters and entanglements. In Pavlov's laboratories, studies were undertaken by co-workers, a mixture of graduate students working towards the completion of their doctoral theses and more established experimenters. Once prepared via surgery, it was common practice for a dog to be assigned to a new co-worker for the duration of their studies (Windholz, 1990, p. 67). In Pavlov's earlier conditioning experiments, human and dog were in the same cramped room, in close proximity, often for eight to ten hours at a time (Todes, 2014, p. 152), some extending to as much as twenty-eight hours (Windholz, 1990, p. 69). Experimenters were expected to keep disruptions to a minimum – any unexpected sound or movement might interfere with the conditioning process and become unwanted 'noise' (Todes, 2014, p. 308). The labour in this space of encounter, for both dog and human, was constraining, monotonous and wearisome, and demanded patience and forbearance on both parts. A key challenge was staying awake – either animal falling asleep at the 'wrong' time was potentially ruinous for the experimental procedure. Boris Babkin, co-worker and subsequently friend and biographer of Pavlov, here recalls the particular form of tedium that characterised conditioning experiments:

> The only action consisted in pressing a bulb, which set up some stimulus, visual, auditory or tactile, every ten or fifteen minutes and writing down the number of drops of saliva secreted in half a minute, then reinforcing them by giving the dog a little meat-and-bread powder when it responded to the stimulation, and again becoming enveloped in silence. It was impossible to read or do anything else, since an interruption of this act then became a conditioned stimulus in itself and might completely obscure the effects of the special stimulation
>
> *(cited in Todes, 2014, p. 309)*

A perfect example of labs as 'highly structured spaces constrain[ing] both the behaviour of the animals *and* the people working there' (Birke, 2010, p. 342; emphasis added). In fact, not every worker could muster the 'great endurance' required indefinitely. As with dogs, there are numerous accounts of human co-workers suffering over-exhaustion, breakdown and even early death (Todes, 2014, p. 152).

This section offers an important corrective to the canonical depiction of Pavlov's experiments as forbearer of a glorious experimental tradition and related representations in which experimenter, animal and apparatus all have their carefully designated place in revealing highly mechanistic and universal psychological processes. They begin to reveal the specific messy and entangled nature of human–animal entanglements at the core of Pavlov's research, in which being human and being animal are mutually involved in situated experiences of co-becoming (Haraway, 2008). In briefly considering the related experiences of human and canine workers, we are also in basic accord with Haraway's aim to avoid morally simplistic rebuttals and defences of animal experiments and her push to attend to the mundane realities of degrees of freedom, co-operation and resistance and its implications for all involved. It is worth remembering this, even as we now consider what are arguably some of the cruellest experiments in Pavlov's career.

The tower of silence

> Pavlov is reported to have been a caring man who never hurt a dog if he could help it and did everything to improve their living conditions
>
> *(Yegorov, 2018, p. 1)*

To temper the idea that attending to the complexity of the human–canine relationships paints a picture of Pavlov as Saint Francis, we can briefly visit an extension of his apparatus, built with significant resources, according to detailed specifications in the early 1920s, but now rarely discussed. The new self-contained and soundproof chambers, dubbed the Tower of Silence, in the grounds of the Institute of Experimental Medicine, were created with the express aim of further verifying Pavlov's typology of higher nervous processes (discussed below). Their construction 'presaged hard times' on the experimental stand, for two dogs in particular – Postrel and Milord (Todes, 2014, p. 501). From 1923-6, Pavlov and his long-time assistant and lover Maria Kapitonovna Petrova experimented on both dogs in the state-of-the-art soundproof chambers at the Institute of Experimental Medicine (Windholz, 1990).

Pavlov and Petrova set out to 'break' the dogs by experimentally eliciting clashes between excitatory and inhibitory 'impulses'. This was achieved by combining electric shocks with force-feeding, increasing the 'severity and duration' of the shocks gradually over a series of experiments, with the aim of facilitating salivation as a conditional response to the shock. Both dogs 'broke' – that is, previously established conditional responses were now erratic, unstructured. Postrel broke in the direction of 'excitation' – excessive and undifferentiated salivation to conditional and neutral stimuli, reflecting 'shattered' inhibitory processes (Todes, 2014, p. 501). Milord, on the other hand, gradually stopped salivating to all positive stimuli as the electric shock increased – evidence, claimed Petrova, of a break towards 'inhibition'.

Hard times indeed. In documenting the use of animals in scientific research many years later, Richard Ryder identified Pavlov's (and, we should add, Petrova's) studies as the starting point for the use of laboratory animals in, as he prosaically put it 'experiments designed to drive them mad... depend[ing] on the simple principle of inflicting pain on animal from which it cannot escape' (Ryder, 1975, p. 113).[14] Although he covers these experiments exhaustively, drawing on Pavlov and Petrova's correspondence and archival material, Todes does not recount any reticence or reservation on their part in undertaking these studies, only fervour (Todes, 2014, pp. 501-3). The results were enthusiastically presented as the experimental production of neuroses (Pavlov, 1928). Whilst Dror argues that Pavlov's approach to his dogs in general reflected a 'benign sensibility', it was 'quite apart from any humanitarian considerations' (Scott, cited in Dror, 1999, p. 226) – always for physiological ends, and therefore revisable in the pursuit of knowledge. Dror insightfully identifies this 'unusual nexus' of sustained interaction at close quarters with animals, and related attempts to create comfort, juxtaposed with the brutal and abrupt utilitarianism that permitted calculated and disinterested killing as a possible explanation for the 'lack of expressed dissonance' in the practitioners of the time, which jars on contemporary reading (ibid). If not indifferent to the suffering of the animals in their care, solicitousness appeared to be readily subsumed within a discourse of scientific progress, as it was routinely in the Tower of Silence.

In terms of 'degrees of freedom', Postrel and Milord found themselves at the extreme end, with perversely reduced options for expressing themselves or contributing to an 'ongoing negotiation'. The experiments conducted in the Tower of Silence are a powerful reminder that the duration and proximity of human–animal relations does not, in itself, guarantee care and compassion. As Haraway points out, 'proximity has a long history of luxuriating brutality' (Potts and Haraway, 2010, p. 326). In psychological experimentation as much as anywhere else, it is the structures and conditions of human–animal proximity that matter. In the realm of the kingdom of dogs, these conditions were constantly shifting and evolving. Whilst the torture of Postrel and Milord represents a nadir, the same theoretical framework which spurred those experiments on reveals yet another dimension of human–canine relations, as the next section examines.

The temperament of a dog

> Lab experiments tend to rest on creating animals as objects, whose experiences are considered unimportant... lab animals are seldom seen as animals. Rather, they tend to exist as numbers, as tools of the trade
>
> *(Birke, 2010, p. 341)*

As noted above, more subtle and yet pervasive forms of canine resistance were also involved – including resistance to Pavlov's carefully constructed theoretical edifice. Paying attention to what dogs actually *did* and how Pavlov and co-workers responded reveals an ongoing 'subject-transforming dance' of a very different kind. In practice, as we have already seen, Pavlov's dogs were not docile and passive conditioned reflex machines. Pavlov was in fact willing to alter his theoretical framework to keep up with the liveliness and unpredictability of his dogs and also accepted it, at least in part, as a consequence of studying 'intact organisms' (2014, p. 169). Todes makes a strong case that Pavlov's later introduction of a personality typology, framed physiologically as a reflection of distinct types of 'higher nervous' processing, was established to interpretively contain experimental results that were in practice highly varied and inconsistent (2014, pp. 529-40).[15] Positing the existence of inherent characteristics – 'nervous types' – is today a much less well-known aspect of Pavlov's oeuvre, but at the time was considered vital to justify otherwise unexplainable variety in conditioned reflexive responses (i.e. timing and quantity of drool produced in response to conditioned stimuli). Thus:

> the co-worker's task went far beyond collecting, measuring and analysing digestive fluids; he also has to assess the normality and personality of his dog and interpret his results accordingly... Such judgements drew upon observations concerning the dog's ease in adapting to the experimental setting... its preference for certain foods... and often the attendant's testimony about its behaviour off the stand
>
> *(Todes, 2014, p. 170–171)*

Interpretive containment of the 'industrial secret' of conditioning experiment variability was made possible by and further encouraged the attentiveness of co-workers, attendants and Pavlov to a dog's behaviour, preferences and character (Dror, 2003; Todes, 1997a,b).

Despite the contemporary image of Pavlov's dogs as interchangeable moving parts in some giant demonstrative machine of stimulus-response learning, co-workers were increasingly encouraged to observe idiosyncrasies in a dogs' behaviour on and off the stand. Such attention became part of experimental protocol by the 1910s, fully endorsed by Pavlov, and exemplified in his own 'anthropomorphic' interpretations of his dogs' behaviour (Todes, 2014, p. 298). Alongside measuring stimuli and response type and timings, a final column was now reserved for 'other observations', in which experimenters remarked on a dog's reactions to the demands of an experiment in terms of 'character'. Dogs were routinely described as 'weak or strong, compliant or independent, passive or impressionable, aloof or sociable, modest or greedy, cowardly or heroic' (2014, p. 495). 'Other observations' were taken extremely seriously, as evidence of experimenters' knowing their dogs and their dispositions, and, from the 1920s, in helping establish a dog's 'nervous type'.[16]

Reading second-hand translated excerpts from more detailed accounts (including correspondence, theses and internal reports), available thanks to the meticulous work of Todes, it is remarkable how seriously dogs' individuality was taken; how attributions of intelligence, character and personality were integral to the everyday work of experiments and how routinely 'assessment of the dog's personality [was] invoked in interpreting experimental data' (Todes, 1997a, p. 240) – in contrast to the tendency noted by Birke in opening this section. We certainly get a sense that dogs were more than objects and numbers: that they behaved and expressed themselves in myriad ways, that they were lively contributors to the work undertaken and that these contributions were noticed, articulated and discussed in the labs. Pavlov revised his understanding of the human condition, including his own, in light of how the dogs responded to life as an experimental animal, and vice versa – for Pavlov, the boundaries between knowledge of people and of dogs were extremely porous, reflected in his 'long-standing practice of interpreting people as dogs and dogs as people' (Todes, 2014, p. 631).

Nor was the dogs' liveliness ever co-opted or made calculable in any final sense. Despite Pavlov's evolving personality typology, and ever-more stringent attempt to control extraneous variables, he was always playing catch-up with the way in which the relational configurations of dogs and co-workers exceeded calculability – much more so than the cautious acknowledgement of 'borderline cases' by his later champions

(Cuny, 1965, p. 94). Ultimately, his quest to systematically understand the psyche via physiological processes 'set him on a three-decade journey to the horizon', whereby 'the ultimate destination continually receded behind an endless landscape of new and perplexing complexities' (Todes, 2014, p. 300). Industrial secrets, interpretive moments and ever-expanding personality typologies point to the liveliness and unpredictability of the dogs on and off the experimenter stand, as observed by Pavlov and his co-workers and to the active engagement of the dogs in expressing their own needs, desires and discomfiture. Whilst dogs were 'significantly unfree partners' in the relational configurations of the lab, we are right to follow Haraway in avoiding absolute categories of freedom versus unfreedom and to instead be drawn to the metaphor of 'degrees of freedom', which always allow for 'unfilled space; something outside of calculation that can still happen' (Haraway, 2008, pp. 72-3). To paraphrase Despret, the system *cannot* fully articulate the animal (Despret, 2004).

In sum, closer attention paid to Pavlov's experiments and the human–animal relations at their core reveals a picture at odds with the one commonly circulating in academic and popular discourses. Borrowing the conceptual lens of the animal turn, they can be profitably framed to reveal a more complex ethics and epistemology. In what follows, the significance of this framing for a psychology of human–animal relations is considered in more detail.

Reversing the moral abandonment of being

The portrait of Pavlov's dogs that emerges from this discussion stands in stark contrast to the standard one found in psychological literature, where they are made visible only as disembodied S-R conduits, saliva-producing apparatuses. In their iconic image, it is in fact the dogs' 'conditioned reflexes' which *stand in* for the dogs. As the countless diagrammatic representations of conditioning attest, they are docile, one-dimensional, animals-as-machines: a necessary but arbitrary component in the Pavlovian equation of conditioning the reflex. We might be tempted to think this is all very well, but interesting only as a historical curiosity. Psychology has moved on in terms of the use of animals in experimentation, evident in, for example, the more stringent codas of the American Psychological Association and British Psychological Society guidelines for working with animals (APA, 2012; BPS, 2012). If this is indeed the case, acknowledgement of earlier fundamental ethical issues to unsettle the teleology of psychology is much needed as a parallel process, as the above discussion of psychology textbooks and other coverage attests.

However, more remains at stake here than 'setting the record straight' for historical accuracy. The ongoing erasure of human–animal ethical and epistemological issues from psychology's past, however habitual and unintentional, impacts on how we understand and articulate psychology's present – in terms of what is prioritised, emphasised, discussed and debated. Here, the recounting of Pavlov's work reifies problematic framings of human–animal relations that are *still* deeply embedded in psychology in general and experimental psychology in particular (Adams, 2018). The result of this perpetual blind spot is a neglect of the 'individuality and species specificity' of the lab animal, the sanctioning of a reductive framing of what a human–animal relationship *is* in the lab and the exclusion of 'any other interspecies relationship [as] a legitimate object of study' (Shapiro, 2010, p. 259). These processes are necessary for constructing Pavlov's dogs retrospectively as docile objects, but they are also alive and well in constructing other historical and contemporary experimental animals in the present. Take a recent psychology textbook account of memory processes:

> When we move on to discuss the relevant evidence, you will notice that the great majority of studies have used monkeys. This has been done because the invasive techniques involved *can only be used* on non-human species. It is generally (but perhaps incorrectly) assumed that basic visual processes are similar in humans and monkeys
> *(Eysenck and Keane, 2015, p. 97; emphasis added)*

The 'can only be used' here implies but does not articulate a logic of human exceptionalism (or speciesism) – it cannot be used on humans because of the 'invasive' nature of psychophysiological research (e.g. Afraz et al., 2006), but it can on rhesus monkeys.[17] Similar processes of erasure accompany uncritical accounts of the 'central' and 'misunderstood' role of animals in psychology experiments in the past and today. Here, Bennett (2012) uses Harlow's 'maternal deprivation' experiments as an example of the ongoing utility of animal experimentation in psychology:

> For example, consider how Harry Harlow's famous monkey studies contributed broadly to social, clinical, developmental, comparative, and biological perspectives on attachment. The

longevity and impact of these studies is evident across disciplines. The animal model developed by Harlow continues to provide the foundation for new discoveries about how early life experiences influence biobehavioral development and health across the lifespan. These studies provide us with controlled, experimental avenues to answer clinically relevant questions that simply could not be addressed with human studies.

This despite the fact that Harlow's studies actually have attracted plenty of retrospective disapprobation for their astounding levels of inventive, pathological cruelty (Blum, 1994; Gluck, 1997; Haraway, 1989). As Birke says of laboratory research with animals more generally, 'this kind of use rests on a moral discontinuity – for we can only justify their use if we believe that non-human lives are ethically less valued than human ones' (2010, p. 342). Notwithstanding moves to make psychology experimentation with animals more ethical, this moral discontinuity is ongoing, a reflection of a still-limited ethical and epistemological framework compared to the developments underway in sister disciplines.

Anthropocene psychology?

> To 'de-passion' knowledge does not give us a more objective world, it just gives us a world 'without us' and therefore without 'them'
> *(Despret, 2004, p. 131)*

Psychology is far from a monolithic beast, incorporating many different tendencies, often at critical odds with each other. In particular, a psychology concerned with human–animal relations continues to emerge and shift, incorporating different ways of working with animals and of conceptually framing human–animal interaction. The flagship APA journal *Psychological Bulletin* published an overview of a 'psychology of human–animal relations' (Amiot and Bastian, 2015), in which the authors lucidly thematise this emerging field. At its heart, though, the understanding of human–animal relations therein is largely untouched by the more radical developments summarised above. In the many studies they cite, emphasis is overwhelmingly placed on human perception of nonhuman animals – the latter are rarely encountered as living beings in methodological procedures, more rarely still as meaningfully contributing to and experiencing interaction and therefore ontologically significant in mutually constitutive ways

(Adams, 2018). It is a parallel issue that in and amongst psychology's canonical timeline, 'classic' studies and ongoing experimental practices, human–animal relations remain an 'absent presence'.

There is great scope to extend the tenets of theoretically curious and critically oriented psychology to the animal turn, and in doing so to radically develop the a psychology of human–animal relations in psychology, opening up the discipline to more interesting stories, past and present. The ethical and epistemological issues raised in this chapter reflect a deeper ontological issue. Basically, if a relational ontology emphasises how 'the relations between entities are ontologically more fundamental than the entities themselves' (Wildman, 2010, p. 55) and 'that entities come to exist through relations' (Collomb, 2011, p. 59), the animal turn extends this premise to human and nonhuman entities. An 'assumption of relationality' (Stanley, 2012, p. 636) is already a central tenet of many versions of critical, constructionist and feminist-oriented psychology, a critical response to the reductive methodological individualism of mainstream psychology. Gergen's version of critical psychology, for example (e.g. 2009, 2011), conceptualises (human) experience as an 'outcome or expression of fundamental relatedness'; displacing the '[human] individual as 'the primary source or ontological foundation of being' (both Gergen and Hosking, cited in Stanley, 2012, p. 636). Within a critical psychology framework, knowledge, power and reality itself all depend on relational dynamics (Gough, 2017) and are accompanied by an ethical commitment to recognising the importance of relational processes in maintaining self and others. Simply put, multi-species and posthuman theory extends the scope of a relational ontology to incorporate other species (Adams, 2018; Smart and Smart, 2017). This is especially salient for social psychology, where to date 'the social' is almost exclusively approached as a human construct, even in critical versions (Adams, 2017).

Finally: recognising relationships

I have attempted to re-examine Pavlov's oeuvre through the everyday experiences of the dogs involved – a form of 'history from below' which takes animals as legitimate historical subjects (Montgomery and Kalof, 2010). Montgomery and Kalof claim that analysing animals as historical subjects 'adds new dimensions and new levels of understanding to a wide range of disciplines' (2010, p. 36) – the subsequent list of disciplines and potential examples does not include psychology, but it clearly could. It is hoped that this chapter has challenged familiar representations of this seminal milestone in psychology's history and its place in the canonical narrative of psychology's (scientific) progress. Closer attention reveals how Pavlov's experiments are spaces of encounter saturated with human–nonhuman interactions – they *are* those interactions. They involve reciprocal relational bonds between the various permutations of humans, dogs, dog-appendages, blood, excretions (saliva, gastric and pancreatic juice), experimental apparatus and physical spaces. Following Haraway's lead, we have attended to entangled subjectivities (2008) and shared interests and dangers, as well as divergent and dissonant experiences and fates.

It has been claimed that the primary flaw in contemporary retellings of Pavlov's experiments with dogs is the lack of recognition *of* a relation, and attendant responsibilities to the other, lost in 'unidirectional relations of use, ruled by practices of calculation and self-sure of hierarchy' (Haraway, 2008, p. 71). In such a partial depiction, important ethical and epistemological issues are routinely erased and therefore remain unaddressed to this day. In terms of ethics, a staging of relationality and responsibility towards (nonhuman) others is notable only by its absence, perpetuating a 'moral abandonment of their being' (Adams, 2010, p. 304). The most significant abandonment ethically here is not, to be clear, Pavlov's, but that found in the contemporary retelling. In terms of epistemology, there is no sense that embodied canine and relational human–canine realities routinely exceeded Pavlov's attempts at interpretation, or that such messiness was an 'industrial secret'. Both are related – not acknowledging canine wilfulness and liveliness permits a two-dimensional perspective, which in turn dissuades scrutiny of the privation and violence meted out – why apply morality to machines?

As an alternative, the experiments can be reframed as a complex form of 'companion species' kinship; if we are willing to stay with the (often violent) trouble of the contradictions and dissonances inherent in that kinship: 'to be in response is to recognize co-presence in relations of use and therefore to remember that no balance sheet of benefit and cost will suffice' (Haraway, 2008, p. 76). The alternative, in other words, is to make Pavlov's dogs *matter* for a psychology that is more actively attuned to the intersection of human and more-than-human worlds. In closing their critical review of Zimbardo's infamous prison studies informed by newly available archival materials, Reicher et al. conclude that 'there is no longer any excuse for repeating a story which is so deeply flawed. We need to get busy rewriting our texts and revising our lectures' (2018, p. 1). The same, surely, can be said of Pavlov's entanglement in the kingdom of dogs. In this case, however, a rewrite has wider implications for who and what counts as psychologically meaningful subjects in relation.

What have Pavlov's labs and his kingdom of dogs got to do with the Anthropocene, an era that at best retrospectively incorporates the times in which he lived on a much more general level? To accept the Anthropocene as invitation is to pay attention to the interpenetration of human and more-than-human worlds. We can do that in the present, engaging, for example, with the 'human-animal worlds' identified at the beginning of this chapter, following Haraway, which includes the laboratory. We can also revisit the past in the present, and it is hoped readers have found value in revisiting a cherished and familiar moment in psychology's history, looking through eyes informed by an Anthropocene imaginary. The established 'facts' of conditional learning built on animal experimentation are revealed as more fluid and contingent, dependent on human–canine co-becomings that the Anthropocene invites us to attend to. In the chapters that follow, this invitation is pursued in more detail, as we venture into other times and places.

Notes

1. An earlier version of this discussion was published as Adams, M. (2019) The kingdom of dogs: Understanding Pavlov's experiments as human-animal relationships. *Theory & Psychology*, DOI: 10.13140/RG.2.2.19245.64483
2. Prefixing animal with nonhuman might better reiterate the fact that humans are of course also animals, and therefore trouble the human–animal distinction as dichotomous. It still depends linguistically on a binary, however, so for the rest of the chapter, 'human' and 'animal' are retained as descriptors.
3. Despret focuses on Oscar Pfungst and Clever Hans (a horse) and Rosenthal's 'dull and bright rats' experiments; both Haraway and Despret discuss Harlow's attachment experiments with rhesus monkeys (Haraway, 1989, pp. 231-243).
4. For example 'Laws governing behavior from studies of pigeons, rats, and other non-human animals—with the assumption that these principles would apply equally to other species, including humans—derived from the behaviourism of Watson, Pavlov, and Skinner' (Melson, 2002, p. 348-9). Though Pavlov did not identify himself as a behaviourist – in fact he was often at pains to disassociate himself from that movement (Todes, 2014).
5. Exposure to general textbook coverage matters to how the discipline is framed and understood, 'because introductory psychology is the most popular psychology course, almost all teachers use textbooks for it, and textbooks play a major role in defining the course for students' (Griggs and Christopher, 2016, p. 108). Within these textbooks, Pavlov has maintained

his position as one of the most cited psychologists (Diener et al., 2014; Griggs and Proctor, 2002) – ninth overall in one recent comprehensive citation analysis (Griggs and Christopher, 2016); sixth across the twentieth century as a whole (Haggbloom et al., 2002).

6. Alongside the growing interdisciplinary field of human-animal studies (Birke and Hockenhull, 2012; DeMello, 2010; Peggs, 2012; Wilkie, 2015), witness attempts to articulate a human-nonhuman relational ontology in fields as diverse as archaeology (Watts, 2013), anthropology (Dugnoille, 2014; Kirksey and Helmreich, 2010; Kohn, 2013), feminism (Adams, 2015; Kemmerer, 2011; Potts, 2010), geography (Whatmore, 2006; Wright, 2015), sociology (Charles, 2014; Cudworth, 2015; McCarthy, 2016; Sanders, 2007; York and Longo, 2017), criminology and legal studies (e.g. Sollund, 2011), philosophy and cultural studies (Haraway, 2003; Litchfield, 2013; Plumwood, 2002) and natural history (Henderson, 2012).

7. Cited in Preece (2006). Bernard was a French physiologist and proponent of vivisection. Mary Midgely recounts how Bernard performed a vivisection on the family's pet dog, to the disgust of his family, and that Marie Francoise, Bernard's wife, subsequently divorced him and became a vocal anti-vivisection campaigner.

8. There is a quote often attributed to Pavlov: 'At that time dogs were collected with the help of street thieves, who used to steal those with collars as well as those without. No doubt we shared the onus of the sin with the thieves' (e.g. Cuny, 1965, p. 30). There are no firm corroborations of the source, in Cuny or elsewhere, so it is unclear when 'that time' was and how out of the ordinary it was as a practice, if pursued at all. Accounts of the use of dogs in late nineteenth- and twentieth-century medical laboratory research suggest that a preference for dogs is at least partly motivated by 'the availability of large numbers of stray and unwanted dogs at low cost' (Scott cited in Giraud and Hollin, 2017, p. 167; Degeling, 2008) and that experimenting on 'street dogs just brought in' does not seem to warrant any further explanation in contemporaneous physiological research (Neilson and Terry, 1906, p. 407).

9. Mikhail Bulkagov's celebrated novella *Heart of a Dog* (1925) is a contemporaneous fictional account of a destitute stray street dog being abducted for the purposes of scientific experimentation. Taken in by Professor Preobrazhensky, a dog (named *Sharik* by the Professor) is operated on and becomes the recipient of a human brain and pineal gland, taken from a recently deceased human. The post-operative Sharik becomes increasingly human in form and character, which Bulkagov largely documents as a downward spiral. The dog becomes increasingly wild and wilfully destructive, whilst using the incipient communist order for his own gain and to get one over on his master. Bulkagov's narrative is more a satire of a corrupt and hypocritical Soviet system than it is a commentary on human versus canine nature – the book was banned from publication until 1968.

10. Though towards the end of his life, Pavlov ran a series of experiments where he contrasted dogs kept in kennels with those allowed to roam freely in the grounds of his science village.

11. It is worth pointing out that although the ages discussed here seem a lot less than a domestic dog's average life expectancy (anywhere from 8–16 years depending on size and breed) today, an urban stray street dog's is more like 1–3 years (Paul et al., 2016) – though there are no reliable figures for the life expectancy of stray dogs at the time.

12. Pavlov referred to condition*al* reflexes (*uslovnyi refleks*) – referred to in English, with a not-insignificant 'Anglo-American distortion' as condition*ed* reflexes (Todes, 2014, p. 1).

13. Less well known still (they are not mentioned by Todes) are parallel experiments conducted by Pavlov's students, exploring, for example, the effects of a severed *corpus callosum* on conditioned reflexes (Bykoff and Speranskii cited in Glickstein and Berlucchi, 2008), which *did* still depend on prior invasive surgery that routinely resulted in extreme suffering and death.

14. In these experiments, at least, Pavlov's apparatus resembles Harry Harlow's infamously cruel 'maternal deprivation' experiments (e.g. Harlow et al., 1966), in which the animal has little opportunity to resist the experimenter's expectations: 'How can a rhesus monkey resist Harlow's experiment? By showing despair? Of course not, that is exactly what is expected of it. By becoming happy? I would not bet on it' (Despret, 2004, p. 124; see also Haraway, 1989).

15. During a visit to London in 1935, Pavlov was received enthusiastically by press and academics alike, and his newer theories reported with headlines like this from the *New York Times* – 'Finds Dogs React Same as Humans: Pavlov Says He Has Proved They Possess Our Four Fundamental Temperaments' (cited in Todes, 2014, p. 689).

16. He initially argued that there were *two* basic nervous processes emanating in waves from the cerebral cortex, excitation and inhibition (Pavlov, 1927; 1932), gradually expanding the number of variations of 'nervous types' to twenty-three (Todes, 2014).

17. In *Uses and Abuses of Psychology*, Richards points this kind of research as 'the most controversial from an animal welfare perspective' (Richards, 2010, p. 240).

References

Adams, C. J. 2010. Why feminist-vegan now? *Feminism and Psychology*, 20(3), 302–317.

Adams, C. J. 2015. *The Sexual Politics of Meat – 25th Anniversary Edition: A Feminist-Vegetarian Critical Theory*. London: Bloomsbury.

Adams, M. 2017. Environment: Critical social psychology in the Anthropocene. In Gough, B. (Ed.), *The Palgrave Handbook of Critical Social Psychology*. London: Palgrave Macmillan, pp. 621–641.

Adams, M. 2018. Towards a critical psychology of human–animal relations. *Social and Personality Psychology Compass*, 12(4), 1–14.

Afraz, S. R., Kiani, R. and Esteky, H. 2006. Microstimulation of inferotemporal cortex influences face categorization. *Nature*, 442(7103), 692–695.

Albuquerque, N., Guo, K., Wilkinson, A., Savalli, C., Otta, E. and Mills, D. 2016. Dogs recognize dog and human emotions. *Biology Letters*, 12(1), 20150883.

American Psychological Association. 2012. *Guidelines for Ethical Conduct in the Care and Use of Nonhuman Animals in Research*. Washington: APA. Accessed 08/07/19 https:// www.apa.org/science/leadership/care/care-animal-guidelines.pdf.

Amiot, C.E. and Bastian, B. 2015. Toward a psychology of human–animal relations. *Psychological Bulletin*, 141(1), 6–47.

Anderson, J., Adey, P. and Bevan, P. 2010. Positioning place: Polylogic approaches to research methodology. *Qualitative Research*, 10(5), 589–604.

Banyard, P., Dillon, G., Norman, C. and Winder, B. (Eds.). 2015. *Essential Psychology*, 2nd ed. London: Sage.

Bennett, A.J. 2012. Animal research: The bigger picture and why we need psychologists to speak out. *Psychological Science Agenda*, April 2012. American Psychological Association. Accessed 08/07/19 https://www.apa.org/science/about/psa/2012/04/animal-research.

Benson, P. Benson, N., Collin, C. Ginsburg, J., Grand, V., Lazyan, M., Weeks, M. and Tomley, S. 2015. *The Psychology Book*. London: Dorling Kingsley.

Birke, L. 2010. Structuring relationships: On science, feminism and non-human animals. *Feminism and Psychology*, 20(3), 337–349.

Birke, L. and Hockenhull, J. (Eds.). 2012. *Crossing Boundaries: Investigating Human–Animal Relationships,* (Vol. 14). New York: Brill.

Bitterman, M. E. 2006. Classical conditioning since Pavlov. *Review of General Psychology*, 10(4), 365–376.

Blum, D. 1994. *The Monkey Wars*. New York: Oxford University Press.

Briggs, R.A. 2014. Coverage of the Stanford Prison Experiment in introductory psychology textbooks. *Teaching of Psychology*, 41, 195–203.

British Psychological Society. 2012. *Guidelines for Psychologists Working with Animals*. Leicester: BPS. Accessed 08/07/19 https://www.apa.org/science/leadership/care/care-animal-guidelines.pdf.

Bruni, C. M., Fraser, J. and Schultz, P. W. 2008. The value of zoo experiences for connecting people with nature. *Visitor Studies*, 11(2), 139–150.

Brysbaert, M. and Rastle, K. 2009. *Historical and Conceptual Issues in Psychology*. London: Pearson Education.

Cederholm, E.A., Björck, A., Jennbert, K. and Lönngren, A. S. 2014. *Exploring the Animal Turn: Human-Animal Relations in Science, Society and Culture*. Lund: Pufendorfinstitutet.

Çevik, M. Ö. 2014. Habituation, sensitization, and Pavlovian conditioning. *Frontiers in Integrative Neuroscience*, 8, 13.

Charles, N. 2014. 'Animals just love you as you are': Experiencing kinship across the species barrier. *Sociology*, 48(4), 715–730.

Cherkaev, X. and Tipikina, E. 2018. Interspecies affection and military aims: Was there a totalitarian dog?. *Environmental Humanities*, 10(1), 20–39.

Clayton, S., Fraser, J. and Burgess, C. 2011. The role of zoos in fostering environmental identity. *Ecopsychology*, 3(2), 87–96.

Collomb, C. (2011). Relational ontology and conceptions of the common. *Multitudes*, 2, 59–63.

Country, B., Wright, S., Suchet-Pearson, S., Lloyd, K., Burarrwanga, L., Ganambarr, R., Ganambarr-Stubbs, M., Ganambarr, B. and Maymuru, D., 2015. Working with and learning from Country: decentring human authority. *Cultural geographies*, 22(2), 269–283.

Country, B., Wright, S., Suchet-Pearson, S., Lloyd, K., Burarrwanga, L., Ganambarr, R., Ganambarr-Stubbs, M., Ganambarr, B., Maymuru, D. and Sweeney, J., 2016. Co-becoming Bawaka: Towards a relational understanding of place/space. *Progress in Human Geography*, 40(4), 455–475.

Cudworth, E. 2015. Killing animals: Sociology, species relations and institutionalized violence. *The Sociological Review*, 63(1), 1–18.

Cuny, H. 1965. *Ivan Pavlov: The Man and His Theories*. Trans. P.S. Eriksson. Greenwich: Fawcett.

Davis, H. E. and Balfour, D. A. 1992. *The Inevitable Bond: Examining Scientist–Animal Interactions*. Cambridge University Press.

Degeling, C. 2008. Canines, consanguinity, and one-medicine: All the qualities of a dog except loyalty. *Health and History*, 10(2), 23–47.

Deleuze, G. and Guattari, F. 1987. *A Thousand Plateaus: Capitalism and Schizophrenia*. London: Bloomsbury Publishing.

DeMello, M. 2010. *Teaching the Animal: Human-Animal Studies across the Disciplines*. New York: Lantern Books.

Despret, V. 2004. The body we care for: Figures of anthropo-zoo-genesis. *Body and Society*, 10(2-3), 111–134.

Diener, E., Oishi, S. and Park, J. Y. 2014. An incomplete list of eminent psychologists of the modern era. *Archives of Scientific Psychology*, 2, 20–32.

Dror, O. E. 1999. The affect of experiment: The turn to emotions in Anglo-American physiology, 1900-1940. *Isis*, 90(2), 205–237.

Dror, O. Y. 2003. Pavlov's physiology factory: Experiment, interpretation, laboratory enterprise. *Journal of the History of Medicine and Allied Sciences*, 58(1), 101–103.

Dugnoille, J. 2014. From plate to pet: Promotion of trans-species companionship by Korean animal activists. *Anthropology Today*, 30(6), 3–7.

Eysenck, M. W. 2004. *Psychology: An International Perspective*. Taylor and Francis.

Eysenck, M.W. and Keane, M.T. 2015. *Cognitive Psychology: A Student's Handbook*, 7th ed. Hove: Psychology Press.

Gibson, S. 2013. Milgram's obedience experiments: A rhetorical analysis. *British Journal of Social Psychology*, 52(2), 290–309.

Giraud, E. and Hollin, G. 2017. Laboratory beagles and affective co-production of knowledge. In Bastian, M., Jones, O., Moore, N. and Roe, E. (Eds.), *Participatory Research in More-Than-Human Worlds*. London: Routledge. Pages 163–177.

Glassman, W. E. and Hadad, M. 2013. *Approaches to Psychology*, 6th ed. Maidenhead: McGraw-Hill.

Glickstein, M. and Berlucchi, G. 2008. KM Bykov and transfer between the hemispheres. *Brain Research Bulletin*, 77(2-3), 117–123.

Gluck, J. P. 1997. Harry F. Harlow and animal research: Reflection on the ethical paradox. *Ethics and Behavior*, 7(2), 149–161.

Gough, B. 2017. Critical social psychologies: Mapping the terrain. In Gough, B. (Ed.), *Palgrave Handbook of Critical Social Psychology*. Basingstoke: Palgrave, pp. 2–16.

Griggs, R. 2015. Psychology's lost boy: Will the real Little Albert please stand up? *Teaching of Psychology*, 42(1): 14–18.

Griggs, R. A. and Christopher, A. N. 2016. Who's who in introductory psychology textbooks: A citation analysis redux. *Teaching of Psychology*, 43(2), 108–119.

Griggs, R. A. and Proctor, D. L. 2002. A citation analysis of who's who in introductory textbooks. *Teaching of Psychology*, 29, 203–206.

Gross, R. 2015. *Psychology: The Science of Mind and Behaviour*, 7th ed. London: Hodder Education.

Haggbloom, S. J., Warnick, R., Warnick, J. E., Jones, V. K., Yarbrough, G. L., Russell, T. M. and Monte, E. 2002. The 100 most eminent psychologists of the 20th century. *Review of General Psychology*, 6(2), 139–152.

Haraway, D. J. 1989. *Primate Visions: Gender, Race, and Nature in the World of Modern Science*. London: Routledge.

Haraway, D. J. 2003. *The Companion Species Manifesto: Dogs, People, and Significant Otherness*. Chicago: Prickly Paradigm Press.

Haraway, D. J. 2008. *When Species Meet*. Minneapolis: University of Minnesota Press.

Haraway, D. (2014, September 5). Anthropocene, Capitalocene, Chthulucene: Staying with the trouble. In *Anthropocene: Arts of living with a Damaged Planet*. AURA: Aarhus University Research on the Anthropocene. https://vimeo.com/97663518

Haraway, D. J. 2016. *Staying with the Trouble*. Minneapolis: University of Minnesota Press.

Harlow, H. F., Harlow, M. K., Dodsworth, R. O. and Arling, G. L. 1966. Maternal behavior of rhesus monkeys deprived of mothering and peer associations in infancy. *Proceedings of the American Philosophical Society*, 110(1), 58–66.

Harré, R. 2006. *Key Thinkers in Psychology*. London: Sage.

Hart-Davies, A. 2018. *Pavlov's Dog: And 49 Other Experiments that Revolutionised Psychology*. London: Modern Books.

Hayes, N. 2000. *Foundations of Psychology*, 3rd ed. London: Thomson.

Head, L. 2016. *Hope and Grief in the Anthropocene: Re-conceptualising Human–Nature Relations*. London: Routledge.

Henderson, C. 2012. *The Book of Barely Imagined Beings: A 21st Century Bestiary*. London: Granta.

Holcomb, R. and Meacham, M. 1989. Effectiveness of an animal-assisted therapy program in an inpatient psychiatric unit. *Anthrozoös*, 2(4), 259–264.

Holmberg, T. 2008. A feeling for the animal: On becoming an experimentalist. *Society and Animals*, 16(4), 316–335.

Ingold, T. 2005. Epilogue: Towards a politics of dwelling. *Conservation and Society*, 3(2), 501–508.

Irvine, L. 2004. A model of animal selfhood: Expanding interactionist possibilities. *Symbolic Interaction*, 27(1), 3–21.

Jarius, S. and Wildemann, B. 2017. Pavlov's reflex before Pavlov: Early accounts from the English, French and German classic literature. *European Neurology*, 77(5-6), 322–326.

Johnson, E. R. 2015. Of lobsters, laboratories, and war: Animal studies and the temporality of more-than-human encounters. *Environment and Planning D: Society and Space*, 33(2), 296–313.

Kazdin, A. E. 2009. Psychological science's contributions to a sustainable environment: Extending our reach to a grand challenge of society. *American Psychologist*, 64(5), 339–348.

Kemmerer, L. A. (Ed.). 2011. *Sister Species: Women, Animals, and Social Justice*. Illinois: UI Press.

Kirk, R. G. 2014. In dogs we trust? Intersubjectivity, response-able relations, and the making of mine detector dogs. *Journal of the History of the Behavioral Sciences*, 50(1), 1–36.

Kirksey, S. and Helmreich, S. 2010. The emergence of multispecies ethnography. *Cultural Anthropology*, 25(4), 545–576.

Kohn, E. 2013. *How Forests Think: Toward an Anthropology Beyond the Human*. Berkeley, CA: California: University of California Press.

Kubie, L. S. 1959. Pavlov, Freud and soviet psychiatry. *Behavioral Science*, 4(1), 29–34.

Latour, B. 2005. *Reassembling the Social: An Introduction to Actor-Network-Theory*. Oxford: Oxford University Press.

Laurier, E., Maze, R. and Lundin, J. 2006. Putting the dog back in the park: Animal and human mind-in-action. *Mind, Culture, and Activity*, 13(1), 2–24.

Litchfield, C. A. 2013. Telling the truth about animals and environments: Media and pro-environmental behaviour. In R. Crocker and S. Lehmann (Eds.), *Motivating Change: Sustainable Design and Behaviour in the Built environment*. London: Routledge, pp. 153–177.

London, I. D. 1949. A historical survey of psychology in the Soviet Union. *Psychological Bulletin*, 46(4), 241.

Lorimer, J. 2010. Elephants as companion species: The lively biogeographies of Asian elephant conservation in Sri Lanka. *Transactions of the Institute of British Geographers*, 35(4), 491–506.

McLeod, K. 2014. Orientating to assembling: Qualitative inquiry for more-than-human worlds. *International Journal of Qualitative Methods*, 13(1), 377–394.

McSweeney, F. K. and Murphy, E. S. (Eds.). 2014. *The Wiley-Blackwell Handbook of Operant and Classical Conditioning.* Oxford: Wiley Blackwell.

McCarthy, D. 2016. Dangerous dogs, dangerous owners and the waste management of an 'irredeemable species'. *Sociology*, 50(3), 560–575.

Martin, A. L. 2017. The development and expression of canine emotion. *Animal Sentience: An Interdisciplinary Journal on Animal Feeling*, 2(14), 10.

Melson, G. F. 2002. Psychology and the study of human-animal relationships. *Society and Animals*, 10(4), 347–352.

Miller, C. 2001. Childhood animal cruelty and interpersonal violence. *Clinical Psychology Review*, 21(5), 735–749.

Montgomery, G. M. and Kalof, L. 2010. History from below: Animals as historical subjects. In DeMello, M. (Ed.), *Teaching the Animal: Human-Animal Studies across the Disciplines.* Brooklyn, NY: Lantern Books, pp. 35–47.

Mullin, M. 2010. Anthropology's animals. In M. DeMello (Ed.), *Teaching the Animal: Human–Animal Studies Across the Disciplines.* New York: Lantern Books, pp. 145–201.

Myers, D. G. and DeWall, C. N. 2018. *Psychology*, 12th ed. New York: Worth Publishers.

Neilson, C. H. and Terry, O. P. 1906. The adaptation of the salivary secretion to diet. *American Journal of Physiology-Legacy Content*, 15(4), 406–411.

Nimmo, R. 2011. Actor-network theory and methodology: Social research in a more-than-human world. *Methodological Innovations Online*, 6(3), 108–119.

Nolen-Hoeksema, S., Fredrickson, B., Loftus, G. R. and Lutz, C. 2014. *Introduction to Psychology.* Cengage Learning.

Opotow, S. 1993. Animals and the scope of justice. *Journal of Social Issues*, 49(1), 71–85.

Paul, M., Majumder, S. S., Sau, S., Nandi, A. K. and Bhadra, A. 2016. High early life mortality in free-ranging dogs is largely influenced by humans. *Scientific Reports*, 6, 19641.

Pavlov, I. P. 1927 [2010]. Conditioned reflexes: An investigation of the physiological activity of the cerebral cortex. *Annals of Neurosciences*, 17(3), 136–141.

Pavlov, I. P. 1928. The reflex of freedom. In Pavlov, I. P. (Ed.), *Lectures on Conditioned Reflexes.* (Transl. by W. H. Gantt.) New York: Liveright Publishing Corp, pp. 282–286.

Pavlov, I. P. 1932. Neuroses in man and animals. *Journal of the American Medical Association*, 99(12), 1012–1013.

Pavlov, I. P. 1941. *Lectures on Conditioned Reflexes.* Vol. 2. Conditioned reflexes and psychiatry. New York, NY: International Publishers.

Peggs, K. 2012. *Animals and Sociology.* New York: Palgrave.

Pettit, M. 2012. The queer life of a lab rat. *History of Psychology*, 15(3), 217–227.

Potts, A. 2010. Introduction: Combating speciesism in psychology and feminism. *Feminism & Psychology*, 20, 291–301.

Potts, A. and Haraway, D. 2010. Kiwi chicken advocate talks with Californian dog companion. *Feminism and Psychology*, 20(3), 318–336.

Plumwood, V. 2002. *Environmental Culture: The Ecological Crisis of Reason.* London: Routledge.

Preece, R. 2006. *Awe for the Tiger, Love for the Lamb: A Chronicle of Sensibility to Animals.* London: Routledge.

Reicher, S., Haslam, S. A. and Van Bavel, J. 2018. Time to change the story. *The Psychologist*, August 2018, 31, 2–3 Accessed 08/07/19 https://thepsychologist.bps.org.uk/volume-31/august-2018/time-change-story.

Richards, G. 2010, *Putting Psychology in its Place: An Introduction from a Critical Historical Perspective*, 3rd edn. Hove: Psychology Press.

Rüting, T. 2007. Ivan Petrovich Pavlov. In Rupke, N. A. (Ed.), *Eminent Lives in Twentieth Century Science and Religion.* London: Peter Lang, pp. 177–195.

Ryder, R. D. 1975. *Victims of Science. The Use of Animals in Research.* London: Davis-Poynter.

Sanders, C. R. and Arluke, A. 1993. If lions could speak: Investigating the animal-human relationship and the perspectives of nonhuman others. *Sociological Quarterly*, 34(3), 377–390.

Safina, C. 2015. *Beyond Words: What Animals Think and Feel.* Connecticut: Tantor Media.

Sanders, C. 2007. The sociology of nonhuman animals and society. In C. Bryant and D. Peck (Eds.), *21st Century Sociology. A Reference Handbook*, Vol. 2. Thousand Oaks, CA: Sage, pp. 2–7.

Serpell, J. A. 2009. Having our dogs and eating them too: Why animals are a social issue. *Journal of Social Issues*, 65, 633–644.

Sevillano, V. and Fiske, S. T. 2016. Animals as social objects. *European Psychologist*, 21(3), 206–217.

Shapiro, K. 2017. Human-animal studies: Fertile ground for qualitative analysis. *Society of Qualitative Investigations in Psychology*, May 25, 2017, Fordham University.

Shapiro, K. J. 1990. Understanding dogs through kinesthetic empathy, social construction, and history. *Anthrozoös*, 3(3), 184–195.

Shapiro, K. J. 2010. Psychology and human-animal studies. In DeMello, M. (Ed.), *Teaching the Animal: Human-Animal Studies across the Disciplines.* Brooklyn, NY: Lantern Books, pp. 254–280.

Smart, A. and Smart, J. 2017. *Posthumanism: Anthropological Insights.* Toronto: University of Toronto Press.

Smith, G. P. 1995. Pavlov and appetite. *Integrative Physiological and Behavioral Science*, 30(2), 169–174.

Sollund, R. 2011. Expressions of speciesism: The effects of keeping companion animals on animal abuse, animal trafficking and species decline. *Crime, Law and Social Change*, 55(5), 437–451.

Specter, D. 2014. Drool: Ivan Pavlov's real quest. *The New Yorker.* November 24th 2014 issue. Accessed 08/07/19 https://www.newyorker.com/magazine/2014/11/24/drool.

Stanley, S. 2012. Mindfulness: Towards a critical relational perspective. *Social and Personality Psychology Compass*, 6(9), 631–641.

Todes, D. P. 1997a. Pavlov's physiology factory. *Isis*, 88(2), 205–246.

Todes, D. P. 1997b. From the machine to the ghost within: Pavlov's transition from digestive physiology. *American Psychologist*, 52(9), 947–955.

Todes, D. P. 2000. *Ivan Pavlov: Exploring the Animal Machine*. Oxford: Oxford University Press.

Todes, D. P. 2002. *Pavlov's Physiology Factory: Experiment, Interpretation, Laboratory Enterprise*. Baltimore: John Hopkins University Press.

Todes, D. P. 2014. *Ivan Pavlov: A Russian Life in Science*. Oxford: Oxford University Press.

Tomley, S. 2012. *The Psychology Book: Big Ideas Simply Explained*. London: Dorling Kinsley.

Train, B. 2007. *Fresh Perspectives: Introduction to Psychology*. Capetown, SA: Pearson.

Tsing, A. L. 2015. *The Mushroom at the End of the World: On the Possibility of Life in Capitalist Ruins*. Princeton, NJ: Princeton University Press.

Tucker, S. D. 2016. *Forgotten Science: Strange Ideas from the Scrapheap of History*. Stroud: Amberley Publishing.

Tully, T. 2003. Pavlov's dogs. *Current Biology*, 13(4), R117–R119.

Tyson, P. J., Jones, D. and Elcock, J. 2011. *Psychology in Social Context: Issues and Debates*. London: John Wiley and Sons.

Watts, C. (Ed.). 2013. *Relational Archaeologies: Humans, Animals, Things*. London: Routledge.

Whatmore, S. 2006. Materialist returns: Practising cultural geography in and for a more-than-human world. *Cultural Geographies*, 13(4), 600–609.

Wildman, W. J. 2010. An introduction to relational ontology. In J. Polkinghorne (Ed.), *The Trinity and an Entangled World: Relationality in Physical Science and Theology*. Grand Rapids, MI: Eerdmans, pp. 55–73.

Wilkie, R. 2015. Multispecies scholarship and encounters: Changing assumptions at the human-animal nexus. *Sociology*, 49(2), 323–339.

Windholz, G. 1990. Pavlov and the Pavlovians in the laboratory. *Journal of the History of the Behavioral Sciences*, 26(1), 64–74.

Windholz, G. 1997. Ivan P. Pavlov: An overview of his life and psychological work. *American Psychologist*, 52(9), 941–946.

Windholz, G. and Lamal, P. A. 1986. Pavlov and the concept of association. *The Pavlovian Journal of Biological Science*, 21(1), 12–15.

Wright, S. 2015. More-than-human, emergent belongings: A weak theory approach. *Progress in Human Geography*, 39(4), 391–411.

Yegorov, O. 2018. Who let the dogs out: 7 of the most famous canine creatures in Russian culture. *Russia Beyond*, January 2 2018. Accessed 08/07/19 https://www.rbth.com/arts/327179-most-famous-russian-dogs.

York, R. and Longo, S. B. 2017. Animals in the world: A materialist approach to sociological animal studies. *Journal of Sociology*, 53(1), 32–46.

3

EATING ANIMALS IN THE ANTHROPOCENE

The broiler chicken, speciesism and vegatopia

What strikes one forcibly is also the reluctance to define cruelty in relation to animals reared and killed for meat. In fact if one person is unkind to an animal it is considered to be cruelty, but where a lot of people are unkind to a lot of animals, especially in the name of commerce, the cruelty is condoned and... will be defended to the last by otherwise intelligent people.

Ruth Harrison

Animals are the main victims of history, and the treatment of domesticated animals in industrial farms is perhaps the worst crime in history.

Yuval Noah Harari[1]

Introduction

The putative Anthropocene Epoch, marking the unprecedented influence of human activity on all forms of planetary life (Steffen et al., 2007), brings human relations to other species into sharp focus. The Anthropocene consolidates the notion of human influence 'on' ecological systems, but it is additionally a way of amplifying the interrelationship and interdependence that define the co-constitution of human and other forms of life. The Human Animal Research Network

Editorial Collective argues that as a discourse, it is paradoxical, capable of both perpetuating and deepening 'a western hierarchy, at the same time that it scrambles and troubles the dualisms on which it rests' (2015, p. ix). Emphasis on the latter is marked by a 're-orientation towards relationality' (ibid) and a 'relational ontology' (Adams, 2018; Lidskog and Waterton, 2018). It is also therefore an invitation to question human-animal and human-nonhuman boundaries and (re)discover and develop models of trans-species reciprocity and interdependence (Adams, 2016b).

Echoing John Rodman's earlier critique of Singer's animal rights agenda, such an invitation envisions a society based on the value of propriety, that is, the principle that 'action should be appropriate to the nature of all parties involved in the transaction, accompanied by the corollary recognition that nonhuman species exist "in their own right" (have their own origin, structure, tendencies, etc.) and not simply "for us"' (Rodman, 1977, p. 109). In fact, Rodman's account pre-empts numerous Anthropocene questions, including 'what does it mean to say that a totally humanized world would diminish us as human beings, to imply that we need nonhuman nature, that we draw sustenance from it, commune with it, find inspiration in its example? Does it not... at least suggest that common principles, common values, animate both it and us and that their loss in either realm is a loss of value?' (Rodman, 1977, p. 116). Taking human-animal relations seriously means addressing how those relations embody and are embedded in intersecting social, political and psychological processes of the Anthropocene and what the possibilities are for imagining and enacting alternative practices collectively. This chapter does so by focusing in on an especially fraught and complex manifestation of those relations – animal agriculture and the problem of meat.

Anthropocene chicken

Geologists of the Anthropocene argue that future evidence of this epoch – its 'sharpest and strongest signals' – will include the fossilised remains of domestic chickens (Zalasiewicz et al., 2010). The remarkably rapid growth in the number and size of chickens over a relatively short period of time means their carcasses are being amassed on an unprecedented scale; their 'skeletons are being fossilised in thousands of landfill sites and on street corners around the world' (Zalasiewicz, cited in Carrington, 2016) and will likely be a prevalent biostratigraphic signal of human activity for any future species that cares to dig deep and deliberate on Earth's geological past (Bennett et al., 2018). First, the size: the chicken has been around for a while and was first domesticated approximately 8,000 years ago (Peters et al., 2016; Potts, 2012). But the modern 'broiler' chicken (meaning young and easily cooked), is notably distinct from even its recent ancestors, especially since the mid-twentieth century (a possible starting point for the Anthropocene), with scientific and technical advances in poultry and egg farming dedicated to the production of larger chickens, more quickly, and on less feed (Siegel, 2014).[2] According to US industry figures (National Chicken Council [US], 2019a), in just under 100 years, the market weight of broiler chickens has more than doubled (from 1.13 to 2.84 kg), while the ratio of feed to chicken has more than halved (from 1:4.7 to 1:1.82).[3] Over the same period, the time it takes to raise a chick from birth to 'market weight', that is, the average lifespan of a chicken, has reduced from 16 weeks to 5–7 weeks.[4] Of course, such efficiency 'gains' depend on intense, mass-scale factory rearing of chickens and the rationalised 'vertical integration' of broiler units, farms, slaughterhouses, processing and packaging plants, marketing and distribution (Bennett et al., 2018). Second, the numbers, which are difficult to comprehend. Although markedly different in size, the domestic chicken would not be a contender for Anthropocene signal were it not for the speed and scale of their (unrequested) global abundance. There are an estimated 23 billion chickens on the planet at any one time, roughly three chickens for every human, by far the most numerous bird species alive today.[5] The vast majority of these are intensely reared broiler chickens or egg-laying hens (Briggs, 2018). Other than fish, chickens are the animals most frequently killed for food (Sanders, 2018). The number slaughtered annually (as of 2016) is estimated by the United Nations at 66 billion (FAO, 2019; Ritchie and Roser, 2017), compared to 1.5 billion pigs and 0.3 billion cattle (Bennett et al., 2018). In the United States alone, over 9 billion broiler chickens were slaughtered in 2018 (National Chicken Council [US], 2019b); 90 million were killed in the United Kingdom in the same year (Farming UK, 2019). The sheer scale of routinised violence and killing of animals that these figures imply is staggering (Cudworth, 2015), a point we return to below.

Whilst astounding in their own right, numbers do not reveal the scale of their impact upon the planet and other forms of life. The rapid growth of broiler chickens inversely parallels a decline in wild birds, the former significantly contributing to habitat loss and species extinction as more land is cleared for livestock, for crops to feed the animals, and more resources are needed to maintain all links in the system of vertical integration it depends upon. Chickens are at the apex of a rapid global spread of farmed animals, reflecting a rising human population's inclination for the consumption of animal protein. More humans, raising and eating more domesticated animals, significantly contribute to the extinction of wild species, habitat loss and greenhouse gas (GHG) emissions (Reynolds, 2013). According to the United Nations, the large-scale industrial farming of animals for meat and related products makes a 'very substantial contribution' to 'climate change and air pollution, to land, soil and water degradation and to the reduction of biodiversity' (Steinfeld et al., 2006, p. iii). In fact, the livestock sector is considered one of 'the top two or three most significant contributors to the most serious environmental problems, at every scale from local to global' (ibid.). To state a few more figures baldly: of all the species on land, domesticated animals now make up the majority, and of all the domesticated animals alive at any moment, 99% are animal agriculture commodities (Cudworth, 2015, p. 1). Farmed animals eat a third of all the food grown on the planet, almost four-fifths of agricultural land is used for the production of animal feed and a quarter of the Earth's ice-free terrestrial surface is used for grazing (Bennett et al., 2018; FAO, 2019; Percival, 2017; Marinova and Bogueva, 2019). Percival provocatively describes the globalised industry of animal farming as a 'double-kill system' (Percival, 2017), following Eschel: 'now we can say, only slightly fancifully: you eat a steak, you kill a lemur in Madagascar. You eat a chicken, you kill an Amazonian parrot' (Eschel, cited in Morell, 2015, p. 1).

Industrialised animal agriculture

Consideration of the broiler chicken forms the basis for an examination of one of the defining features of the Anthropocene – the raising and killing of animals for meat and related by-products. If we provisionally accept the suggested start date as the 'Great Acceleration' of the 1950s, this also coincides with the emergence and then rapid rise of intensive, industrial animal agriculture. Since the Anthropocene was first defined, human–animal relations have figured centrally. Crutzen and Stoermer (2000) included the growth of global cattle populations; species extinction rates and the rise of industrial fisheries as key markers, alongside GHG emissions and the now-familiar carbon spheres emitted by power stations, radioactive elements from nuclear bomb tests, plastic pollution, concrete and nitrogen and phosphate (from fertilisers) in soils are other signals (Waters et al., 2016). Whilst it has many travelling companions then, the humble broiler chicken is a powerful signifier of the Anthropocene story – 'a striking example of a human reconfigured biosphere' (Bennett et al., 2018, p. 2). It offers a prime example of the normalisation of animals as domesticated, the ones we consume usually out of everyday sight (at least whilst alive). Absolute and per capita chicken slaughter continues to increase on all continents (Sanders, 2018), and, despite variations, so does meat production more generally, a trend set to continue well into the mid-century (Alexandratos and Bruinsma, 2012; Godfray et al., 2018). Chakrabarty is partly right, then, in stating that 'as an idea, the Anthropocene represents the makers of geology inscribing themselves into their own rock record' (2009, p. 207). But it is not just one species we are inscribing, it is our relations to other species – systematised and institutionalised – as they are reflected in the distinct corporeality of amassed carcasses and skeletal remains. Nowhere is the Anthropocene story more visceral than in the nature and scope of our consumption of animals as meat.

As an exemplar of human and more-than-human entanglement, the broiler chicken also speaks to the Anthropocene as an invitation, as has been articulated in this book. As our entwinement with other species reaches a fever pitch of accelerating harms, risks and potential remedies, it is an invitation to bear witness and reflect, to consider our ethical obligations to nonhuman others, multi-species interdependency, and what it means to live a liveable and meaningful life, in relation. It is a specific manifestation of Anthropocene narrative as confronting culturally embedded ideologies of human exceptionalism and speciesism (Cole and Morgan, 2011a), challenging our collective imagination to reconsider ideas about what constitutes a good life for multiple species on a planetary scale. Industrialised animal agriculture, and the human consumption of meat, are relations between the human and more-than-human world that profoundly impact upon its protagonists, both human and animal, and our broader planetary habitat and ecology. Here, we begin our own inquiry with recent attempts to shine a light on the psychological processes involved in eating meat, especially in the context of environmental, health and ethical counter-imperatives.

As our introductory discussion of the broiler chicken might lead one to guess, the most significant point of human–animal interaction in terms of global scale and scope is animal agriculture, allied with the slaughter and butchery industries (Cudworth, 2015; Hamilton and McCabe, 2016; Potts and Haraway, 2010). Yet in established coverage of human-animal relations as a psychological topic, the chains of interaction that constitute industrial agriculture are only beginning to feature as points of contact, with an emphasis on individuals who eat meat (Bastian and Loughnan, 2017; Dhont and Hodson, 2014) – pets, therapy, zoos, parks and wilderness are much more likely focal points (cf. Clayton and Myers, 2015). If we are to accept, in responding to the Anthropocene invitation, the 'growing call for an acknowledgment of the role of animals in human lives and for a broadening of psychology beyond the human ingroup' (Amiot and Bastian, 2015, p. 32), then we must attend to the problem of the slaughter of animals for meat. How do we approach animal agriculture and the production and consumption of meat in the Anthropocene as a topic for psychology? My intention here is to eschew theory and research concerned with the dynamics of meat-eating as factors and variables of the individual alone, but to still maintain a grounding in individual experience. To this end, we begin with a relatively recent example of an approach rooted in psychology, whilst attempting to understand eating of meat as a manifestation of complex human–animal relations mediated by configurations of biology, culture, history and politics.

The never explicitly stated fact

Bastian and Loughnan's analysis takes the psychological interior as its starting point and works from there outwards to sociocultural dynamics, the latter scaffolded on the demands of the former. They begin with the assumption that the meat-eating individual is commonly beset by a discomforting 'moral conflict', which they label 'the meat paradox' – 'whilst the majority of people the world over eat meat... many of these same people experience discomfort when the meat on their plate is linked to the death of animals' (2017, p. 278). This is 'the never explicitly stated fact: that meat eaters fear having to sacrifice their enjoyment in eating (his hamburger, her chicken, their fishes) to respond to the scandal that is meat eating' (p. 312). The 'scandal' here is the violence and suffering experienced by nonhuman animals in becoming meat. That we go out of our way to deny it is an established premise (Mussgnug, 2019; Harrison, 1964). In 2002, for example, Derrida described the industrialisation of the production and consumption of meat in the following terms:

However one interprets it, whatever practical, technical, scientific, juridical, ethical, or political consequence one draws from it, no one can deny this event any more, no one can deny the *unprecedented* proportions of this subjection of the animal… Neither can one seriously deny the disavowal that this involves. No one can deny seriously, or for very long, that men [sic] do all they can in order to dissimulate this cruelty or to hide it from themselves, in order to organize on a global scale the forgetting or misunderstanding of this violence that some would compare to the worst cases of genocide
(Derrida and Wills, 2002, p. 294; emphasis in the original)

Echoing Derrida, Bastian and Loughnan argue that the discomfort provoked by eating meat runs so deep, the majority are motivated to make it 'vanish into the commonplace and everyday' (2017, p. 278). Adopting what might be referred to as a psychosocial framework, the authors claim that the drive to resolve this discomfort runs virally through social networks via the shaping of habits, descriptive and injunctive social norms and the prejudicial and discriminatory pathways of objectification and dehumanisation. Once established in cognitive patterns, interpersonal networks, rituals, institutions and ideologies, these structures of thinking and feeling in turn deliver 'their citizens from [the] discomfort associated with their own moral conflicts' (p. 278). The authors extensively describe the circuitous route taken to resolve the meat paradox, which is now explored in more detail (see also Chapter 6).

The concept of cognitive dissonance originates in Leon Festinger's fascinating work (Festinger et al., 1956; Festinger and Carlsmith, 1959). Broadly defined, it refers to a felt sense of discomfort that arises from attempting to hold two or more contradictory beliefs, ideas or values, or from engaging in action/behaviour that contradicts the beliefs, ideas or values we hold (Cooper, 2017). Furthermore, humans are fundamentally driven or motivated to reduce that dissonance; we have, Festinger claimed, a proclivity to seek consistency. The concept has been applied, critiqued and debated ever since (e.g. Draycott and Dabbs, 1998; Greenwald and Ronis, 1978; McGrath, 2017), but what interests us more generally here are the intriguing patterns in the way we attempt to reduce dissonance, first formulated by Festinger, and utilised extensively by Bastian and Loughnan to explore the 'meat paradox'.[6]

There are issues in presenting the meat paradox as an applied example of cognitive dissonance, especially in terms of the way it reduces the complexities of the practice of eating meat to a behaviour (eating meat) and a belief or attitude (eating meat is wrong, scandalous). Despite, or perhaps because of, that reductionism, however, it is worth pursuing their logic for the issues it raises. If our behaviour contradicts our beliefs, as it supposedly does in experiencing the meat paradox, dissonance can be resolved simply by aligning one's behaviour with one's beliefs – we can stop eating meat. Like a long line of psychologists before and after, however, Festinger highlights how rational resolution of conflict is rarely our strong suit. If we find giving up the behaviour too challenging a prospect, Festinger argues, we often seek the least effortful ways of reducing dissonance, instead finding different ways to modify our beliefs, ideas or values to justify the behaviour. Building on Festinger's insights, Bastian and Loughnan claim that there are three major pathways through which dissonance appears and is resolved: harm, responsibility and identity: 'by minimizing harm, denying responsibility, and diffusing the identity-relevant implications of their actions, people reduce dissonance and enable their consumption of meat' (2017, p. 280).

The idea that by eating meat we are unjustifiably causing the unnecessary suffering of others is claimed to be an affront to most people's values and therefore a source of dissonance (Graça et al., 2015; Rothgerber, 2014). In response, we minimise the harm involved by making those we eat less morally relevant: they do not have the capacity to experience pain, suffer, understanding – the amount of perceived suffering is minimised. The animals we eat have a good life, are happy, are treated 'humanely' - a perception which again minimises the suffering experienced by the animals we eat; and such perceptions are reinforced by the use of categorisation processes emphasising the uniqueness of humans compared to other animals (Bastian et al., 2012; Bilewicz et al., 2011; Loughnan et al., 2010, 2014). Similarly, in denying responsibility for eating meat, choice over our actions is removed from the equation and conflict is dissolved. Pointing to the ubiquity and normality of meat consumption, positing one's individual behaviour as inconsequential in the wider context and endorsement of the well-known '3 Ns' of meat-eating rationalisation (Joy, 2011) – it is normal, necessary and natural: all help diffuse a sense of responsibility for the harm done to animals.[7] The final pathway incorporates more varied and creative processes utilised to 'buffer' established identities – presumably an amalgam of beliefs, ideas and values – from the implied negative consequences of the behaviour in question. This might involve creative accounting to self and others – underreporting or highlighting selective or moderate consumption (I don't eat meat very often; very little red meat) (Loughnan et al., 2014). Bastian and Loughnan also highlight in-out group processes here – categorising others (avid carnivores *and* vegans) as 'extreme' and related stereotypes of vegans and vegetarians (Cole and Morgan, 2011b; Twine, 2014).

Resolving dissonance becomes habitual, goes viral, gets outsourced

Again following Festinger, these 'active' processes can enable and *increase* a commitment to the behaviour in question – meat eating. In itself, accounting for these dynamics is little help in addressing broader questions relating to human–animal relations in the Anthropocene. It is where they take it next that makes Bastian and Loughnan's analysis interesting, however. As the 'active' strategies noted here are repeated, they are translated into 'passive' processes that further serve to reduce dissonance and reinforce meat eating – they become habitual, go viral and get outsourced. Habit, by definition, is behaviour followed on a plane of reduced awareness, the purposiveness of which has become taken for granted, subsumed into a rarely reflected-upon 'practical consciousness' (Giddens, 1991). Helped along initially by active processes, the behaviour settles into embodied competencies in routinised settings, reducing awareness of conflict involved, and with it the need for active strategies. Habituation thus contributes to meat eating as a routinely unquestioned social practice (Shove et al., 2012). Active dissonance reduction leads to habits developing around meat-eating, which in turn protect us from having to actively consider harm and suffering caused by the practice and reduces experiences of dissonance.

Habits are formed in interpersonal and social contexts that reinforce them. For Bastian and Loughnan, the 'spread' of habitual behaviours through social norms and networks amounts to dissonance reduction strategies 'going viral'. An 'active' individual view of animals as objects, less-than-human or 'dumb', for example, meets a wider cultural framing of farmed animals as a particular outgroup, with attendant stereotypes (Sevillano and Fiske, 2016), which profoundly 'interact with our readiness to eat them' (Amiot and Bastian, 2015, p. 27). These processes underpin habits and overlap with other established discourses. Here, their analysis connects with insights from cultural theory emphasising culture, ideology and intersectionalism in the production of 'meat cultures' (Adams, 2015; Potts, 2016). In terms of gender, for example, 'farmed animals are commonly thought to exhibit a cluster of traits that patriarchal society has filed under "feminine," and that the "stupidly female" nature of these traits is a key a factor in the degraded moral status of these animals' (Parry, 2010, p. 383, citing Davis, 1995).

Stereotypical framing of vegetarians and vegans is also considered part of dissonance reduction going viral. Again extending this point into insights from social and cultural theory, individual and interpersonal categorisation becomes written into wider cultural dynamics of stigmatisation and othering, firming up one's own identity against the denigrated other – as, for example, extreme, unnatural, (too) liberal and excessively feminine (Cole and Morgan, 2011b; Corrin and Papadopoulos, 2017; Markowski and Roxburgh, 2019; Rothgerber, 2013, Ruby and Heine, 2011). In the context of a drive to reduce dissonance, the viral spread of ideologies of carnism and speciesism offer something akin to scripts, which we can be read off to legitimise meat eating and avoid experiencing the uncomfortable conflict at the heart of the meat paradox. As people utilise these scripts, recruit self and others to the practice of meat-eating and derogate those who defer or oppose, points of view further diverge, engendering wider polarisation in society more generally, amplifying cultural support and bolstering the world view of eating meat as normal, necessary and natural. The more we adhere to culturally supported rationalisations, the more *not* eating meat becomes abnormal, deviant, doubtful and suspicious.

So far, we have followed the argument that a drive for dissonance reduction shapes internal, interpersonal and group processes. In Bastian and Loughnan's final step, they consider how it 'may also shape social structures in ways that work to further avoid dissonance' (2017, p. 285). They describe how dissonance reduction is further 'outsourced' to cultural practices and norms through processes of *institutionalisation* and *ritualisation*. The former refers to the ways in which the meat *production* process is obscured by the numerous institutions directly or indirectly benefitting from it: farms, advertising and branding companies, supermarkets, local and national governments. Echoing established accounts of commodity fetishism in consumer societies, the realities of the production process are hidden to enable the flesh consumed to exist in a magical and internally referential world of signs and symbols (Billig, 1999). Here, the task is specifically to protect people from experiencing the immorality of their meat-eating behaviour. This is achieved by an array of practices including cultural obfuscation, evident in the imagery and language used in the advertising and packaging of meat; the (lack of) visibility of farmed animals in the mass media and in a material distancing, whereby animal agriculture and slaughterhouse industries are physically remote from consumers (Gillespie, 2011; Pilgrim, 2013; Worthy, 2013): 'hidden away in... factory farms, slaughtered at mass disassembly plants and transformed into sanitized packages of meat' (Mussgnug, 2019, p. 122). All of which makes it possible for individuals to eat meat 'without necessarily connecting it to the animals from which it came' (Bastian and Loughnan, 2017, p. 286). As culturally contingent 'ways that things are done', rituals tend to be pursued without much questioning of their origins and consequences, and are therefore considered to work on reducing dissonance in a similar way to habituation. Preparing and eating is meat is central to many holiday, leisure, family and religious traditions, from Thanksgiving, Christmas and Eid al-Adha to the Sunday roast, the barbeque and so on. Vitally, ritualisation is also a path via which meat 'becomes symbolic of a large number of cultural identities' (p. 286) such as masculinity (Ruby and Heine, 2011; Sobal, 2005), but also specific national, ethnic and class identities (de Morais Sato et al., 2016; Heinz and Lee, 1998). Through ritualisation, people's sense of morality is protected by embedding dissonant behaviour within the ready-made consensus and legitimacy that stem from identification with a group.

In sum, the active and passive dynamics of a drive to reduce dissonance serve to reinforce and enhance meat eating practices, throwing 'a powerful veil over immoral behaviour' (Bastian and Loughnan, 2017, p. 287). They entrench habits, routines and rituals that revolve around meat eating as an individual and social practice, initiate and maintain socially organised discourses and ideologies and material infrastructure that *successfully* minimise a sense of harm, diffuse responsibility and buffer one's identity against the discomfort arising from knowing about animal suffering: 'When immorality reappears, people are not lost for ways to defend their psychological equanimity; they just seldom feel the need to' (Bastian and Loughnan, 2017, p. 287). In fact, this comment points to the fact that, in a culture so good at facilitating avoidance, the dissonance-inducing paradox is rarely experienced *as* a paradox. In a 'meat culture' – the representations and discourses, practices and behaviours, diets and tastes that generate shared beliefs about, perspectives on and experiences of meat – alternative narratives are always already available that pre-empt and therefore nullify it (Potts, 2016). In the final analysis, then, experiences of individual dissonance are not the primary driver of meat culture, but a complex material–social–cultural–political–psychological–historical assemblage frames meat in ways which make it palatable. A less cumbersome term to capture some of these intersecting dynamics is *speciesism*.

Speciesism and beyond

As is evident in the work referenced in the previous section, a wealth of literature in related disciplines broadly supports and extends Bastian and Loughnan's analysis – in often more sophisticated cultural analyses at the level of discourse and ideology (e.g. Adams, 2015; Potts, 2016). A prevalent focal point is speciesism, which Potts defines as 'the taken-for-granted belief that humans are superior to and have the right to dominate all other creatures, and that "humanity" alone bears the hallmarks of intelligence and sentience' (Potts, 2010, p. 292). As a pervasive discourse, speciesism is arguably what runs through and connects the active and passive dynamics of dissonance reduction Bastian and Loughnan describe. In fact, Bradshaw and Watkins (2006, p. 7) describe speciesism as something as fundamental as 'a primary cultural organizing principle. Human–animal differencing comprises much of what defines western human collective identity and an ego construct based on what animals are presumed to lack'. Starting from individual drives and working outwards perhaps blunts the radical implications of Bastian and Loughnan's analysis, unnecessarily psychologising and individualising the processes involved (Scotton, 2018), overly reductive in suggesting we are motivated primarily by an individual drive to resolve dissonance. Nonetheless, it adds some welcome specificity and richness to the generality of cultural theoretical approaches asserting the prevalence of speciesism, and helps make sense of the banality and stubborn pervasiveness of speciesist logic.[8]

There are more detailed discussions of speciesism as ideology and its intersections with other powerful social categorisations and overlapping and interdependent systems of discrimination, disadvantage and violence (e.g. Adams, 2015; Cudworth, 2014, Glasser, 2011; Monteiro et al., 2017). In the context of this chapter, combined with Bastian and Loughnan's analysis, the piling up of chicken carcasses as Anthropocene signal, and at a global level a rising average per capita and total consumption of meat, a greater proportion of which is processed prior to purchase (FAO, 2018; Godfray et al., 2018), paints a bleak and inescapable picture of the ongoing plight of industrially farmed animals and our willingness to eat them. However, in stressing the Anthropocene as an *invitation*, the guiding principle of this book, are there signs of a new or resurgent reassessment of meat as a human–animal relation?

Although some of the negative environmental impacts of animal agriculture are long established, the growing recognition of a climate, species loss and ecological crisis has been accompanied by attempts to identify the most destructive global practices. As described at the beginning of this chapter, these have included highlighting the greenhouse gas emissions involved in animal agriculture, and related demands on land and water (FAO, 2019). The UN, many NGOs, scientists, campaign groups, political parties and media organisations now explicitly support measures encouraging a reduction in meat production and/or consumption (e.g. Green Party UK, 2019; Greenpeace, 2019; Machovina et al., 2015). In terms of the now familiar lists of 'environmentally friendly' changes we can make as individuals, consuming less meat now features prominently; it is common to emphasise in parallel the health benefits of reduced consumption of processed meat as a double-win (Carrington, 2019). *Food in the Anthropocene* (Willett et al., 2019), for example, a report from an international collaboration of scientists, focuses on how although they currently threaten both, 'food systems have the potential to nurture human health and support environmental sustainability' (p. 1). As is common in this health-environment focus, however, there is no mention of human responsibility for the lives or welfare of farmed animals in the Anthropocene. Such narratives result from a reconsideration of human impact on the environment, but they are not necessarily about, or primarily concerned with, an ethical commitment to other species.

In other words, it might be argued that these developments do *not* fundamentally threaten the meat paradox, and speciesism as a primary cultural organising principle remains intact in the Anthropocene imaginary to date. Following the twin environment-health logic, if the carbon footprint of animal agriculture could miraculously be reduced, and processed meat made healthier for human consumption, there would be presumably be no further problem. But, of course, there has always been an explicitly ethical counter-narrative, challenging the system of industrial farming and the ideology of speciesism, the defence of animal rights stretching back further still (e.g. Salt, 1892). Ruth Harrison's *Animal Machines* (1964), a quote from which opens this chapter, was a pivotal moment in the development of that narrative, a response to new systems of industrial agriculture that were emerging, at a time many now consider as a contender for the beginning of the Anthropocene (Bellio, 2015). She clearly and candidly revealed the lives and deaths of industrially farmed animals. At the time, the book generated a sizeable public reaction, a Ministry of Agriculture investigation and subsequently the Brambell report and an Act of Parliament designed to govern farm animal welfare in this rapidly growing industry. It was also significant in the emergence of a new wave of animal advocacy, with an essay from Harrison opening an important edited collection from a group of British scholars (Godlovitch et al., 1971), in which Richard Ryder first used the term 'speciesism'. However, animal advocacy did not feature heavily in the development of environmentalist narratives from that time onwards. *Animal Machines* was published only two years after Rachel Carson's *Silent Spring* and featured a foreword by her, but it is now largely forgotten.[9] As Carol Adams points out, it is a shame Harrison's book did not share the spotlight with Carson's in shaping the perspective of environmental activists to include industrial agriculture (Adams, 2016a) and today is largely absent from human–animal studies teaching and scholarship (e.g. DeMello, 2010). Perhaps it is a reflection of just how psychologically and culturally embedded the meat paradox really is.[10]

Nonetheless, Harrison has been followed by many attempts to draw attention to the ethical issues pertaining to industrial farming and meat. Forty and more years later, on the back of 'robust theory and activism' spurred on by feminist thinking (Adams, 2016a), established and emerging fields tackling the issues involved include critical animal studies, ecofeminism, trans-species psychology, multi-species ethnography, posthumanities and sociologies of violence (e.g. Adams and Donovan, 1995; Adams and Gruen, 2014; Best et al., 2007; Bradshaw and Watkins, 2006; Cudworth, 2015; Haraway, 2013; Kirksey and Helmreich, 2010). Whilst often opposed to 'any sense of generic human responsibility' (Connolly, 2017, p. 33), a number of these developments embrace the Anthropocene as a framework for a profound reconsideration of human and nonhuman animal entanglement, some of which addresses farmed animals (e.g. Bovenkerk and Keulartz, 2016; Donaldson and Kymlicka, 2011; Gabardi, 2017; Human Animal Research Network Editorial Collective, 2015; Sexton, 2018).

Greater attention is also being paid to the emotional and psychological costs for *humans* working in these industries, especially the 'dangerous and demoralizing' work in slaughterhouses (Blanchette, 2015, 2019;

Blaznik, 2018; Hamilton and McCabe, 2016; jones, 2010; Muller, 2018; Wasley, 2015). Ethnographers, for example, have documented human–animal entanglement in the 'surge in the speed of industrial slaughterhouses, with their concomitant increase in both the quantities of animal carcasses they generate and the human workers' bodies that they reshape through repetitive motion injuries' (Blanchette, 2018, p. 186; Ribas, 2016). The demands of this work in contemporary factory farming systems on the scale described earlier, so often hidden as part and parcel of the material distancing of meat consumption and production highlighted by Bastian and Loughnan, are gradually being revealed (e.g. Food Empowerment Project, 2019). Increased line speeds and 'efficiency' measures demand an enormous amount of killing under severe time pressures – a 'pig-sticker', for example, will cut up to 1,100 throats an hour in an industrial abattoir (Percival, 2017). Numerous opportunities for mistakes mean animals are inadvertently injured, partially severed, burnt or boiled – also harrowing experiences for workers (Potts, 2012). In Europe and the United States, workers are often undocumented, on temporary contracts, low-paid, in unsafe environments and unaware of their rights or how to complain (Wasley and Heal, 2018). We are confronted with a historically contingent biopower – 'an explosion of numerous and diverse techniques for achieving the subjugations of bodies and the control of populations' (Foucault, 1976, p. 140) that operates simultaneously across 'asymmetrically valued' human–human *and* human–nonhuman populations (Cavanagh, 2014, p. 273).[11] Bluntly stated, 'vulnerable animals are often slaughtered by some of society's most vulnerable humans' (Newkey-Burden, 2018).

Such developments are gaining increasing visibility and arguably represent a piercing of the veil of meat culture, encouraging more of us to bear witness and mount a critical challenge. However, in the context of the analysis above, is it a movement as yet beyond the reach of a psychosocial proclivity to reduce dissonance as it intersects with meat culture and speciesism as a primary cultural organising principle, and therefore one that is unlikely to challenge the habitual, culturally viral and socially structured outsourced dynamics of the meat paradox? If taken alone, perhaps, but this resurgent and growing interdisciplinary emphasis is mirrored elsewhere, in an increasingly vocal, indignant and creative activism, arguably manifesting as a more or less explicit acceptance of the Anthropocene as invitation (Adams, 2016b). This book documents resurgent attention to human and more-than-human relations placing 'a fresh emphasis on the subjectivity and agency of organisms whose lives are entangled with humans' (Kirksey and Helmreich, 2010, p. 545). It is grounded in serious consideration of multi- and inter-species ethics, care and conviviality, spurred on by critical engagement with an Anthropocene imaginary. It is also evident in contemporary farmed animal advocacy and activism.

Disclosing cultural secrets of systemic violence

In addressing animal agriculture in the Anthropocene, of great interest are 'the possibilities of narrative to disturb and disclose cultural secrets of systemic violence' (Boyde, 2018, p. 9). Attempts to document the practices of animal agriculture, the scale of the violence and suffering involved, have become increasingly sophisticated, as has the ability to communicate such attempts. Reliable global figures and statistical analysis are part of this documentation, but also the actions of NGOs, charities and campaign groups adeptly combining media and communication with the ability to share rapidly and widely through social media networks. This includes the use of high production techniques in producing imagery and film and the adoption of developing media technologies such as virtual reality (VR).[12]

An example of the former is Last Chance for Animals' short film *Casa de Carne* (Brown, 2019a). Set in the near future, the film opens in a high-end restaurant, at a table of three friends. The waiter introduces himself with the line 'Welcome to Casa de Carne. We take the dining experience full circle'. For one of the friends, this is their first visit, and they choose 'baby back ribs'. As the narrative unfolds, the meaning of 'full circle' becomes apparent (spoiler alert) – the diner is led away to a back room of the restaurant, handed a butcher's knife and informed he must slaughter the pig himself. Sumptuously shot in the style of a contemporary horror/thriller, the denouement is shocking. The film has won numerous industry awards and was viewed over 2 million times in the first year of its release. The writer and director's comments are illustrative of the film's intended impact:

> I'd like this film to make people think and question their everyday reality. Now more than ever, we need stories that expand our circle of empathy and allow us to see the world through a more compassionate lens. It's easy to use our differences as starting points for conflict: different race, different religion, different

country… different species. And yet, we're all sharing this planet.
Our similarities far outweigh our differences

(Brown, 2019b)

Thanks to a combination of smartphones, cardboard glasses and video
software development, readily accessible, immersive, perspective-
taking videos are also increasingly being produced. The wedding of
emerging VR technology with environmental and sustainable behaviour
campaigning is at a very early stage, but a recent example of VR being
utilised in relation to the ethics of animal agriculture is *ianimal*,
developed by the charity Animal Equality.[13] Narrated by 'compassionate
celebrities', the films allow users to take the perspective of a farmed
animal – pigs, chickens, calves and cows at time of writing – via a 360°
'tour', revealing the conditions of life and death in the factory. The
campaigning logic is simple – such technology viscerally confronts
participants with the living and dying conditions of the animals in
question – the power of the immersive, perspective-taking VR
experience means participants make a more direct experiential
connection with the animals in question. Outreach events, ready
availability on social media, the relative simplicity of the additional
technology and the ubiquity of the smartphone mean that developments
such as this have an enormous potential audience.

Vegatopia?

If these examples share the intention of conscientisation and encouraging a
behavioural shift in ways that reflects greater empathy for farmed animals,
clearly there is the potential for them backfiring if we adopt Bastian and
Loughnan's conceptual frame. Confronting us with the morally troublesome
practice of eating meat might amplify discomfort, whereby we double
down on dissonance reduction strategies, increasing our commitment to
meat eating, an endorsement of speciesism, and a further polarisation of
positions. Bastian and Loughnan explicitly state that attempts like this to
make individuals aware of the immorality of cherished behaviours are 'like
a drop in the ocean when habits, institutions, and rituals provide a powerful
anchor for people to avoid dissonance' (2017, p. 281). Whilst still marginal
as artefacts of popular culture and limited in terms of social influence, other
inroads are being made into habits, institutions and rituals, developments
suggesting at least a loosening of that anchor.

Alongside narratives of disturbance and disclosure, there is also a distinctly hopeful, even utopian, element to contemporary approaches to the posthuman and more-than-human (Wadiwel, 2018). In pursuing the Anthropocene imaginary as invitation in the context of animal agriculture and meat, one specific and situated acceptance of this invitation has been the push to reduce the production and consumption of meat and an accompanying pull of veganism and adoption of plant-based lifestyles for a growing number of citizens nurtured in a meat culture (Potts, 2016). Whether through collective pressure on policy makers and businesses, or more individualised 'how to take effective climate action' lists, animal agriculture is now featuring more prominently as a culturally legitimate concern. There is a proliferation of calls to incentivise plant-based diets through taxes, to stop or consume fewer animal products and the growing cultural presence and practice of veganism and vegetarianism, if against a backdrop of persistent speciesism (Cole and Morgan, 2011a).

Explicit identification with veganism, vegetarianism and 'flexitarianism' (intentionally reducing meat consumption) has grown rapidly in the early twenty-first century in countries including Australia, China, South Africa, United Arab Emirates, the United States and much of Europe, an increase especially marked among younger people and set to continue – with the fastest-growing markets forecast for China, the United Arab Emirates and Australia. The Asia–Pacific region has long maintained the highest number of vegetarians and vegans, a reflection of the historical influence of Buddhist and Hinduist religious practices.[14] Many institutions, organisations, supermarkets and government at different levels reflect and drive this shift, adopting practices which encourage reduced meat consumption. In 2018, for example, it was reported that the German government had removed meat from official functions for 'environmental reasons' (Huggler, 2017). Whilst ostensibly driven by growing recognition of the environmental and health impacts of the livestock sector globally, part of this shift is a broader, resurgent inquiry into the complex meanings and practices of eating and not eating meat – in terms of one's own health, environmental impacts, animal rights *and* welfare (Greenebaum, 2012; Radnitz et al., 2015).

Despite the growth in veganism and vegetarianism, it remains a niche practice, much vilified and ridiculed (Stewart and Cole, 2018). The visibility of such practices might well be accompanied by more derision and outrage from many commentators, perhaps supporting

Bastian and Loughnan's counter-intuitive assertion that being confronted with the cause of dissonance can amplify both one's commitment to meat eating and encourage hostility towards those drawing attention to the source of one's discomfort. As Adams puts it, 'discovering a feeling of guilt or uneasiness in themselves, they assume it is we who have placed it there. In other words, since it is assumed that I am going to make you feel uneasy, and you discover that indeed you do feel uneasy, then I must have done it' (Adams, 2010 p. 313). However, the combination of growing support from animal science, creative approaches to campaigning, artistic endeavours and increased academic attention, increasingly framed within the political and existential ferment that is the Anthropocene, meat production and consumption are increasingly being questioned from all sides.

Might these changes perhaps encourage shifts at various points along the networks of influence described by Bastian and Loughnan, chipping away at defensive responses to the meat paradox at micro, meso and macro levels? A revived sociology of practise, particularly developments in social practice theory (e.g. Shove et al., 2012), argues that it is often subtle shifts across these multiple levels of experience – cultural conventions, materials and embodied competencies – that facilitate 'defection' from established practices and 'recruitment' to alternatives, including from meat eating to veganism (Twine, 2014, 2018). Thus, Twine describes the greater visibility of vegan products in mainstream supermarkets, and especially substitute products, an expanded vegan network and community of practice facilitated by social media (sharing advice on recipes, ingredients, sources) and the reinforcing experiences of experimentation and new tastes: all contributing to the nascent social normalisation of veganism despite the dominance of meat culture (Twine, 2018).

One attempt to *imagine* more widespread social normalisation, also perhaps a more complex example of conscientisation, is the feature-length film *Carnage*, commissioned not by a campaign group but, perhaps surprisingly, the BBC (2017). *Carnage* is a 'mockumentary' (i.e. depicting fictional events but presented as a documentary), written and directed by British comedian and writer Simon Amstell. The film depicts a 2067 utopia where humans no longer raise animals for consumption. A Bill of Animal Rights has been passed, abattoirs have become repurposed as museums to honour past horrors, whilst 'older generations are suffering the guilt of their carnivorous past' (BBC, 2017). It intersperses life in 2067 with a history of how the social transition from carnism to veganism came about, stretching back to the mid-twentieth century. By switching between archive television footage of TV chefs, factory farm practices, fast food advertising, the BSE crisis and the 'present day' of the utopian future, the film cleverly creates an 'outside' standpoint from which the factory farming of animals and the consumption of meat is freshly framed as ethically abhorrent. Though comedic in its various representations of vegans, utopian ideals and resistant meat eaters, *Carnage* is powerful and provocative. In what we might refer to as a counterfactual portrayal of a possible future (Pargman et al., 2017; Todorova, 2015), a basis is provided for a reinterpretation of the past and present within a different narrative frame (Adams, 2017).

It is interesting to ask here how Bastian and Loughnan themselves envisage significant social change coming about, considering the extent to which their analysis embeds a majority in a speciesist meat culture. The answer is that the authors give scant consideration to the possibility of widespread change; in fact, they conclude by reiterating how the various 'forces' they described 'interlock' (2017, p. 293). They tackle the issue once, briefly, as follows (p. 288):

> If widespread change does occur, it is likely to be catastrophic, where acute circumstances raise the experience of dissonance within large segments of a given population simultaneously. As the process of social influence reverses and collective soul searching leads to the deconstruction of protective social norms, feelings of unresolved dissonance will motivate a push toward prohibition and behavior change.

A series of 'catastrophic' and 'acute' circumstances followed by 'collective soul searching' is precisely what *Carnage* integrates into its counterfactual narrative. Whilst change is portrayed as gradual at first, a combination of climate crisis, disease and regicide provokes a vegan 'revolution' after which a plant-based diet becomes the norm and meat is prohibited, though there is still dissent (debate subsequently comes to an end with the invention of a 'Thought Translator', which allows humans to understand and communicate with animals). Leading up to the 'present day' (the year 2067), collective soul searching is depicted extensively via characters' televised confessions, psychotherapy and group support sessions.

Whether cataclysm of one kind or another is the only likely instigator of radical change is uncertain. Whilst pessimistic, at times the optimism of utopian visions of more-than-human or posthuman can, in contrast, seem unwarranted. In relation to the scientific knowledge mentioned above, for example, trans-species psychologist Gay Bradshaw claims unconvincingly that 'by recognizing a shared psychobiology, science [has] catalysed a move from anthropocentrism to ecocentrism' (2009, p. 160). Bastian and Loughnan are not alone in pointing to the persistence and complexity of human exceptionalism, materially, ideologically, culturally and psychologically. That said, it would be wrong to imagine the various developments described here as taking root in isolation. Narratives drawing on environmental, health and ethical rationalisations for challenging the practices of animal agriculture or reducing meat consumption may well cross-fertilise and mutually encourage a more culturally supportive context for their flourishing, whether or not they explicitly recognise the logic and symbolism of each other. jones [sic] here describes a link between environmental and ethical imperatives at the level of the psyche: 'To eat those burgers, we have to tune out not only the FAO [Food and Agriculture Organization of the United Nations – warns us that animal agriculture contributes more to climate change than any other industry] but also the bellowing fear of cows forced onto the killing floor. Could there be a connection between these two kinds of not listening?' (jones, 2010, p. 366). To ask a related question, could listening to one help us hear the other?

Killing without making killable

This is not to suggest that greater attentiveness to and empathy for human and nonhuman life at the heart of animal agriculture leads normatively to a collective adoption of veganism (Potts and Haraway, 2010). Bastian and Loughnan's analysis brackets out difficult issues of when and how the killing of animals *is* justifiable. By implying that eating meat and knowing about suffering and violence are incommensurable, all psychological and social rationalisations of killing animals are already ascribed to the category of 'strategy to reduce dissonance'. However, animal agriculture and meat eating *are* morally defensible – in that people defend it as such, in ways that cannot readily be reduced to a by-product of a drive to reduce dissonance. Donna Haraway's consideration of the possibility of 'killing without making killable' is a case in point (Haraway, 2008, 2003; Potts and Haraway, 2010). The phrase refers to Haraway's assertion that the killing of others and being killed is a relationship and an unavoidable aspect of living and dying on Earth. When killing is framed as 'the act of a subject done to an object' (Haraway, in Potts and Haraway, 2010, p. 329), a sense of relationship and responsibility is denied. This is what Carol Adams, Bastian and Loughnan and many others point to as aiding and abetting the normalisation of eating meat – the objectification of the animal and related categorisations which justify it. Yet Haraway resists collapsing all killing of animals for meat within this frame (p. 329):

> I am in every way opposed to and active against many – most – contemporary industrial factory-farming human–animal entanglements, both locally and globally. However, I am appalled by the notion that the myriad domestic working animals, individuals and kinds, should not exist except as rescue, pet, or heritage remnants, and by the related position that all these diverse human–animal ways of living, dying, nurturing, and killing should be banished from our presents and futures. I am appalled by the lack of respect for human–animal labor implied in what to me seem to be right to life positions in some versions of animal liberation thinking on animal factory farming.

Haraway considers whether killing *without* making killable is possible, and defensible, in relation to numerous human–animal relational domains, including 'breeding, raising and killing working food and fiber animals' (p. 330). Haraway only lightly sketches what this might involve as a practice – acknowledgement of the co-evolving webs in which humans and domestic animals are enmeshed, and violence and killing as unavoidably constituent of those networks; respect for human–animal labour; deconstructing categories that make animals 'killable' – elements which together equate to a clear-sighted responsibility for the act of killing and any pain and cruelty involved. 'In short, symbiogenetic living and dying in asymmetric company with co-diners, in pleasure and terror, is the name of earth's evolutionary and historical cats-cradle patterns' (p. 330). Haraway's approach has been subject to some debate (e.g. Giraud, 2013; Singh and Dave, 2015), but whatever position we take, it seems nonsensical to reduce such arguments to psychological attempts to resolve uncomfortable experiences of dissonance.

Veganism as decolonial act?

Though the main focus of this chapter has been academic work and activism in the West and/or Northern Hemisphere, the issues raised are being taken up globally (Feliz Brueck, 2017; Worth, 2010). Just as meat cultures are plural and historically contingent, challenges, both new and established, are plural, and, as noted above, can trace roots in many cultural and religious traditions (Harper, 2010a). Alternative practises, rituals and institutions exist and emerge in different places, sometimes at far remove from each other, but also, in a globalised world, as entangled and hybrid forms. Kirsty Dunn (2019) thoughtfully interweaves a personal account of indigenous and vegan identity with an analysis of wider attempts to address the perceived incompatibility of Māoritanga (meaning Māori culture, practices, way of life) and veganism. Dunn describes some of the barriers, or perceived barriers, to adopting veganism as a Māori. Whilst there are numerous parallels with Western meat culture described above, there are also important specific and situated differences. Perceived incompatibility arises in part from the limited scope of vegan praxis to date, largely positioned and represented as a white Euro-American, privileged, luxury, consumerist lifestyle choice (Harper, 2010b), and in part from the apparent intransigence of authentic and legitimate expressions of indigenous beliefs and practices, including those integral to Māoritanga. In terms of the former, Dunn describes a lack of availability of and access to relevant products, and the physical and virtual spaces of vegan praxis as excluding in their (white) cultural and racial normativity. In terms of the latter, against the backdrop of a long history of colonial occupations and displacements, 'the careful and thoughtful provision of food' remains a vital component of Māoritanga, and 'practices relating to food are key ways in which we can assert ourselves as Māori' (Dunn, 2019, p. 46). Abandoning Māori knowledge and practices that involve killing and using different animal species can be considered a concession to Western, colonial norms, a perceived 'cultural failure'.

Despite these barriers, Dunn is keen to explore how if and how they are overcome, in attempts to integrate veganism and Māoritanga in everyday practices. What she finds, in an analysis of online presentation and discussion of Māori veganism, is an outflowing of creative and constructive rapprochement of veganism and Māoritanga. She discerns both widespread acknowledgement of the challenges veganism poses to some customary practices and accounts of how Māoritanga nonetheless offers a valuable resource for establishing culturally contingent vegan ethics. The latter include drawing on elements of Māori culture emphasising respect and *kaitiakitanga* (care and guardianship) for 'the land, the sea, the plants the people, alive or dead'; 'I took lessons [...]

from my people and extended it to include animals' (p. 51). Dunn argues that kaitiakitanga underpins opposition to both the exploitation of animals and ecological degradation wrought by industrialised agriculture – both common concerns of established veganism. Vegan praxis is also contingently enhanced through *whakapapa* (see Chapter 6) – the genealogies of descent, lineage and relations that incorporate multiple species and fundamentally inform Maori beliefs and practices: 'In light of our whakapapa, our connectedness, there is scope for conceptualising our relationships with other animals, the environments in which we share, and the wider world in nuanced and complex ways' (p. 48). As a practice, whakapapa also translates into 'health discourses of veganism, but enriches it with a conceptualisation of spiritual health and wellbeing, entangled with the possibilities of a plant-based diet as 'a decolonial act' (p. 54).[15]

Finally

None of this is to suggest that some form of pluralist veganism is the ready-made answer to the multiple challenges posed by the Anthropocene. Veganism does not fully address the globally structured asymmetries of power dramatically and unjustly dividing responsibility for, and the effects of, anthropogenic impacts, nor does it necessarily challenge parallel asymmetries in terms of food production outside of animal agriculture (Harper, 2010b). But as we hurtle forwards in an Anthropocene defined by an acceleration of human–animal violence, academic work, art, journalism, social movements and campaign groups are coalescing around a different narrative. They are contributing to a collective imagination that in one way or another accepts the Anthropocene as an invitation - confronting and articulating the scope of violence, noticing attachments, expanded and more nuanced debates, the telling of human–animal entanglement stories. Solnit reminds us that 'great public moments' – protests, marches, uprisings – ushering in genuine change are 'not the planting but the harvest of a change in public imagination' (Solnit, 2019).

This chapter began with the broiler chicken as geological signal of the Anthropocene. It offered a starting point for understanding the scope of industrialised animal agriculture and its acceleration from post-war to the present day. Whilst explanations for how and why violence on this scale continues unabated can rely on demographics, economics, geographical, social, historical and cultural analysis, we began with social psychology, in particular, Bastian and Loughnan's conceptualisation of the 'meat paradox' working its way through individual motivation and reasoning processes, interpersonal and group dynamics, social norms, cultural conventions and spatial-material infrastructure. Their elaborate framework offered a way to consider how 'meat culture' is maintained psychologically, socially, culturally. The causal logic here was one way – from individual to societal. Active strategies 'promote the formation of habits, which themselves shape cultures in ways that ultimately protect people from feelings of dissonance associated with morally troublesome action' (2017, p. 283). But of course we are always already cultural beings, born into cultures which dynamically shape and construct 'drives', habits, beliefs and practices – as sociological and cultural studies orientations make plain. Cultural analyses of speciesism and meat culture add sophistication to the detail of those ideologies, how they intersect with others to shape permissible and desirable practices, identities, competencies, even as they miss some of the psychological and interpersonal work involved. On combining these levels of analysis, however imperfectly, one might suggest individuals are 'locked in' to particular forms of human–animal relations, exemplified here by meat culture. However, in accepting the Anthropocene as invitation, we also witness a new and resurgent willingness to lift the veil on that culture and our own embroilment in it.

The loss of biodiversity, decimation and destruction of countless species and the wider ecological devastation that herald the Anthropocene are reflections of the profound interrelatedness of human-nonhuman and point to the necessity of finding ways to foster more equitable, just, and sustainable relations (Abell, 2013; Bekoff and Bexell, 2010). The challenge is formidable, but 'we must somehow... reinvent the conditions for multispecies flourishing... in a time of human-propelled mass extinctions and multispecies genocides that sweep people and critters into the vortex' (Haraway, 2016, p. 130). Percival, in reflecting on the life of factory-farmed pigs, envisages a day when 'the worry and misery and fear, the unanswered question in billions of minds – *Why like this?* – have all receded, and she is rooting where she wills' (2017, p. 69).

Notes

1. From http://www.theguardian.com/books/2015/sep/25/industrial-farming-one-worst-crimes-history-ethical-question.
2. *The Chicken of Tomorrow*, a US educational film presented by the 'National Chicken of Tomorrow Committee' captures the cultural significance of

this shift towards mass production and consumption of chickens and eggs at its inception https://archive.org/details/Chicken01948 (see Shrader, 1952)

3. Though studies of wider broiler populations suggest as much as a fivefold increase in individual biomass over similar period (Havenstein et al., 2003; Zuidhof et al., 2014).

4. The rearing conditions and artificially enhanced size of broiler chickens result in multiple osteo-pathologies and organ function complications: 'if left to live to maturity, broilers are unlikely to survive' (Bennett et al., 2018, p. 8).

5. The passenger pigeon is considered the most common *wild* bird in human history, with an estimated population of 3–5 billion in the 1800s. It is now extinct (Hung et al., 2014).

6. See Cooper (2017) for a clear overview and reflection on Festinger's work and legacy in this area. The concept of the 'meat paradox' has also been subject to further study and scrutiny (e.g. Dowsett et al., 2018; Oleschuk et al., 2019; Panagiotou and Kadianaki, 2019).

7. Piazza et al. (2015) add a fourth 'N': niceness, as in, 'Meat is delicious', 'Meat adds so much flavor to a meal it does not make sense to leave it out', 'The best tasting food is normally a meat-based dish' (p. 118) – a prominent, if 'very weak' moral defence.

8. The concept of 'banal speciesism' could be developed from Michael Billig's seminal work on 'banal nationalism' (1995). Billig's influential account established the foundations of critical psychological approaches to nationalism and identity, drawing 'attention to the powers of an ideology which is so familiar that it hardly seems noticeable' (1995, p. 12).

9. A tribute to Harrison following her death in 2000 reports the following: 'She sent her completed manuscript to Rachel Carson, whom she had never met, and asked her to write the foreword. So stunned by what she read, Rachel asked a mutual friend, Christine Stevens, 'Could it be true?' Christine replied, 'Indeed, it is true' and encouraged her to write the foreword. In it, Rachel expressed hope that the book would 'provoke feelings of dismay, revulsion and outrage' and called for a consumers' revolt (Free, 2000, p. 14).

10. One can only speculate as to why a number of the scholars involved, including Richard Ryder, have become synonymous with philosophical and political discussion of animal rights, and whether it reflects at some level the intersection of sexism and speciesism established so forcibly by Adams (2015). The idea that 'the animal welfare movement's foundations stem from Peter Singer and Tom Regan's call for a more equitable world of multispecies rights' (Ogden et al., 2013, p. 19) misses completely Harrison's contribution and suggests the narrative needs to be revisited and corrected.

11. Cavanagh claims that in the context of the Anthropocene, there is a commonality across these two forms of biopower, distinguishing "species life' – bonded by their interdependencies under capital – from those uninsured forms of life who are construed as 'surplus under global political-economic-ecological relations' (2014, p. 278).

12. Recent examples other than the ones described here include the Netflix-funded feature-film *Okja* (Director: Bong, 2017) https://www.imdb.com/title/tt3967856/; the documentaries *Cowspiracy* (Directors: Andersen & Kuhn, 2014), *Dominion* (Director: Delforce, 2018) https://www.imdb.com/title/tt5773402/?ref_=tt_rec_tti, *Earthlings* (Director: Monson, 2005) https://www.imdb.com/title/tt0358456/, *Eating Animals* (Director: Quinn, 2017) https://www.imdb.com/title/tt2180351/ and *Lucent* (Director: Delforce, 2014) https://www.imdb.com/title/tt4134784/?ref_=tt_rec_tti and photodocumentaries such as Timo Stammberger's project *Making the Connection* (2016) https://www.timostammberger.com/making-the-connection and Jo-Anne MacArthur's ongoing *We Animals* project http://www.weanimals.org.

13. The films are accessible here https://ianimal.uk.

14. As reported by the Vegan Society; accessed here https://www.vegansociety.com/news/media/statistics#worldwidestatistics; Statista, accessed here https://www.statista.com/topics/3377/vegan-market/.

15. If, as Dunn claims, when animals are consumed, 'whakapapa mitigates the reduction of these narratives to simplistic exemplars of meat consumption and animal exploitation' (2019, pp. 47–8), might whakapapa embody a form of 'non-innocent' killing, which Haraway holds onto speculatively as a necessary response to the totalising perspective of veganism? It is at least conceivable that whakapapa functions to bypass meat culture dynamics of objectification, fragmentation and consumption that render 'animals being-less through technology, language, and cultural representation' (Adams, 2010, p. 304).

References

Abell, J. 2013. Volunteering to help conserve endangered species: An identity approach to human–animal relationships. *Journal of Community & Applied Social Psychology*, 23(2), 157–170.

Adams, C. J. 2010. Why feminist-vegan now? *Feminism & Psychology*, 20(3), 302–317.

Adams, C. J. 2015. *The Sexual Politics of Meat: A Feminist-Vegetarian Critical Theory*. USA: Bloomsbury Publishing.

Adams, C. J. 2016a. Feminism and the politics of meat. Discover Society. Issue 30 March 1 2016. Accessed https://discoversociety.org/2016/03/01/feminism-and-the-politics-of-meat-2/.

Adams, C. J. and Donovan, J. 1995. *Women and Animals: Feminist Theoretical Explorations*.

Adams, C. J. and Gruen, L. (Eds.). 2014. *Ecofeminism: Feminist Intersections with Other Animals and the Earth*. USA: Bloomsbury Publishing.

Adams, M. 2017. Carnage imagines a vegan utopia where animals live as equals – could it happen? *The Conversation*, March 21st 2017. Accessed https://theconversation.com/carnage-imagines-a-vegan-utopia-where-animals-live-as-equals-could-it-happen-73982

Adams, M. 2016b. *Ecological Crisis, Sustainability and the Psychosocial Subject: Beyond Behaviour Change.* London: Palgrave Macmillan.

Adams, M. 2018. Towards a critical psychology of human–animal relations. *Social and Personality Psychology Compass*, 12(4), 1–14.

Alexandratos, N. and Bruinsma, J. 2012. *World agriculture towards 2030/2050: the 2012 revision* (Vol. 12, No. 3). FAO, Rome: ESA Working paper. Accessed http://www.fao.org/fileadmin/templates/esa/Global_persepctives/world_ag_2030_50_2012_rev.pdf.

Amiot, C. E. and Bastian, B. 2015. Toward a psychology of human–animal relations. *Psychological Bulletin*, 141(1), 6-47.

Bastian, B. and Loughnan, S. 2017. Resolving the meat-paradox: A motivational account of morally troublesome behavior and its maintenance. *Personality and Social Psychology Review*, 21(3), 278–299.

Bastian, B., Loughnan, S., Haslam, N. and Radke, H. M. 2012. Don't mind meat? The denial of mind to animals used for human consumption. *Personality and Social Psychology Bulletin*, 38, 247–256. http://dx.doi.org/10.1177/014616721142429.

BBC. 2017. *Simon Amstell: Carnage.* Accessed https://www.bbc.co.uk/programmes/p04sh6zg.

Bellio, D. 2015. Did the Anthropocene Begin in 1950 or 50,000 Years Ago? *Scientific American*. April 2 2015 Accessed https://www.scientificamerican.com/article/did-the-anthropocene-begin-in-1950-or-50-000-years-ago/?redirect=1.

Bekoff, M. and Bexell, S. M. 2010. Ignoring nature: Why we do it, the dire consequences, and the need for a paradigm shift to save animals, habitats, and ourselves. *Human Ecology Forum*, 17, 70–74.

Bennett, C. E., Thomas, R., Williams, M., Zalasiewicz, J., Edgeworth, M., Miller, H., Coles, B., Foster, A., Burton, E. J. and Marume, U., 2018. The broiler chicken as a signal of a human reconfigured biosphere. *Royal Society Open Science*, 5(12), 180325.

Best, S., Nocella, A. J., Kahn, R., Gigliotti, C. and Kemmerer, L. 2007. Introducing critical animal studies. *Journal for Critical Animal Studies*, 5(1), 4–5.

Bilewicz, M., Imhoff, R. and Drogosz, M. 2011. The humanity of what we eat: Conceptions of human uniqueness among vegetarians and omnivores. *European Journal of Social Psychology*, 41, 201–209. http://dx.doi.org/10.1002/ejsp.766.

Billig, M. 1995. *Banal Nationalism.* London: Sage.

Billig, M. 1999. Commodity fetishism and repression: Reflections on Marx, Freud and the psychology of consumer capitalism. *Theory & Psychology*, 9(3), 313–329.

Blanchette, A. 2015. Herding species: Biosecurity, posthuman labor, and the American industrial pig. *Cultural Anthropology* 30(4):640–669.

Blanchette, A. 2018. Industrial meat production. *Annual Review of Anthropology*, 47, 185–199.

Blanchette, A. 2019. *Porkopolis: American Animality, Standardized Life, and the 'Factory' Farm.* Durham, NC: Duke Univ. Press.

Blaznik, M. 2018. Training young killers: How butcher education might be damaging young people. *Journal of Animal Ethics*, 8(2), 199–215.

Bovenkerk, B. and Keulartz, J. 2016. *Animal Ethics in the Age of Humans.* Dordrecht: Springer.

Boyde, M. 2018 The dairy issue: 'Practicing the art of war'. *Animal Studies Journal*, 7(2), 9–24. Available at: https://ro.uow.edu.au/asj/vol7/iss2/3.

Bradshaw, G. A. 2009. Transformation through service: Trans-species psychology and its implications for ecotherapy. In Buzzell, L. and Chalquist, C. (Eds.), *Ecotherapy. Healing with Nature in Mind.* Sierra Club Books.

Bradshaw, G. A. and Watkins, M. 2006. Trans-species psychology: Theory and praxis. *Psyche & Nature*, 75, 69–94.

Briggs, H. 2018. 'Planet of the chickens': How the bird took over the world. BBC News. 12 December 2018. Accessed https://www.bbc.co.uk/news/science-environment-46506184.

Brown, D. Director. 2019a. *Casa de Carne.* Last Chance for Animals. Accessed https://www.youtube.com/watch?v=c1DcFmUrxUQ.

Brown, D. 2019b. 'Casa De Carne': My Short Film That Explores a Restaurant Where Customers Have to Kill Their Own Food'. Bored Panda. https://www.boredpanda.com/casa-de-carne-short-film-animal-rights-dustin-brown/?utm_source=google&utm_medium=organic&utm_campaign=organic.

Carrington, D., 2016. The Anthropocene epoch: scientists declare dawn of human-influenced age. *The Guardian*, 29th August, 2016. Accessed https://www.theguardian.com/environment/2016/aug/29/declare-anthropocene-epoch-experts-urge-geological-congress-human-impact-earth

Carrington, D. 2019. New plant-focused diet would 'transform' planet's future, say scientists. *Guardian*. 16 January 2019 Accessed https://www.theguardian.com/environment/2019/jan/16/new-plant-focused-diet-would-transform-planets-future-say-scientists.

Cavanagh, C. J. 2014, May. Biopolitics, environmental change, and development studies. *Forum for Development Studies* 41(2): 273-294.

Chakrabarty, D. 2009. The climate of history: Four theses. *Critical Inquiry*, 35(2), 197–222.

Clayton, S. and Myers, G. 2015. *Conservation Psychology: Understanding and Promoting Human Care for Nature.* John Wiley & Sons.

Cole, M. and Morgan, K. 2011a. Veganism contra speciesism: Beyond debate. *The Brock Review*, 12(1), 144–163.

Cole, M. and Morgan, K. 2011b. Vegaphobia: Derogatory discourses of veganism and the reproduction of speciesism in UK national newspapers 1. *The British Journal of Sociology*, 62(1), 134–153.

Connolly, W. E. 2017 *Facing the Planetary: Entangled Humanism and the Politics of Swarming.* London: Duke University Press.

Cooper, J. 2017. Cognitive dissonance. Revisiting Festinger's end of the world study. In Smith, J. R. and Haslam, S. A. (Eds.), *Social Psychology: Revisiting the classic studies*, 2nd ed. London: Sage.

Corrin, T. and Papadopoulos, A. 2017. Understanding the attitudes and perceptions of vegetarian and plant-based diets to shape future health promotion programs. *Appetite*, 109, 40–47.

Crutzen, P. J. and Stoermer, E. F. 2000. The Anthropocene. *Global Change Newsletter*, 41, 17–18.

Cudworth, E. 2014. Beyond speciesism: Intersectionality, critical sociology and the human domination of other animals. In N. Taylor and R. Twine (Eds.), *The Rise of Critical Animal Studies: From the Margins to the Centre*. London: Routledge, pp. 19–35.

Cudworth, E. 2015. Killing animals: Sociology, species relations and institutionalized violence. *The Sociological Review*, 63(1), 1–18.

Davis, K. 1995. Thinking like a chicken: Farm animals and the feminine connection. In C. J. Adams. and J. Donovan (Eds.). *Animals and Women: Feminist Theoretical Explorations*. Durham, NC: Duke University Press, pp. 192–213.

DeMello, M. 2010. *Teaching the Animal: Human-Animal Studies Across the Disciplines*. Lantern Books.

de Morais Sato, P., Gittelsohn, J., Unsain, R. F., Roble, O. J. and Scagliusi, F. B. 2016. The use of Pierre Bourdieu's distinction concepts in scientific articles studying food and eating: A narrative review. *Appetite*, 96, 174–186.

Derrida, J. and Wills, D. 2002. The animal that therefore I am (more to follow). *Critical Inquiry*, 28(2) (Winter, 2002), 369–418.

Dhont, K. and Hodson, G. 2014. Why do right-wing adherents engage in more animal exploitation and meat consumption? *Personality and Individual Differences*, 64, 12–17.

Donaldson, S. and Kymlicka, W. 2011. *Zoopolis: A Political Theory of Animal Rights*. Oxford: Oxford University Press.

Dowsett, E., Semmler, C., Bray, H., Ankeny, R. A. and Chur-Hansen, A. 2018. Neutralising the meat paradox: Cognitive dissonance, gender, and eating animals. *Appetite*, 123, 280–288.

Draycott, S. and Dabbs, A. 1998. Cognitive dissonance 1: An overview of the literature and its integration into theory and practice in clinical psychology. *British Journal of Clinical Psychology*, 37(3), 341–353.

Dunn, K. 2019. Kaimangatanga: Maori perspectives on veganism and plant-based kai, *Animal Studies Journal*, 8(1), 42–65. Available at: https://ro.uow.edu.au/asj/vol8/iss1/4.

FAO. 2018. FAOSTAT. Accessed www.fao.org/faostat/en/?#data.

FAO. 2019. Animal production. Accessed http://www.fao.org/animal-production/en/.

Farming UK. 2019. Broilers UK. Accessed https://www.farminguk.com/MarketData/Poulsl/Broilers-UK_79.html.

Feliz Brueck, J. 2017. Introduction. In Feliz Brueck, J. (Ed.), *Veganism in an Oppressive World: A Vegans of Color Community Project*. Sanctuary Publishers. pp. 1–33.

Festinger, L. and Carlsmith, J.M. 1959. Cognitive consequences of forced compliance. *Journal of Abnormal and Social Psychology*, 58, 203–210.

Festinger, L., Riecken, H. and Schachter, S. 1956. *When Prophecy Fails*. New York: Harper.

Food Empowerment Project. 2019. Slaughterhouse workers. Accessed https://foodispower.org/human-labor-slavery/slaughterhouse-workers/.

Foucault, M. 1976. *The Will to Knowledge: The History of Sexuality Volume 1* (trans. R Hurley, 1998). New York: Pantheon Books.

Free, C. 2000. A tribute to Ruth Harrison. *Animal Welfare Institute Quarterly*, 49(4), 14–15.

Gabardi, W. 2017. *The Next Social Contract: Animals, The Anthropocene, and Biopolitics*. Temple University Press.

Giddens, A. 1991. *Modernity and Self-Identity*. Cambridge: Polity Press.

Gillespie, K. 2011. How happy is your meat? Confronting (dis) connectedness in the 'alternative' meat industry. *The Brock Review*, 12(1), 100–128.

Giraud, E. 2013. 'Beasts of burden': Productive tensions between Haraway and radical animal rights activism. *Culture, Theory and Critique*, 54(1), 102–120.

Glasser, C. L. 2011. Tied oppressions: An analysis of how sexist imagery reinforces speciesist sentiment. *The Brock Review*, 12(1), 51–68.

Godfray, H. C. J., Aveyard, P., Garnett, T., Hall, J. W., Key, T. J., Lorimer, J., Pierrehumbert, R. T., Scarborough, P., Springmann, M. and Jebb, S. A. 2018. Meat consumption, health, and the environment. *Science*, 361(6399), eaam5324.

Godlovitch, S., Godlovitch, R. and Harris, J. (Eds.) 1971. *Animals, Men and Morals*. London: Gollancz.

Graça, J., Calheiros, M. M. and Oliveira, A. 2015. Attached to meat? (Un)willingness and intentions to adopt a more plant-based diet. *Appetite*, 95, 113–125.

Greenebaum, J. 2012. Veganism, identity and the quest for authenticity. *Food, Culture & Society*, 15(1), 129–144.

Green Party UK. 2019. Animal rights. January 2019 Accessed https://policy.greenparty.org.uk/ar.html.

Greenpeace. 2019. Dirty meat is destroying the planet. Its time for us all to step up and act. Accessed https://lessismore.greenpeace.org.

Greenwald, A. G. and Ronis, D. L. 1978. Twenty years of cognitive dissonance: Case study of the evolution of a theory. *Psychological Review*, 85(1), 53.

Hamilton, L. and McCabe, D. 2016. 'It's just a job': Understanding emotion work, de-animalization and the compartmentalization of organized animal slaughter. *Organization*, 23(3), 330–350.

Haraway, D. J. 2003. *The Companion Species Manifesto: Dogs, People and Significant Other-Ness*. Chicago: Prickly Paradigm Press.

Haraway D. J. 2008. *When Species Meet*. Minneapolis: University of Minnesota Press.

Haraway, D. J. 2013. *When Species Meet* (Vol. 3). University of Minnesota Press.

Haraway, D. J. 2016. *Staying with the Trouble: Making Kin in the Chthulucene*. Durham, NC: Duke University Press.

Harper, A. B. 2010a (ed.) *Sistah Vegan: Black Female Vegans Speak on Food, Identity, Health, and Society*. Lantern Books.

Harper, A. B. 2010b. 'Race as a 'feeble matter' in veganism: Interrogating whiteness, geopolitical privilege, and consumption philosophy of 'cruelty-free' products. *Journal for Critical Animal Studies*, 8(3), 5–27.

Harrison, R. 1964. *Animal Machines: The New Factory Farming Industry*. London: Vincent Stuart.

Havenstein, G. B., Ferket, P. R. and Qureshi, M. A. 2003. Growth, livability, and feed conversion of 1957 versus 2001 broilers when fed representative 1957 and 2001 broiler diets. *Poult. Sci.* 82, 1500–1508. (doi:10.1093/ps/82. 10.1500).

Heinz, B. and Lee, R. 1998. Getting down to the meat: The symbolic construction of meat consumption. *Communication Studies*, 49(1), 86–99.

Huggler, J. 2017. Discord in Angela Merkel's government after environment ministry bans meat at official functions. *The Telegraph*, 21 July 2017. Accessed https://www.telegraph.co.uk/news/2017/02/21/discord-angela-merkels-government-environment-ministry-bans/.

Human Animal Research Network Editorial Collective. 2015. *Animals in the Anthropocene: Critical Perspectives on Non-Human Futures*. Sydney: Sydney University Press.

Hung C. M., Shaner P.-J. L., Zink R. M., Liu W.-C., Chu T.-C., Huang W.-S., Li S.-H. 2014. Drastic population fluctuations explain the rapid extinction of the passenger pigeon. *Proceedings of the National Academy of Sciences of the United States of America*, 111, 10 636–10 641. (doi:10.1073/pnas. 1401526111).

jones, p. 2010. Roosters, hawks and dawgs: Toward an inclusive, embodied eco/feminist psychology. *Feminism & Psychology*, 20(3), 365–380.

Joy, M. 2011. *Why We Love Dogs, Eat Pigs, and Wear Cows: An Introduction to Carnism*. Conari Press.

Kirksey, S. and Helmreich, S. 2010. The emergence of multispecies ethnography. *Cultural Anthropology*, 25(4), 545–576.

Lidskog, R. and Waterton, C. 2018. The Anthropocene: Its conceptual usage and sociological challenges. In Boström, M. and Davidson, D. (Eds.). *Environment and Society: Concepts and Challenges*. Basingstoke: Palgrave, pp. 25–46.

Loughnan, S., Bastian, B. and Haslam, N. 2014. The psychology of eating animals. *Current Directions in Psychological Science*, 23, 104–108.

Loughnan, S., Haslam, N. and Bastian, B. 2010. The role of meat consumption in the denial of moral status and mind to meat animals. *Appetite*, 55(1), 156–159.

Machovina, B., Feeley, K. J. and Ripple, W. J. 2015. Biodiversity conservation: The key is reducing meat consumption. *Science of the Total Environment*, 536, 419–431.

Marinova, D. and Bogueva, D. 2019. Planetary health and reduction in meat consumption. *Sustainable Earth*, 2(1), 3.

Markowski, K. L. and Roxburgh, S. 2019. 'If I became a vegan, my family and friends would hate me:' Anticipating vegan stigma as a barrier to plant-based diets. *Appetite*, 135, 1–9.

McGrath, A. 2017. Dealing with dissonance: A review of cognitive dissonance reduction. *Social and Personality Psychology Compass*, 11(12).

Monteiro, C. A., Pfeiler, T. M., Patterson, M. D. and Milburn, M. A. 2017. The Carnism Inventory: Measuring the ideology of eating animals. *Appetite*, 113, 51–62.

Morell, V. 2015. Meat-eaters may speed worldwide species extinction, study warns *Science*. August 11 2015. Accessed https://www.sciencemag.org/news/2015/08/meat-eaters-may-speed-worldwide-species-extinction-study-warns.

Muller, S. M. 2018. Zombification, social death, and the slaughterhouse: US industrial practices of livestock slaughter. *American Studies*, 57(3), 81–101.

Mussgnug, F. 2019. Species at war? The animal and the Anthropocene. *Paragraph*, 42(1), 116–130.

National Chicken Council [US]. 2019a. US broiler performance https://www.nationalchickencouncil.org/about-the-industry/statistics/u-s-broiler-performance/.

National Chicken Council [US]. 2019b. Broiler chicken industry key facts 2019. Accessed https://www.nationalchickencouncil.org/about-the-industry/statistics/broiler-chicken-industry-key-facts/.

Newkey-Burden, G. 2018. There's a Christmas crisis going on: no one wants to kill your dinner. *The Guardian* 19 November 2018. Accessed: https://www.theguardian.com/commentisfree/2018/nov/19/christmas-crisis-kill-dinner-work-abattoir-industry-psychological-physical-damage.

Ogden, L. A., Hall, B. and Tanita, K. 2013. Animals, plants, people, and things: A review of multispecies ethnography. *Environment and society*, 4(1), 5–24.

Oleschuk, M., Johnston, J. and Baumann, S. 2019. Maintaining meat: Cultural repertoires and the meat paradox in a diverse sociocultural context. *Sociological Forum*, 34.

Panagiotou, E. and Kadianaki, I. 2019. From cognitive dissonance to cognitive polyphasia: A sociocultural approach to understanding meat-paradox. *Journal for the Theory of Social Behaviour*, 49.

Pargman, D., Eriksson, E., Höök, M., Tanenbaum, J., Pufal, M. and Wangel, J. 2017. What if there had only been half the oil? Rewriting history to envision the consequences of peak oil. *Energy Research & Social Science*, 31, 170–178.

Parry, J. 2010. Gender and slaughter in popular gastronomy. *Feminism & Psychology*, 20(3), 381–396.

Percival, R. 2017. Pig rhythm. In confronting the Cthulhucene. In Hine, D. and Wheeler, S. (Eds.), *Dark Mountain Issue 12: Sanctum*. Dark Mountain Project.

Peters, J., Lebrasseur, O., Deng, H. and Larson, G. 2016 Holocene cultural history of red jungle fowl (*Gallus gallus*) and its domestic descendant in East Asia. *Quat. Sci. Rev.* 142, 102–119. (doi:10.1016/j.quascirev.2016.04.004).

Piazza, J., Ruby, M. B., Loughnan, S., Luong, M., Kulik, J., Watkins, H. M. and Seigerman, M. 2015. Rationalizing meat consumption. The 4Ns. *Appetite*, 91, 114–128.

Pilgrim, K. 2013. 'Happy cows,' 'happy beef': A critique of the rationales for ethical meat. *Environmental Humanities*, 3(1), 111–127.

Potts, A. 2010. Introduction: Combating speciesism in psychology and feminism. *Feminism & Psychology*, 20, 291–301.

Potts, A. 2012. *Chicken*. London: Reaktion Books.

Potts, A. 2016. What is meat culture? In A. Potts (Ed.), *Meat culture*. Brill, pp. 1–30.

Potts, A. and Haraway, D. 2010. Kiwi chicken advocate talks with Californian dog companion. *Feminism & Psychology*, 20(3), 318–336.

Radnitz, C., Beezhold, B. and DiMatteo, J. 2015. Investigation of lifestyle choices of individuals following a vegan diet for health and ethical reasons. *Appetite*, 90, 31–36.

Reynolds, L. 2013. Agriculture and Livestock Remain Major Sources of Greenhouse Gas Emissions. Worldwatch Institute. Accessed http://www.worldwatch.org/agriculture-and-livestock-remain-major-sources-greenhouse-gas-emissions-0.

Ribas V. 2016. *On the Line: Slaughterhouse Lives and the Making of the New South*. Berkeley: University of California Press.

Ritchie, H. and Roser, M. 2017. *Meat and Seafood Production & Consumption: Empirical view*. Our world in data, August 2017. Accessed https://ourworldindata.org/meat-and-seafood-production-consumption.

Rodman, J. 1977. The liberation of nature? *Inquiry*, 20, 83–131.

Rothgerber, H. 2013. Real men don't eat (vegetable) quiche: Masculinity and the justification of meat consumption. *Appetite*, 14, 363–375.

Rothgerber, H. 2014. Efforts to overcome vegetarian-induced dissonance among meat eaters. *Appetite*, 79, 32–41.

Ruby, M. B. and Heine, S. J. 2011. Meat, morals, and masculinity. *Appetite*, 56(2), 447–450.

Salt, H. 1892/1980. *Animal Rights*. New York: Macmillan.

Sanders, B. 2018. *Global Chicken Slaughter Statistics and Charts*. Faunanalytics. Accessed https://faunalytics.org/global-chicken-slaughter-statistics-and-charts/.

Scotton, G. 2018. Metaphors and maladies: Against psychologizing speciesism. *Animaladies: Gender, Animals, and Madness*, 101.

Sevillano, V. and Fiske, S. T. 2016. Warmth and competence in animals. *Journal of Applied Social Psychology*, 46(5), 276–293.

Sexton, A. E. 2018. Eating for the post-Anthropocene: Alternative proteins and the biopolitics of edibility. *Transactions of the Institute of British Geographers*, 43(4), 586–600.

Shove, E., Pantzar, M. and Watson, M. 2012. *The Dynamics of Social Practice: Everyday Life and How It Changes*. London: SAGE.

Shrader, H. L. 1952. The Chicken-of-Tomorrow Program; its influence on 'meat-type; poultry production. *Poultry Science*, 31(1), 3–10.

Siegel, P. B. 2014. Evolution of the modern broiler and feed efficiency. *Annu. Rev. Anim. Biosci.*, 2(1), 375–385.

Singh, B. and Dave, N. 2015. On the killing and killability of animals: Nonmoral thoughts for the anthropology of ethics. *Comparative Studies of South Asia, Africa and the Middle East*, 35(2), 232–245.

Sobal, J. 2005. Men, meat, and marriage: Models of masculinity. *Food and Foodways*, 13(1–2), 135 158.

Solnit, R. 2019. Every protests shifts the world's balance. June 1st 2019, *The Guardian*. Accessed https://www.theguardian.com/books/2019/jun/01/rebecca-solnit-protest-politics-world-peterloo-massacre

Steffen, W., Broadgate, W., Deutsch, L., Gaffney, O. and Ludwig, C. 2015. The trajectory of the Anthropocene: The Great Acceleration. *The Anthropocene Review*, 2, 81–98.

Steffen, W., Crutzen, P. J. and McNeill, J. R. 2007. The Anthropocene: Are humans now overwhelming the great forces of nature? *AMBIO: A Journal of the Human Environment*, 36(8), 614–621.

Steinfeld, H., Gerber, P., Wassenaar, T. D., Castel, V. and de Haan, C. 2006. *Livestock's Long Shadow: Environmental Issues and Options*. United Nations: Food & Agriculture Organisation.

Stewart, K. and Cole, M. 2018. Vegans: why they inspire fear and loathing among meat eaters. *The Conversation*, October 31 2018. Accessed https://theconversation.com/vegans-why-they-inspire-fear-and-loathing-among-meat-eaters-106015.

Todorova, M. 2015. Counterfactual construction of the future: Building a new methodology for forecasting. *World Future Review*, 7(1), 30–38.

Twine, R. 2014. Vegan killjoys at the table—Contesting happiness and negotiating relationships with food practices. *Societies*, 4(4), 623–639.

Twine, R. 2018. Materially constituting a sustainable food transition: The case of vegan eating practice. *Sociology*, 52(1), 166–181.

Wadiwel, D. 2018. Animal utopia: Liberal, communitarian, libertarian or...? [Review Essay] Wayne Gabardi. The next social contract: Animals, the Anthropocene, and biopolitics. *Animal Studies Journal*, 7(1), 304–318.

Wasley, A. 2015. UK chicken farming puts workers and food safety at risk. *The Guardian*. 22 December 2018. Accessed https://www.theguardian.com/sustainable-business/2015/dec/22/uk-chicken-farming-puts-workers-and-food-safety-at-risk.

Wasley, A. and Heal, A. 2018. Revealed: Shocking safety record of UK meat plants. *The Bureau of Investigative Journalism*. 29th July 2018. Accessed https://www.thebureauinvestigates.com/stories/2018-07-29/uk-meat-plant-injuries

Waters, C. N., Zalasiewicz, J., Summerhayes, C., Barnosky, A. D., Poirier, C., Gałuszka, A., Jeandel, C. et al. 2016. The Anthropocene is functionally and stratigraphically distinct from the Holocene. *Science* 351, aad2622. (doi:10.1126/science.aad2622).

Willett, W., Rockström, J., Loken, B., Springmann, M., Lang, T., Vermeulen, S., Garnett, T. et al. 2019. Food in the Anthropocene: The EAT–Lancet Commission on healthy diets from sustainable food systems. *The Lancet*, 393(10170), 447–492.

Worth, R. 2010. Activist Relies on Islam to Fight for Animal Rights. *The New York Times*, 21 November 2010 https://www.nytimes.com/2010/11/22/world/africa/22egypt.html.

Worthy, K. 2013. *Invisible Nature: Healing the Destructive Divide between People and The Environment.* Buffoal, NY: Prometheus Books.

Zalasiewicz, J., Williams, M., Steffen, W. and Crutzen, P. 2010. The new world of the Anthropocene. *Environment Science and Technology,* 44, 2228–2231.

Zuidhof, M. J., Schneider, B. L., Carney, V. L., Korver, D. R. and Robinson, F. E. 2014. Growth, efficiency, and yield of commercial broilers from 1957, 1978, and 2005. *Poultry Science* 93, 2970–2982. (doi:10.3382/ps.2014-04291).

4

CRAFTING NEW HUMAN–ANIMAL ATTACHMENTS

Do Anthropoceneans dream of eclectic sheep?[1]

> *We are a knot of species coshaping one another in layers of reciprocating complexity all the way down. Response and respect are possible only in those knots, with actual animals and people looking back at each other, sticky with all their muddled histories*
>
> *(Haraway, 2008, p. 42)*

> *The cosmos emerges, again and again, out of diverse ways of composing worlds, of crafting attachments and connections that link soil and earth, compost, humus, mud, grass, dogs, sheep, humans and more*
>
> *(Despret and Meuret, 2016, p. 35)*

Introduction

The Anthropocene era is defined by the profound impact of one species – *homo sapiens* (or at least some members of it) – on countless other species, mainly in terms of extinction and displacement. It is also defined by the mass-scale organisation of other species' lives, especially farm animals: 'bending the biorhythmic impulses of 45 billion sentient beings so that they acquiesce to a pre-specified production schedule' (Percival, 2017, p. 67), *and* the subsequent planetary impacts of the processes involved. As documented in previous chapters, animal agriculture now operates on a scale of Anthropocene proportions – an estimated one-third of all food grown on the planet, on one-third of all arable land, is eaten by farmed animals, whilst a quarter of the Earth's ice-free terrestrial surface is used for grazing

(FAO, 2018). Since it was first defined, significant Anthropocene impacts have included the growth of global cattle populations, the rise of industrial fisheries, multiple species habitat loss and extinctions (Crutzen & Stoermer, 2000). In terms of greenhouse gases, the animal agriculture sector produces more than the entire global transport system (Reynolds, 2013). In significantly contributing to 'climate change and air pollution, to land, soil and water degradation and to the reduction of biodiversity' (Steinfeld et al., 2006, p. iii), there is little doubt that the farming of domesticated animals is a key component of the Anthropocene.

What, then, is the nature of our relationship with the 'domesticated' animals that make up the 45 billion today? The answer will, of course, depend on the specifics of culture, geography and economics – where and how one lives. The Anthropocene is not homogenously experienced, nor are the human–animal and multi-species relations within it. Nonetheless, it is a safe bet that for the majority of the readership of this book, as for me, it is difficult to imagine our contact with chickens, pigs, sheep, cows, salmon *as* a relationship, in any meaningful sense. In fact, many commentators have claimed that contemporary life is defined in part by the day-to-day separation of human and nonhuman animals, with the important exception of companion animals, as a result of interrelated changes wrought by science and technology, industrialisation and urbanisation (Franklin, 1999; Vining, 2003).[2] In terms of farmed animals, that distance is simultaneously physical, social and psychological. The business of animal agriculture, such as breeding, housing and slaughter, is commonly located away from the routines of everyday life, certainly for a growing urban population. Even for those living in closer proximity, the 'vertical integration' of large-scale factory farming, joining up farms, slaughterhouses, processing and packaging plants, marketing and distribution, renders the animals themselves routinely invisible, other than as meat (Bennett et al., 2018; though see Levitt, 2019). Socially and culturally, the lives of farmed animals are commonly mediated through the advertising, packaging and consumption of meat and by-products, culturally embedding an experiential distance as routine (Bastian and Loughnan, 2017; see Chapter 3 for more detailed discussion). At a related but more individual level, personal and intra-personal psychological mechanisms involved in managing the moral and social status of farmed animals to rationalise eating them are well documented (e.g. Joy, 2011).

This chapter engages with some salient aspects of the human relationship with one particular farmed animal – the sheep. Following Haraway, a first step in developing a more response-able and respectful multi-species perspective is to make the 'knots' of reciprocating complexity that constitute human–sheep relations in the Anthropocene, and their antecedents, explicit. Reflecting this call, the first section offers a general historical consideration of human–sheep relations, attempting a brief 'muddled history' of species coshaping. Framing that relational history within the Anthropocene, as noted above, the processing of animals, including sheep, as meat, is foremost. What else is possible? In accepting the Anthropocene as invitation, I also explore what other opportunities there might be for developing response-ability and respect. The second half of this chapter is a reflection on a project involving 'actual animals and people looking back at each other' – a volunteer urban shepherding programme. I do not approach that relationship in isolation, but as one iteration of 'layers of reciprocating complexity', 'sticky' with muddled multi-species histories. Nonetheless, I consider the nature of this encounter, how it is experienced and the extent to which, echoing Despret and Meuret, the crafting of new attachments and connections becomes possible.

Human–sheep histories

> As the etymology of the word reminds us, to protest means above all to testify. And that is precisely where sheep's problem lies: they have never been able to testify to what interests them since whatever it is that might interest them has been offered no affordance, no possibility of articulation with what interests those who attest on their behalf
>
> *(Despret, 2006, p. 363)*

Sheep (*Ovis aries*) have long been associated with the development of human societies and are often claimed to be the first species, besides dogs, to be domesticated by humans (Armstrong, 2016). The possible origins of that domestication, beginning around 11,000 years ago, deepen a sense of entanglement. Successfully domesticating wild sheep must have required significant and early 'imprinting' prior to weaning – the transfer of a within-species maternal bond to a sheep–human attachment, as a basis for establishing dependency. With no other sources of milk available, it is considered likely that lambs may have been suckled by humans, elsewhere documented as a human–animal practice (Armstrong, 2016; Haraway, 1989). The suggestion that the first domesticated sheep were suckled rather than milked is intriguing. It unsettles origin myths of human–animal entanglement involving dominance, entrapment and hunting; and, by hinting at expressions of compassion and intimacy, at least momentarily challenges those strategies which hold farmed animals at a psychological distance (Davis, 2019). It is a possibility which 'reminds us, perhaps uncomfortably, of the intimacy and mutuality of our kinship with animals' (Armstrong, 2016, p. 31).

Over multiple generations, domestication allowed sheep's milk and wool to be utilised by humans, and eventually meat. Sheep subsequently contributed to various forms of self-subsistent husbandry throughout ancient and early medieval cultures. To take Britain as our focus here, by the time of the 1086 Domesday Book census, sheep were more numerous than all other livestock combined, a reflection, by this point, of a shift away from self-subsistent husbandry to an established and still-developing wool industry (Armstrong, 2016).[3] The independence and hardiness of sheep, and their plasticity in terms of selective breeding, rapidly made them the definitive feature of many and varied landscapes, not least across Britain (Franklin, 2007, p. 74). Whilst the size of the global flock has fluctuated historically, reflecting contingencies such as war, climactic change and disease (Stone, 2003), the overall picture is of sheep increasing in number and size over the last millennia (Grau-Sologestoa and Albarella, 2019). The production and export of wool became a primary driver of the economy by the twelfth century and was central to England's ascendancy to the status of a global power. Over the next 500 years, wool helped create a new class of wealth and status, radically changed the structure and organisation of market towns, underpinned political and economic power and, as a result of extensive trading routes and connections across Europe, played a significant role in social and cultural changes (Rose, 2017). It is without hyperbole, then, that one material can be claimed to play a central role in the shift to business and commercial contours of modernity – wool, and therefore one animal – the sheep (Salisbury, 2012). These are the beginnings of a 'bigger story about human beings' growing power to manipulate organic life on a large scale' (Armstrong, 2016, p. 79), accelerating towards the present, culminating in our understanding of the current era as the Anthropocene. Though there are numerous contenders, just three more key elements of the history of human–sheep relations are briefly considered here, which exemplify the sticky, muddled histories of our Anthropocene entanglement: enclosure, colonialism and industrial revolution.

Enclosure, colonialism and industrial revolution

Enclosure refers to the 'conversion of commonable lands, whether on wastes, commons, or village fields, into exclusively owned parcels, and the concomitant extinction of common rights, of which the most important was that of pasture' (Blomley, 2007, p. 2). England has a history of enclosure going back at least 900 years, but it is in the early modern period from the sixteenth century onwards that enclosure accelerated in pace and scope. This reorganisation of agricultural land was frequently imposed, and by force, if legally, and was often resisted (Armstrong, 2016; Hentschell, 2016).[4] Whereas peasant-farmed small holdings and common land permitted small-scale crop growing and care of livestock, enclosure allowed favoured landowners to create large estates. They promptly populated the newly enclosed spaces with sheep, for the wool market, converting more and more land to pasture and requiring little human labour (Armstrong, 2017). Marx argued that the 'primitive accumulation' epitomised by enclosure, and the way of farming sheep it permitted, was a vital harbinger of capitalism (Fornäs, 2014). The surplus of English wool and low labour costs created consistent profit margins, whilst the eviction of peasants created a landless, surplus labour force. With little alternative as more and more land was enclosed, these were the class of people later drafted to work in the new industries established in the north of England, producing, amongst other things, cloth derived from the wool of sheep on enclosed land (De Angelis, 2001).

Turning to our second element, the practice of enclosure also subsequently functioned for the British Empire as a model for colonialism (Armstrong, 2016, p. 22). As with the highland clearances in Scotland, the colonisation of Australia and Aotearoa New Zealand was accompanied by the introduction of species domesticated back 'home'. Sheep became the 'agents of the expansion of white settlement' (ibid. p. 23). As well as dispossessing and displacing indigenous populations, the introduction of sheep and the rapid expansion of flocks radically transformed the landscape (Brooking and Pawson, 2010). In Australia, for example, sheep killed off groundcover and compacted soils, leading to less rain and reducing the land's ability to absorb moisture, increasing erosion. Many native plants and animal habitats were decimated, and with it, indigenous knowledge and practice – leaving local populations little choice but to participate in coloniser-related employment, including pastoralism (Armstrong, 2016; 2017; Franklin, 2007). These converging dynamics, which Crosby refers to as 'ecological imperialism' (2004), all accomplished by 'flocks of imported sheep nibbling imported grasses' (Armstrong, 2017, p. 24), indicate the extent to which colonialism inserts itself into the interconnection of human and more-than-human worlds at the heart of the Anthropocene.[5]

Finally, I now turn to the radical changes in manufacturing methods and technologies that marked the unfolding Industrial Revolution in Britain and the rise of modernity across the eighteenth and nineteenth centuries. Sheep are again essential characters, but the dynamics of colonialism, enclosure and industrialism are now tightly woven into a single thread. New wool technologies developed in the context of emerging industrialism drove the building of wool mills in the north of England, dramatically increasing the speed and scale of spinning and weaving, erasing any last vestiges of the production of wool as a household business, which had been undertaken alongside the production of subsistence crops. This population must increasingly seek employment in the factories and food and shelter in the cities expanding around them. As finer wool is increasingly imported from the colonies, British sheep are increasingly used (and selectively bred) for meat, especially as demand grows, not least from a hungry urban workforce. From the late 1880s, frozen mutton and lamb are shipped back as cargo from Australia and New Zealand, and the dynamic shifts again (Armstrong, 2017). Human–sheep relations, in sum, have been central to the rise of modernity and, more specifically, to a modern 'commitment to the large-scale reorganization of territories, peoples, environments and species as dictated by the idea of industrial, capitalist and imperialist "progress"' (Armstrong, 2016, p. 111).

Today, in many ways, sheep are the archetypal domesticated animals of the Anthropocene. Whilst they might not be bred, raised and killed on the same scale as chickens or pigs (see Chapter 3), they are valued for their fleece, flesh and milk. Worldwide, there are approximately 1.15 billion sheep and lambs alive at any one time (Common Objective, 2018; FAO, 2014; National Sheep Association, 2019). About 1,160 million kilograms of clean wool are produced from the global sheep population annually (Common Objective, 2018). Whilst only responsible for about 1% of global totals (FAO, 2019), about 10 million tonnes of sheep milk (used to make cheese) is still produced every year (FAO, 2011; 2019). Their flesh is readily consumed. Over 500 million sheep (the vast majority as lambs) are slaughtered for human consumption globally every year (Sentient Media, 2019; Thornton, 2019), close to 15 million in the United Kingdom alone (Humane Slaughter Association, 2019).[6]

As creatures regularly put out to pasture, then and now, one might readily assume a relatively sedate and positively uneventful existence, compared to the plight of some other farmed animals, whatever the landscape they find themselves in. Compared to the intensive conditions of many factory-farmed animals, the 'extensive' methods of pastoralism mean that sheep spend at least a portion of life outdoors without much interference from humans (Caroprese et al., 2009). Measures of public opinion suggest that sheep are indeed perceived to be living a 'natural life' (Goddard et al., 2006). However, reiterating plenty of animal scholarship, Richmond et al. (2017) point out extensive management of farmed animals does not necessarily equate with high welfare and poses contingent problems: greater risk of predation, exposure to extreme weather and health and welfare complications following long periods of neglect. The risks of exposure are amplified by early shearing – the animal welfare charity PETA estimates 1 million sheep are sheared 'too young' in the season (at peak of wool density) and die of exposure as a result. Others document live transportation (2 m a year from Australia alone, often in cramped conditions), forced ovulation, mistreatment including hasty and careless shearing and mulesing (the cutting of skin from around a sheep's anus) (Armstrong, 2016; PETA, 2019). As we enter the present day, then, sheep, like other farmed animals, are a profitable component of systematised mass-scale confinement, extraction and killing that defines the global industrial-agricultural system (Armstrong, 2016). It is that system, certainly in the global North, which most prominently shapes human–sheep relations and human perceptions and experiences of sheep.

How we see sheep

Just as with people, the cultural and psychological perceptions of animals matter in terms of how we treat them, individually and collectively (Sevillano and Fiske, 2016). Observation and analysis have revealed some of the related social, cultural and psychological dynamics and implications of a cultural and psychological distancing from farmed animals, including sheep (e.g. Cole and Stewart, 2016; Piazza et al., 2015), much of which have been engaged with elsewhere in this book. It is broadly argued that a lack of daily and routine physical and spatial contact with wild and many types of domesticated animals reflects both a historical and psychological split, in the sense that 'human relationships with animals that were based on proximity to them gradually changed to relations based on separateness' (Vining, 2003, p. 89). In this denuded relational space, the primary contemporary interaction – eating animals and consuming their by-products – becomes less morally troubling (Bastian et al., 2012; Morgan and Cole, 2011). Cultural stereotypes that legitimatise the inferiority of farmed animals can more readily take root, intersect with other powerful discourses and shore up cherished identities (Rothgerber, 2013) and further allay any psychological and cultural dissonance experienced in relation to the practices of animal agriculture (Bastian and Loughnan, 2017; see Chapter 3). Hence, common stereotypes of sheep are that they are docile, pliant, meek and stupid (Armstrong, 2016; Marino and Merskin, 2019).

Social perceptions and psychological representations are symbiotically related to the histories described above. Sevillano and Fiske deepen an appreciation of this interrelatedness, making the important point that animal stereotypes have a fundamentally self-fulfilling dimension – routine depictions of farm animals as inoffensively passive and timid and judged with indifference are reinforced by the material conditions of being intensively farmed by humans (2016, p. 277). Embedded in factory-like production systems, intensively managed, passively co-operative, perceptions of sheep as lesser, and therefore consumable, are confirmed (Sevillano, 2019). Here, physical remoteness, material conditions and psychological and social perceptions of animals interconnect with the advertising imagery, packaging and language of 'meat culture' (Potts, 2016), combining to 'conceal suffering, prevent empathy, and promote indifference' (Sevillano and Fiske, 2016; Plous, 2003). In sum, the Anthropocene figure of the sheep is psychosocially constructed through relations of production and consumption and attendant dynamics of fragmentation, objectification and commodity fetishism (Adams, 2004; Gouveia and Juska, 2002; Heinz and Lee, 1998; Potts, 2016).

It is questionable then whether our perception of sheep reflects sheep 'as they really are', if that perception is reciprocally shaped by, and recursively legitimises, the conditions in which we keep them. Further complexity arises from the fact that the bodies, psychology and sociality of domesticated sheep have been fashioned and distorted by generations of selective breeding in line with shifting human demands – for hardiness, timidity, wool or meat – and by impositions on the constitution of flocks reflected in, for example, the routine slaughtering of lambs and the removal of males. Unless studying 'wild' breeds, any study of sheep 'mentality', and any perception grounded in observation and contact, is a reflection of that distortion. Nonetheless, the more we pay attention to and ask questions about the intelligence of sheep, whilst recognising the specific and situated contingencies of their existence, the more complexity is revealed. Attentiveness reveals alert and socially intelligent creatures, with an 'elaborate communicative repertoire' (Armstrong, 2016, p. 32), a skill for species-distinction, strong connections to place, a tight social structure and complex social lives in which bonding, attachment and long-term relationships endure, all facilitated by active cognitive and memory processes (Despret, 2006; Gray, 2014; Kendrick et al., 2001; Rowell and Rowell, 1993; Webster, 2019). A recent comprehensive review of research on sheep behaviour, affect, cognition, and personality asserted in conclusion that 'they are complex, individualistic, and social' beings (Marino and Merskin, 2019, p. 1), to an extent, the authors argued, that should prompt a reconsideration of 'the use of sheep as commodities in modern agricultural production and in invasive research' (p. 16; see also Davis, 2019; Haraway, 2008, pp. 41–2; Horback, 2019; Vonk, 2019).

Knowledge such as this can challenge stereotypes, but the majority of encounters with sheep continue to be as fleece and flesh, as meat consumption grows around the world (Ritchie and Roser, 2018). As a form of human–animal relation, if we follow comprehensive analyses of meat culture (Bastian and Loughnan, 2017; Potts, 2016), everything – habits, thought processes, rituals, institutions – appears fixed, and 'forces interlock' to make changes to our physical, psychological and social relations with sheep and other domesticated animals unlikely, unless societies experience 'acute circumstances' of catastrophic proportions, provoking 'collective soul searching' and a subsequent reversing of social norms (Bastian and Loughnan, 2017, p. 288). Whilst many have cared for, and learnt in encounter with, sheep, the dominant perception with the greatest impact on lives of sheep is that they 'are negligible in themselves, but valuable in so far as they can be treated as a mass of raw material, to be used in whatever way yields the most benefit and profit to humans' (Armstrong, 2016, p. 144; Sevillano, 2019). Such a pessimistic analysis is clearly justified, echoing much of our account of the broiler chicken in the previous chapter. However, if we are to pursue the Anthropocene as an invitation to reconsider human–animal and multi-species interconnections and interdependencies, whilst addressing specific and situated human and more-than-human encounters, there is perhaps more still to be said. What if an opportunity arose for narrowing the physical and psychological distance between humans and sheep? Might proximity and contact pull at the thread of entangled Anthropocene histories and begin their unravelling, so that we might craft new attachments and connections?

Situating human–sheep encounters

Following the lead of human–animal studies, I have become increasingly interested in theory and research which attempts to place the life of animals in the spotlight (Johnson, 2015, p. 299) and the dynamics of human–animal relations (see Adams, 2018) evident in the previous chapters in this book. A fascinating and evolving field is dedicated to researching these relations empirically, incorporating novel research methods such as multi-species ethnography. As the field evolves, it is also addressing the many epistemological, methodological and ethical challenges of inter- or multi-species research (e.g. Collard, 2015; Wolch and Emel 1998). Much of the remainder of this chapter offers some reflections on a modest attempt to engage with this field empirically, as it relates to the themes of this chapter. A more systematic approach is taken to methodology, data collection and analysis elsewhere.[7]

Over two summers, the first of which working alongside a colleague and a student researcher, I conducted a number of 'walk-along' interviews with volunteer urban shepherds, referred to as 'lookerers' in the local vernacular, whilst accompanying them on their 'shift'.[8] The interviews took place on council–owned land on the edges of a city on the United Kingdom's south coast. Sheep have been introduced there as part of a low-intensity livestock conservation grazing project, the express logic of this being that their grazing habits help create more biodiverse landscapes compared to human management (chopping, mowing etc.) or abandonment (for details on landscape benefits, see Grazing Animals Project, 2018). This local project reflects wider recognition of low-intensity livestock (including horses, cattle, deer, goats and sheep) grazing as a viable component of conservation strategies across Europe in recent years, to help positively shape heterogeneous vegetation and flourishing multi-species habitats (DeGabriel et al., 2011; Dostálek and Frantík, 2008; Evans et al., 2006).

The project involves the city council leasing sheep (and now ponies) from local farms. Council-employed park rangers work with farmers to manage the number of sheep involved and co-ordinate the project. Multiple flocks of various sizes are out to pasture at any one time and rotated around a number of sites on the edges of the city. Sheep so close to the city are deemed to require more regular checks – twice-daily – than flocks further into the countryside. Since its inception over a decade ago, the scheme has relied on lookerers to regularly check on the welfare of the sheep, see whether the site is secure and undertake other tasks like watering. Volunteers first undertake a two-day training programme, where they learn the basics of sheep management. The work of volunteers is coordinated by the rangers – they sign up for 'shifts' via an online system, whilst every flock's location is kept up to date via a grazing map, which is publicly available. The grazing sites variedly occupy the urban fringes, buttressed between housing estates, municipal parks, roads, golf courses, parking lots and downland. The volunteer scheme has proved very popular – there is now an extensive waiting list, and the overwhelming majority of lookering slots are filled throughout the year.

We approached the project openly – as a small, internally funded exploratory study. Our decision to interview volunteers obviously meant we were firmly on the human 'side' of the human–animal relationship. When it came to the sheep's experiences, we were confident only in what we lacked – 'the methodological tools to establish how sheep experience their role' (Hamilton and Mitchell, 2018, p. 349) – if reassured by the fact that previous researchers had obviously felt the same. Nonetheless, we incorporated a few tentative steps into our methods that we hoped might at least raise awareness of the sheep's contribution, informed by recent developments in human–animal studies and related scholarship (e.g. DeMello and Shapiro, 2010; Wilkie, 2015). First, the decision was made to carry out 'walk-along' interviews, accompanying lookerers as they observed the sheep and their environs, to allow for the for the presence of the sheep (and any other critters) to more readily intrude into the interview, physically and figuratively.[9] Second, although only loosely structured, we made sure we asked participants *about* the sheep – what they knew about them, how they thought and felt about them. Third, we valued both Armstrong's call for a respectful 'attentiveness to specificity', in that 'every flock – indeed, every individual sheep – embodies an entirely specific relation to place' (2017, p. 17), and Shapiro's broader insistence that 'the investigator must become a historian of the individual animal or animals under study. In effect, he or she develops a biographical account' (1990, p. 187). To achieve this third goal, in addition to researching a general history, a version of which is offered above, we set out to find out as much about these specific sheep as we could – especially their life outside the moment of the lookerer-sheep (and researcher-lookerer-sheep) encounter. Even a partial consideration of where the sheep have come from and where they end up necessarily moves us beyond the 'comfortable intellectual and ethical spaces' of multi-species encounters in the moment (Kopnina, 2017, p. 335), by allowing wider ethical, social and political issues to infiltrate that space. All these elements, we hoped, would help avoid reducing the sheep to the role of object, in our own approach, in the questions we ask our participants and in how we observe, listen and interpret. That said, to reiterate, we accepted that our methods remained anthropocentric in orientation.

The sheep: a pen portrait[10]

The sheep are an assortment of 'rare and ancient' breeds: Herdwicks, blue-faced Leicester, Scottish black face and mules (mixed breeds) were all identified by the council ranger responsible for the programme.[11] The sheep are rented from a local farmer, who regularly purchases them from livestock markets in Cumbria, in the north of England. As 'he [the farmer] can bring them down here in spades you know loads of them', they are presumably transported by lorry from here to the south coast in significant numbers. The breeds are apparently selected to combine 'grazers' – who eat mainly grasses – and 'browsers' who will also eat leaves from shrubs and thickets such as hawthorn and bramble. The number of sheep involved has grown substantially since the programme began over a decade ago, and the ranger estimates that there approximately 1,000 sheep out at any one time, across multiple sites on the edges of the city, in different-sized flocks. Whilst those sites are varied in terms of size, location and landscape, all are within the city environs, roughly 5 miles square. Sheep remain out on the downland all year round. Flocks are shepherded on to different sites every 3–4 weeks and moved to and from the farm they are leased from as part of a co-ordinated grazing programme. All the leased sheep are supposed to be 'empty' (not pregnant) ewes and ewe lambs. Rams and pregnant ewes are excluded because of the additional management and welfare expertise involved. Key elements of the sheep farming cycle such as breeding (from around October), lambing (5-month gestation period, peak lambing time March–April), shearing (summer months) and slaughter (ongoing) take place at the farm. Wool from these sheep today is apparently not commercially viable – the cost of shearing (required legally for welfare reasons) is greater than the market value of the wool. Whilst the programme might retain the same sheep on and off the site 'quite regularly for two or three years', all sheep are eventually slaughtered and sold for meat by the farmer, as lamb or mutton (lambs intended for meat are generally sent for slaughter at 5 to 8 months old).

The identity of the actual sheep on any one site at any one time, and over time, therefore, changes regularly.

The immediate environment the sheep inhabit whilst grazing is characterised by a diverse array of biota. This includes varied flora, much of which incorporates the sheeps' diet, including downland plant species establishing themselves in symbiosis with the sheep's activities (grazing, defecating, trampling and so on). Those identified comprise mixed grasses, pyramidal orchids, common broomrape, kidney and horseshoe vetch, rosehips and blackberries, whilst stands and thickets include ash, oak, beech, sweet chestnut and yew. Moths, butterflies and dragonflies are regularly spotted, and many other insects are apparently encouraged in this habitat. Birds seen and heard by lookerers (and many by us) include skylarks, pigeons, peregrines, buzzards, green woodpeckers, pheasants and herons. A regular sight was magpies or starlings sitting on the backs of sheep, picking ticks, maggots and other parasites (more species!) off the sheep – a nice example of a mutually symbiotic relation. Other fauna include frogs and newts, horses (and their riders) passing through, the occasional glimpse of a deer, rabbits, dogs, and other features of the landscape such as snow, dewponds and hoarfrost. The human is represented in the guise of dogwalkers, golfers, farmers, rangers, walkers, runners, travellers, 'lads from the estate' and 'the public'. The majority of the biota listed here are those described by lookerers and/or encountered and named on our trips out – no doubt there are many other species. On the sites we have visited, within fenced enclosures (often electrified), the sheep have plenty of space, access to water and shade and varied terrain, mostly hilly and on relatively high ground, with expansive views down to the English Channel, as well as municipal parks, caravan sites and housing estates. All have public access with various gated entry and exit points and are criss-crossed by footpaths.

Much of a sheep's day is taken up eating and digesting grass. They are often stationary, standing, chewing the cud, urinating or defecating, or lying, nearly always in groups of various sizes. That said, a common sight is a group on the move, presumably to graze elsewhere, perhaps for a change of scene or in response to a threat. On our approach, they often amble away unhurriedly, though sometimes dash off with apparent urgency, or even hold their ground. The sheep are out in all seasons, and in very cold weather they huddle together in denser groups, whilst in the heat they also gather in larger groups, but for shade. In groups, sheep nuzzle, push and butt each other, gambol, scratch their backs on trees and posts and appear to form an orderly queue for the water trough. They bleat and baa intermittently, individually, sometimes interchangeably – as if in conversation, and also at times in unison. These are the kinds of actions and activities we witnessed with the lookerers – they reported others. Sheep die in the fields, become injured, ill, trapped, lost, end up on the 'wrong' side of the fence, escape, give birth and be born (errors in scanning for pregnant ewes are apparently fairly common), are worried and sometimes killed by dogs, but on the whole are left to their own devices. A more general knowledge of sheep, as outlined above, variations of which are often drawn upon in lookerers' talk, supplements this sketch. I might add, for example, that the sheep we encounter can recognise each other (and human faces), are communicating in sophisticated ways and are in the process of forming and maintaining strong bonds and social attachments. What we know about the wider impositions of agricultural domestication in general also bears significantly on sheep's experience in particular – being regularly relocated, many lambs and rams removed from the flock and so on.

Going further, it is important to reiterate that though this multi-species site is the place of encounter for lookerers and sheep, it is not the only one, or necessarily the definitive one, for the sheep. They are steered through other human–animal and multi-species environments, incorporating multiple sites (farm, lorry, pen, abattoir), activities (shearing, slaughter, reproduction, pregnancy, suckling) and others (farmers, drivers, slaughterhouse workers, vets). In advancing multi-species scholarship, it is vital to locate the immediate encounters that are the focus of research – more 'comfortable intellectual and ethical spaces' – within these wider historical, material and social networks, that often involve more hidden forms of nonhuman violence and abuse (Kopnina, 2017, p. 351). It is especially important for avoiding a consideration of the psychological dynamics of volunteering and 'helping behaviour' in pristine isolation from more complex material, social and ethical concerns. Nonetheless, guardianship, as both a sense of responsibility for something and being in a position to care for, protect or defend that same something, emerged as in important element of lookering for our participants. Exploring guardianship in a little more detail in the context of the lookering experience allows us to consider what possibilities for respect and response are offered in this context and what kinds of attachments and connections, if any, are crafted.[12]

Learning to looker

> What does it mean to try and look at sheep as they really are, rather
> than to remain content with seeing them as we have made them?
>
> *(Armstrong, 2016, p. 171)*

Every trip accompanying volunteers on their shift was a fascinating and
unique experience. Each relayed the bare bones of the practicalities of
their role in fairly similar ways, with some of the received wisdom of
the training programme echoing across the recounting of duties –
checking the fence, testing the battery, looking for limpers, escapees,
identifying common problems. But in and amongst the expediencies
were plenty of moments where nothing was said, 'oohs' and 'ahhs',
gestures, gesticulations and shared moments of attention. Plenty of this
attentiveness was bestowed on sheep – a key aspect of the job in a sense,
of course, but a deeper consideration, too. On these trips, there was
often a willingness to challenge or qualify what were asserted to be
established understandings of sheep. Our human participants offered
alternative perceptions, the outcome of attentiveness, even if these were
accompanied by later rebuttals, qualifications, ambivalence or
contradictions. Regular proximity permitted greater attention to sheep
'as they really are', and on the whole a greater appreciation of their
intelligence and complexity, which was contrasted with received ideas
about their stupidity and passivity. Lookerers told sheep stories that
highlighted their character as, for example, determined, seeking
companionship, communicative, considerate, sensible and wily. Some
volunteers described how lookering provoked them to learn more about
sheep in general, knowledge which recursively informed further
observation and deepens attentiveness. Such talk shifted easily back and
forth between accounts of a sense of duty and a desire to protect or care
for the sheep – both clearly informed each other, just as wider scholarship
suggests perceptions of animal sentience and intelligence are negatively
correlated with our willingness to morally harm them (Caviola, Everett
and Faber, 2019; Loughnan, Haslam and Bastian, 2010; Piazza and
Loughnan, 2016).

That lookerers appear to be motivated to help by a sense of
responsibility and a duty of care is perhaps unsurprising, as the lookering
role is explicitly one of watching over a flock, reporting potential threats
(such as broken fences where sheep might escape or predators enter) and
ensuring sheep are watered and in good health.[13] However, related,
more subtle, aspects of guardianship were also evident. As noted above,

the character of sheep was defended against imagined others who might belittle or underestimate them, rendering them in the process as matters of care and concern rather than mute objects. This in itself is a form of guardianship – a warding off of demeaning myths and stereotypes. What some lookerers referred to as 'PR work' was another form of guardianship – explaining the presence of the sheep as part of a conservation grazing programme to 'the public', appeasing curious or irate dog-walkers, local residents or anyone who might feel the presence of sheep and the fencing of land as an affront to their freedom to roam, for example. The labour of guardianship is extended here, to incorporate walking, observing, reporting and the practicalities of a shift; the psychological effort to reconsider and defend what it is to be a sheep and the public work of defending the presence of the sheep and its wider ecological value. Lookerers regularly described the importance of the sheep's capacities for work – valuing their grazing as important labour in contributing to conservation and biodiversity. Just as Hamilton and Mitchell consider sheep and shepherding a form of shared work, 'inextricably tied together', and traversing 'extant subject distinctions' (2018, p. 359; p. 349), lookering might also be articulated as both human and nonhuman labour, valuably combined in the pursuit of the programme's goals of conservation and multi-species flourishing. Echoing Hamilton and Mitchell, in this context, human–animal relationships are clearly valued in ways that surpass economic exchange or consumption. However, in our example, located in wider human–sheep entanglements, I would not follow them in claiming here that 'sheep and humans co-constitute a process of work in which neither party is a clear and separate agent' (p. 358), nor that the value invested in this shared labour extends to a form of 'interspecies solidarity' (p. 355; see also Coulter, 2016), for reasons detailed below.

Lookerers explicitly valued playing a part, with the sheep, in contributing to the flourishing of the places in which they lookered. Whilst this value was often attached to goals of conservationism or environmentalism, it was also articulated in terms of the pleasure they derive from being in and amongst the place and its cohabitants. Many participants expressed a positive and personal connection not just to the sheep but to the place and the species that constitute it. They talked of the joy of noticing the changes wrought by the seasons, the play of shadows on the hills, the movement of the grasses in the wind, the song of a skylark or of simply sitting and watching and having a moment's reverie. Expressions of love for the places they lookered were often emphatic. After talking to lookerers, Gray's assertion that 'in analyzing human–animal relations we should always be ready to include a third dimension—place' (p. 220) makes good sense (but extends to human-species-place – not just the animal in question). His ethnographic work with hill sheep farms in the Scottish Borders offers a richly detailed account of sheep–shepherd entanglement in a particular place. The long multi-generational history of sheep farming he studies is obviously a very different human–animal prospect, one in which it does not seem hyperbolic to observe 'a relational configuration of sheep and shepherds in their movements through the landscape as mutual acts of emplacement… an intertwining of lives that transforms the very being of sheep and people so that attachment to land is "in the blood"' (p. 220). As Gray argues, human–animal relations *always* take place in specific, situated places, to the extent that it makes sense to talk of human-animal-place co-constituting each other in a trinary, rather than a binary human–animal relation (p. 221).

In describing shepherding, Gray uses the term 'emplacement' to describe the embodied process and sense of a person becoming embedded in place, which 'happens in the sensuous act of walking and biking over the landscape' (p. 228; see also Ingold and Vergunst 2008). In their more modest volunteer commitment, lookerers nonetheless routinely walk (and pause) in particular places, often over weeks and years. Our go-along method was well suited to attending to the significance of walking for lookerers as integral to a sense of emplacement, tied with their attentiveness to sheep, and with it, other forms of life that constituted place – an ongoing triad of human-species-place. Lookerers establish particular routes and paths, adapting to where sheep are and to the specifics of the hilly terrain, inculcating cherished pausing places. Lookerers were also emplaced via memories of where things had happened – a bird spotted, a dog attacked, a sheep had escaped – all nicely evoked in talk by the walk-along method. Emplacement was evident in plenty of descriptions of situated and specific connections and positive feelings in relation to seeing and being with sheep, birds, flowers and other features of the landscape. It was also evident in unspoken ways, in being there, with the lookerers and sheep. It is reflected in long pauses, expressive verbal gestures, moments of low murmuring and inaudible exchanges and the presence of other sounds – the wind, boots on the ground, the movement or voices of sheep, dog barks, other people and greetings, traffic, gates opening and closing. Of course, this is difficult, perhaps impossible, to analyse as 'data'. It is normally missing from standard interviews in a room, or at best bracketed out as extraneous, the better to sharpen one's focus on words. This is all perfectly understandable in the research traditions we inherit, but there is something vital (in both senses of the word) in the specific and situated human and more-than-human encounter that what is said cannot fully capture. But it is briefly recounted here to convey a felt sense of emplacement as it is enacted and experienced in the moment, and all its attendant liveliness. It hints at the significance of Gray's emphasis on the triad of human-animal-place for human–animal scholarship.

Enacting the dream of a flourishing multispecies community?

If the above discussion suggests a uniform embrace of lookering as a progressive human–animal encounter, a final theme unsettles such a notion. Another account of animal guardianship – van Dooren and Rose's account of Hawaiian monk seals (2016) – offers some interesting parallels to the human–sheep encounter in a way that makes an ambivalence at the heart of lookering more apparent. Hawaiian monk seal numbers are in severe decline, close to extinction. Seals regularly 'haul-out' onto shore for mating, resting and tending to their young, where they are effectively defenceless. As well as the general threats such as ship strikes, pollution and net entanglement, they are 'not infrequently subject to deliberate and violent attack by people, beaten to death on the beach' (van Dooren and Rose, 2016, p. 78). A depressing scenario, but van Dooren and Rose find room for optimism:

> Into this environment of violence and loss some local people are injecting narratives and practices of care. When a seal hauls out on a beach in an inhabited part of the islands, volunteers are called. They go to the reported site and set up a perimeter with stakes and plastic tape; they put up signs of warning, make sure the event is reported, and stay. They are not as much police as educators, so while they make sure that people respect the sleeping seal's need to be left alone, they also answer questions about monk seal biology, history, future, and behavior. Although the official literature does not put it this way, volunteers are ambassadors for monk seals. Their response, their commitment to being there, is in itself an ethical statement
>
> *(2016, p. 79)*

For van Dooren and Rose, these seal ambassadors or guardians provide a blueprint: 'Through these grounded acts of care, of witnessing and careful storytelling, these volunteers help daily to enact the dream of a flourishing multispecies community on the beaches of Hawai'i' (p. 79). Whilst a very different example, it might be tempting to consider the attentive guardianship of lookerers in a similar vein, helping to enact the dream of a flourishing multispecies community on the downlands of Southern England. However, a final 'moment' we were drawn to in our research with lookerers portrays a more complex dynamic.

For many lookerers, physical proximity and a deeper attentiveness encouraged recognition of sheep complexity and a sense of duty and guardianship, which sometimes extended into more explicit expressions of love and care. Others noticeably retreated from such expressiveness after stating a version of it. This was noticeable in a common 'moment' – talk of sheep intelligence, sentience or character was often hedged with hesitancy or nervous laughter – perhaps a residue of cultural inappropriateness in 'sentimentalising' or 'anthropomorphising' farm animals, of appearing foolish for recognising intelligence in animals culturally legitimated as dumb, inferior? Especially, but not only, where reticence to 'talk up' sheep was more explicit in lookerer's narratives, there might follow warnings (to us as researchers, to other lookerers, 'lady lookerers' – this was gendered, to no one in particular?) not to get 'too close' to sheep, and to never name them, or bestow too much affection on them. But there was an interesting consequence in raising a warning here. It begged a question, and was felt as a momentary pause, a blip, to be answered or not, in terms of why, precisely, they should not be sentimentalised. These other fates were often described more reticently and ambiguously, closed off as 'something we don't like to think about' or passed over as 'just the way things are'. Nonetheless, all of us, as researchers, felt there was a discomfort, which we shared, in these moments. Unlike the monk seals, these sheep are farmed animals, and other places of their lives and fates outside of the field of encounter remain relatively opaque – in our lookerers' talk and in more general discourse. Paying attention to the chain of encounters beyond this immediate environment (see the pen portrait above) troubles any easy notion of 'guardianship' or 'emplacement' as unequivocal and straightforward. For domesticated farm animals, anyhow, it is likely to be partial, a palatable encounter or 'moment' in individual and collective sheep trajectory.

Imagine, for example, the experiences of veterinary students visiting an abattoir for the first time, whose encounters with farmed animals also reflect the reality of the latter's experience, part of the same trajectory, seeing them 'as they really are', but giving rise to very different affective responses and sensibilities and unequivocally, viscerally, revealing very different fates (Pedersen, 2013). After travelling by bus through 'beautiful natural surroundings', the students disembark in the slaughterhouse grounds. After a break and various protocols and practices in the outer-office facilities, the group head for the slaughterhouse itself – for the majority of students, their first visit.

> The moment we enter this passageway marks a shift of character in our study visit, a shift from detached discussions of animal protection measures and productivity figures to a physical experience with the animals going to their slaughter. In the narrow passageway we proceed slowly side by side with them, at a similar pace, with only a low fence between us that allows for eye contact between us and them. Physically, the distance between us is only a few decimetres, but in all respects... [w]e and the cows enter parallel universes. The radical species-coded separation, demarcating who of us will be killed at the end of the line and who will not, makes the momentary intimacy between us and them appear almost obscene
>
> *(Pedersen, 2013, p. 723)*

This is not an always evolving multi-species co-becoming, in which relational meaning emerges as an ongoing embodied negotiation. It ends, abruptly, in death for one species. Physical proximity here exacerbates a sense of the depth of human and nonhuman entanglement, but if the shared 'zooethnographic' space of the slaughterhouse facilitates a 'blurring of ontological lines', it also forces a radical separation: 'in a certain sense, the end of the (animal) research subject's existence marks the limits, the edges, of our knowing' (ibid.). This is precisely why it is vital to situate multi-species research in relevant times and places beyond the immediate encounter, 'sticky with all their muddled histories' (Haraway 2008, p. 42). It has been attempted here via the wider trajectory of our pen portrait, wider still in the muddled history of human–sheep entanglement.

Finally

Echoing the quotes that opened this chapter, we have, if briefly, become 'sticky' with the muddled histories of human–sheep relations, and entertained a contemporary possibility for 'crafting attachments and connections' anew. Whilst it might be impossible to fully encounter sheep, or any animal, 'as they are', accepting the Anthropocene as invitation encourages us to hone in on our entanglements, and in particular the crafting of attachments and connections that might more readily provoke care and compassion.

In a sense, our study was asking, indirectly, what happens when routine contact with unfamiliar domestic animals, *especially*, perhaps, those we rear for meat on an industrial scale, is (re)instated. Are existing social perceptions and stereotypes of sheep confirmed or challenged? However modest as an example, involvement in such grazing schemes explicitly relies on narratives of conservation, biodiversity and multi-species flourishing, whilst facilitating routine experiences of human–animal proximity. Lookering as a practice *troubles* understandings of sheep as 'raw materials' and 'negligible in themselves' amidst an ambivalent cultural milieu of normalised meat consumption, distance from farmed animals and ecological threat.

In sum, as a specific and situated example of a human–animal encounter, lookering engenders a sense of animal complexity that challenges existing myths and stereotypes, a multi-faceted form of guardianship and shared labour and an embodied sense of emplacement – relating person to place. In doing so, such experiences amount to a crafting of new attachments and acknowledge multi-species interdependencies that mark the Anthropocene as invitation, with all sorts of attendant possibilities. That said, perceptual opacity and degrees of ambivalence endure, visible once we embed situated encounters in wider chains of contact. In the spirit of staying with the trouble of human–sheep encounters as we find them, these stickier moments must remain in focus, to meet Haraway's conditions for 'actual animals and people looking back at each other' with response and respect.

Notes

1. Head defines 'Anthropoceneans' as 'the well-off citizens of the modern world who, having contributed so much to the problems, have to try and remake ourselves and our worlds' (Head, 2016, p. 167).
2. 'Companion animals' refers to species with which we commonly share a home, and have regular daily contact with therein, such as dogs and cats, but also birds, horses, rabbits, goats, snakes, gerbils, rats, mice, fish, amphibians and other species.

3. The focus here is Britain, as reflected in the specific historical examples of enclosure, colonialism and the industrial revolution. In *Dolly Mixtures*, Sarah Franklin offers a comprehensive and engaging history of sheep breeding and the pastoral tradition in a British context (2007, pp. 73-117). However, distinct but parallel processes incorporate sheep and other animals into the spread of European colonial power across the globe (see, for example, Anderson, 2006; Greer, 2012; Melville, 1997; Skabelund, 2013).

4. As Blomley (2007, p. 14) recounts, resistance in the early 1600s 'saw the first use of the terms leveler and digger, later deployed in the revolutionary risings of the mid seventeenth century... In a remarkable document entitled 'The Diggers of Warwickshire to All Other Diggers', a group of 'poor delvers and day labourers' issued a call to others to join the rising, in a condemnation of the 'devouring encroachers': 'We as members of the whole do feel the smart of these encroaching tyrants [i.e. enclosers], which would grind our flesh upon the whetstone of poverty ... so that they may dwell by themselves in the midst of their herds of fat wethers [sheep]' (Bending and McRae, 2003: 147).

5. Might the extent of impacts warrant a consideration of a case for the Pastoralocene as alternative to Anthropocene, Capitalocene, Plantationocene?

6. By comparison, approximately 2.6 million cattle, 10 million pigs, 80 million fish and 950 million birds are slaughtered for human consumption every year in the UK (Human Slaughter Association, 2019).

7. Bringing animals 'in' as research subjects – rather than objects – has been identified as posing huge but important challenges for scholarship (Wolch and Emel 1998). Those challenges include how to become attuned to animal capacities for communication; how to take seriously the agency and subjectivity of animals as well as humans in the process of their co-constitution; how to attend to the capacity of humans and nonhumans to be affected by, and to respond to, each other across species boundaries, all whilst attending to 'radically asymmetrical relations of power' (Haraway 2008, 216; see also Greenhough and Roe 2011; Wolfe 2003).

8. 'Lookering' captures the distinction from shepherding in that volunteers rarely 'herd' the animals, but merely observe their well-being.

9. The 'walk-along' or 'go-along' interview is a relatively novel method, particularly well suited for studying engagements with place (e.g. Carpiano, 2009), and, potentially at least, human-animal relations in place (Campbell et al., 2016; Springgay and Truman, 2017).

10. Pen portraits are a research device developed by Hollway and Jefferson (2000) to make 'the person [research participant] come alive for a reader' (2000, p. 70). They suggest portraits should be 'largely descriptive and provide enough information against which subsequent interpretations could be assessed. In a way, a pen portrait serves as a substitute "whole" for a reader who will not have access to the raw data but who needs to have a grasp of the person who figures in a case study if anything said about him or her is going to be meaningful' (ibid.). Whilst making the

move from human to nonhuman animal, I am nonetheless taking anthropocentric liberties here in eschewing sheep individuality and portraying 'the sheep' collectively. After my colleague and co-researcher James Ormrod suggested pen portraits for our human participants, I thought it would be interesting and in the spirit of human-animal studies to provide one for the sheep.

11. All quotes used in this sheep portrait are taken from an interview with the council ranger who has overall responsibility for the lookering programme, in the summer of 2018. Additional information from National Sheep Association (undated) *Year on a Sheep Farm*. Accessed 25 July 2019 https://www.nationalsheep.org.uk/know-your-sheep/year-on-a -sheep-farm/

12. The key themes identified in the research, and reflections on the novel methodological approach, are detailed elsewhere – what follows is not a summary of those findings or reflections.

13. Lookerers reported occasions where they handled sheep – rescued them from bramble or lifted them over fences. However, on the whole, their work rarely involved physical contact, experiences of which are considered to be 'an important feature of feeling compassion for another agent, human or otherwise' (Abell, 2013, p. 161), and 'touch is the primary sense for communicating concern and welfare in humans' (p. 163; see also Goetz et al., 2010). Yet regular proximity and observation appeared to be sufficient for establishing an important bond, deriving significant meaning and a sense of identity from the volunteering role.

References

Abell, J. 2013. Volunteering to help conserve endangered species: An identity approach to human–animal relationships. *Journal of Community & Applied Social Psychology*, 23(2), 157–170.

Adams, C. J. 2004. *The Pornography of Meat*. New York: Bloomsbury.

Adams, M. 2018. Towards a critical psychology of human-animal relations. *Social and Personality Psychology Compass*, 12(4), p. e12375.

Anderson, V. D. 2006. *Creatures of Empire: How Domestic Animals Transformed Early America*. USA: Oxford University Press.

Armstrong, P. 2016. *Sheep*. London: Reaktion Books.

Armstrong, P. 2017. Sheep-shaped. In J. Bull, T. Holmberg, C. Åsberg (Eds.), *Animal Places: Lively Cartographies of Human-Animal Relations*. London: Routledge, pp. 17–32.

Bastian, B. and Loughnan, S. 2017. Resolving the meat-paradox: A motivational account of morally troublesome behavior and its maintenance. *Personality and Social Psychology Review*, 21(3), 278–299.

Bastian, B., Loughnan, S., Haslam, N. and Radke, H. R. 2012. Don't mind meat? The denial of mind to animals used for human consumption. *Personality and Social Psychology Bulletin*, 38(2), 247–256.

Bending, S. and McRae, A. 2003. Property and oppression: Voices from the margins. In Bending, S. and McRae, A. (Eds.), *The writing of rural England, 1500-1800* (p. xxxiv276). New York: Palgrave Macmillan, pp. 145–178.

Bennett, C.E., Thomas, R., Williams, M., Zalasiewicz, J., Edgeworth, M., Miller, H., Coles, B., Foster, A., Burton, E.J. and Marume, U. 2018. The broiler chicken as a signal of a human reconfigured biosphere. *Royal Society Open Science*, 5(12), 180325.

Blomley, N. 2007. Making private property: Enclosure, common right and the work of hedges. *Rural History*, 18(1), 1–21.

Brooking, T. and Pawson, E. 2010. *Seeds of Empire: The Environmental Transformation of New Zealand* (Vol. 4). IB Tauris.

Campbell, K., Smith, C. M., Tumilty, S., Cameron, C. and Treharne, G. J. 2016. How does dog-walking influence perceptions of health and wellbeing in healthy adults? a qualitative dog-walk-along study. *Anthrozoös*, 29(2), 181–192.

Caroprese M, Annicchiarico G, Schena L, Muscio A, Migliore R and Sevi A. 2009. Influence of space allowance and housing conditions on the welfare, immune response and production performance of dairy ewes. *The Journal of Dairy Research*. 76, 66–73. doi:10.1017/S0022029908003683

Carpiano, R. M. 2009. Come take a walk with me: The 'go-along' interview as a novel method for studying the implications of place for health and well-being. *Health & Place*, 15(1), 263–272.

Caviola, L., Everett, J. A. and Faber, N. S. 2019. The moral standing of animals: Towards a psychology of speciesism. *Journal of Personality and Social Psychology*, 116(6), 1011.

Cole, M. and Stewart, K. 2016. *Our Children and Other Animals: The Cultural Construction of Human-Animal Relations in Childhood*. Routledge.

Collard, R. C. 2015. Ethics in research beyond the human. In Perreault T., Bridge G. and McCarthy J. (Eds.), *The Routledge Handbook of Political Ecology*. London, UK: Routledge, pp. 127–139.

Common Objective 2018. Global Wool Production and Sustainable Standards. Accessedhttps://www.commonobjective.co/article/global-wool-production-and-sustainable-standards

Coulter, K. 2016. *Animals, Work, and the Promise of Interspecies Solidarity*. London: Palgrave Macmillan.

Crosby, A. W. 2004. *Ecological Imperialism: The Biological Expansion of Europe, 900–1900*. Cambridge University Press.

Crutzen, P. J. and Stoermer, E. F. 2000. The Anthropocene. *Global Change Newsletter*, 41, 17–18.

Davis, H. 2019. Our disparaging view of sheep is indeed based on cognitive inadequacy: Unfortunately, it's ours. *Animal Sentience*, 4(25), 20.

De Angelis, M. 2001. Marx and primitive accumulation: The continuous character of capital's enclosures. *The Commoner*, 2(01), 1–22.

DeGabriel, J. L., Albon, S. D., Fielding, D. A., Riach, D. J., Westaway, S. and Irvine, R. J. 2011. The presence of sheep leads to increases in plant diversity and reductions in the impact of deer on heather. *Journal of Applied Ecology*, 48(5), 1269–1277.

DeMello, M. and Shapiro, K. 2010. The state of human-animal studies. *Society & Animals*, 18(3), 307–318.

Despret, V. 2006. Sheep do have opinions. In Weibel P. and Latour B. (Eds.), *Making things public. Atmospheres of democracy.* Cambridge: MIT Press, pp. 360–370.

Despret, V. and Meuret, M. 2016. Cosmoecological sheep and the arts of living on a damaged planet, *Environmental Humanities*, 8(1): 24–36.

Dostálek, J. and Frantík, T. 2008. Dry grassland plant diversity conservation using low-intensity sheep and goat grazing management: Case study in Prague (Czech Republic). *Biodiversity and conservation*, 17(6), 1439–1454.

Evans, D. M., Redpath, S. M., Elston, D. A., Evans, S. A., Mitchell, R. J. and Dennis, P. 2006. To graze or not to graze? Sheep, voles, forestry and nature conservation in the British uplands. *Journal of Applied Ecology*, 43(3), 499–505.

FAO 2011. *Sheep milk (whole, fresh) Production (tonnes)*, FAO Statistics Division 2011, Accessed http://www.fao.org/faostat/en/#data/QL

FAO (Food and Agricultural Organization of the United Nations) 2014. *Data.* Accessed 24/08/19 www.fao.org/faostat/en

FAO (Food and Agricultural Organization of the United Nations) 2018. *Animal production.* Accessed 24/08/19 http://www.fao.org/animal-production/en/

FAO (Food and Agricultural Organization of the United Nations) 2019. *Dairy Animals.*http://www.fao.org/dairy-production-products/production/dairy-animals/en/

Fornäs, J. 2014. *Capitalism: A Companion to Marx's Economy Critique.* London: Routledge.

Franklin, A. 1999. *Animals and Modern Cultures: A Sociology of Human-Animal Relations in Modernity.* London: Sage.

Franklin, S. 2007. *Dolly Mixtures: The Remaking of Genealogy.* Durham, NC: Duke University Press.

Goddard, P., Waterhouse T., Dwyer, C., Stott, A. 2006 The perception of the welfare of sheep in extensive systems. *Small Ruminants Research*, 62, 215–225.

Goetz, J. L., Keltner, D. and Simon-Thomas, E. 2010. Compassion: An evolutionary analysis and empirical review. *Psychological Bulletin*, 136, 351–374.

Gouveia, L. and Juska, A. 2002. Taming nature, taming workers: Constructing the separation between meat consumption and meat production in the US. *Sociologia Ruralis*, 42(4), 370–390.

Grau-Sologestoa, I. and Albarella, U. 2019. The 'long' sixteenth century: A key period of animal husbandry change in England. *Archaeological and Anthropological Sciences*, 11(6), 2781–2803.

Gray, J. 2014. Hefting onto place: Intersecting lives of humans and sheep on Scottish hills landscape. *Anthrozoös*, 27(2), 219–234.

Greenhough, B. and Roe, E. 2011. Ethics, space, and somatic sensibilities: Comparing relationships between scientific researchers and their human and animal experimental subjects. *Environment and Planning D: Society and Space*, 29(1), 47–66.

Greer, A. 2012. Commons and enclosure in the colonization of North America. *The American Historical Review,* 117(2), 365–386.

Hamilton, L.A. and Mitchell, L. 2018. Knocking on the door of human-animal studies: The value of work in interdisciplinary perspective. *Society and Animals,* 26(4), 347–366.

Haraway D. J. 2008. *When Species Meet.* Minneapolis: University of Minnesota Press.

Haraway, D. J. 1989. *Primate Visions: Gender, Race, and Nature in the World of Modern Science.* London: Routledge.

Head, L. 2016. *Hope and Grief in the Anthropocene: Re-conceptualising Human–Nature Relations.* London: Routledge.

Heinz, B. and Lee, R. 1998. Getting down to the meat: The symbolic construction of meat consumption. *Communication Studies,* 49(1), 86–99.

Hentschell, R. 2016. *The Culture of Cloth in Early Modern England: Textual Constructions of a National Identity.* London: Routledge.

Hollway, W. and Jefferson, T. 2000. *Doing Qualitative Research Differently: Free Association, Narrative and the Interview Method.* London: Sage.

Horback, K. 2019. Applied cognition research to improve sheep welfare. *Animal Sentience,* 4(25), 18.

Humane Slaughter Association 2019. General information. Accessed 24/08/19 https://www.hsa.org.uk/faqs/general

Ingold, T. and Vergunst, J. L. (Eds.). 2008. *Ways of Walking: Ethnography and Practice on Foot.* Farnham: Ashgate.

Johnson, E. R. 2015. Of lobsters, laboratories, and war: Animal studies and the temporality of more-than-human encounters. *Environment and Planning D: Society and Space,* 33(2), 296–313.

Joy, M. 2011. *Why We Love Dogs, Eat Pigs, and Wear Cows: An Introduction to Carnism.* Conari Press.

Kendrick, K. M., da Costa, A. P., Leigh, A. E., Hinton, M. R. and Peirce, J. W. 2001. Sheep don't forget a face. *Nature,* 414(6860), 165.

Kopnina, H. 2017. Beyond multispecies ethnography: Engaging with violence and animal rights in anthropology. *Critique of Anthropology,* 37(3), 333–357.

Levitt, T. 2019. The smell, the noise, the dust: My neighbour, the factory farm. *The Guardian* 24 July 2019. Accessed 24 July 2019 https://www.theguardian. com/environment/2019/jul/24/the-smell-the-noise-the-dust-my-neighbour-the-factory-farm

Loughnan, S., Haslam, N. and Bastian, B. 2010. The role of meat consumption in the denial of moral status and mind to meat animals. *Appetite,* 55(1), 156–159.

Marino, L. and Merskin, D. 2019. Intelligence, complexity, and individuality in sheep. *Animal Sentience,* 4(25), 1.

Melville, E. G. 1997. *A Plague of Sheep: Environmental Consequences of the Conquest of Mexico.* Cambridge: Cambridge University Press.

Morgan, K. and Cole, M. 2011. The discursive representation of nonhuman animals in a culture of denial. In *Human and Other Animals.* London: Palgrave Macmillan, pp. 112–132.

National Sheep Association 2019. *Sheep facts.* Accessed https://www. nationalsheep.org.uk/know-your-sheep/sheep-facts/

Pedersen, H. 2013. Follow the Judas sheep: Materializing post-qualitative methodology in zooethnographic space. *International Journal of Qualitative Studies in Education*, 26(6), 717–731.

People for the Ethical Treatment of Animals (PETA) 2019. *The wool industry.* Accessed 23/08/19 https://www.peta.org/issues/animals-used-for-clothing/wool-industry/

Percival, R. 2017 Pig rhythm. In confronting the Cthulhucene. In Hine D. and Wheeler S. (Eds.), *Dark Mountain Issue 12: Sanctum.* Padstow: Dark Mountain Project., pp. 58–69.

Piazza, J. and Loughnan, S. 2016. When meat gets personal, animals' minds matter less: Motivated use of intelligence information in judgments of moral standing. *Social Psychological and Personality Science*, 7(8), 867–874.

Piazza, J., Ruby, M. B., Loughnan, S., Luong, M., Kulik, J., Watkins, H. M. and Seigerman, M. 2015. Rationalizing meat consumption. The 4Ns. *Appetite*, 91, 114–128.

Plous, S. 2003. Is there such a thing as prejudice toward animals? In Plous S. (Ed.), *Understanding Prejudice and Discrimination.* Boston, MA: McGraw-Hill, pp. 509–528.

Potts, A. 2016. *Meat Culture.* New York: Brill.

Reynolds, L. 2013. *Agriculture and Livestock Remain Major Sources of Greenhouse Gas Emissions.* Worldwatch Institute. Accessed http://www.worldwatch. org/agriculture-and-livestock-remain-major-sources-greenhouse-gas-emissions-0

Richmond, S. E., Wemelsfelder, F., de Heredia, I. B., Ruiz, R., Canali, E. and Dwyer, C. M. 2017. Evaluation of animal-based indicators to be used in a welfare assessment protocol for sheep. *Frontiers in Veterinary Science*, 4, 210.

Ritchie, H. and Roser, M. 2018. Meat and seafood production & consumption. Our World in Data. Accessed https://ourworldindata.org/meat-and-seafood-production-consumption

Rose, S. 2017. *The Wealth of England: The Medieval Wool Trade and Its Political Importance 1100–1600.* Oxford: Oxbow Books.

Rothgerber, H. 2013. Real men don't eat (vegetable) quiche: Masculinity and the justification of meat consumption. *Psychology of Men & Masculinity*, 14(4), 363.

Rowell, T.E. and Rowell, C.A. 1993. The social organization of feral *Ovis aries* ram groups in the pre-rut period. *Ethology*, 95: 213–232.

Salisbury, J. 2012. *The Beast within: Animals in the Middle Ages.* London: Routledge.

Sentient Media 2019 How Many Animals Are Killed for Food Every Day? Accessed 24/08/19 https://sentientmedia.org/how-many-animals-are-killed-for-food-every-day/

Sevillano, V. 2019. Our ambivalent stereotypes of sheep. *Animal Sentience*, 4(25), 35.

Sevillano, V. and Fiske, S. T. 2016. Warmth and competence in animals. *Journal of Applied Social Psychology*, 46(5), 276–293.

Skabelund, A. 2013. Animals and imperialism: Recent historiographical trends. *History Compass*, 11(10), 801–807.

Springgay, S. and Truman, S. E. 2017. *Walking Methodologies in a More-Than-Human World: WalkingLab*. Routledge.

Steinfeld, H., Gerber, P., Wassenaar, T. D., Castel, V. and de Haan, C. 2006. *Livestock's Long Shadow: Environmental Issues and Options*. Food & Agriculture Organisation, United Nations.

Stone, D. 2003. The productivity and management of sheep in late medieval England. *The Agricultural History Review*, 51(1), 1–22.

Thornton, A. 2019. This is how many animals we eat each year. *World Economic Forum.*Accessedhttps://www.weforum.org/agenda/2019/02/chart-of-the-day-this-is-how-many-animals-we-eat-each-year/

Van Dooren, T. and Rose, D. B. 2016. Lively ethography: Storying animist worlds. *Environmental Humanities*, 8(1), 77–94.

Vining, J. 2003. The connection to other animals and caring for nature. *Human Ecology Review*, 10(2), 87–99.

Vonk, J. 2019. Pulling the wool from our eyes. *Animal Sentience*, 4(25), 3.

Webster, J. 2019. Sentient animals do not just live in the present. *Animal Sentience*, 4(25), 10.

Wilkie, R. 2015. Multispecies scholarship and encounters: Changing assumptions at the human-animal nexus. *Sociology*, 49(2), 323–339.

Wolch, J. R. and Emel, J. (Eds.). 1998. *Animal Geographies: Place, Politics, and Identity in the Nature-Culture Borderlands*. London: Verso.

Wolfe, C. (Ed.). 2003. *Zoontologies: The Question of the Animal*. Minnesota: University of Minnesota Press.

5

HEARTBREAKING LOSSES IN REAL PLACES

Losing and finding solace in the Anthropocene

Introduction: bearing small dispatches

Like the rest of this book, this chapter explores some of the ways in which we, as human beings, are entangled in the Anthropocene and the intersecting psychological, emotional and social consequences, all of which impact varyingly in terms of their reach, pace, extent, observability and tangibility. It offers a critical counterpoint to approaches to the Anthropocene framed in technical-managerial terms, which can perpetuate dichotomous, colonialist, human exceptionalist perspectives on 'mitigation' and 'adaptation'. It embraces multiple, heterogeneous, often marginalised perspectives, with the intention, to paraphrase Campbell et al. (2018, p. 3), to explore the terrain not as 'conquistador mapmakers' of the Anthropocene, 'but as bearers of small dispatches'. Anthropocene psychology is about coming to terms with an actually and anticipated radically changing world, which means we are looking for ways to approach the 'complex linkages between environmental transformations, lives and livelihoods, cultural identity, and mental, emotional, and spiritual well-being' (Tschakert et al., 2013, p. 14).

Across environmental psychology, medical and health geographies, places have been defined as 'local environments imbued with meaning and significance by those associated with them' (Ellis and Albrecht, 2017, p. 161). Relatedly, the conceptualisation of the psychological and social significance of a 'sense of place' has been central to an emerging field dedicated to 'the analysis of the cultural, personal and mental health risks posed by a changing climate' (ibid; Adger, 2016; Berry et al., 2011). These risks include a threatened sense of place on multiple scales, incorporating home, neighbourhood, local habitat, landscape and ecosystem, but also the more distal spatial scale of region, nation, continent or the whole earth (Devine-Wright, 2013).[1] Across all scales, place attachment and sense of place are theorised as integral to human development, health and identity, a position now supported by many studies (e.g. Cummins et al., 2007; Fresque-Baxter and Armitage, 2012; Hess et al., 2008; Cunsolo Willox., 2012). Disruptions to place from a changing climate can therefore run deep, engendering environmentally induced psychological distress and 'psychoterratic' syndromes rooted in experience of place (Albrecht, 2011).

In this chapter, the focus is on place, as the situated and specific context through which Anthropocene realities are known and articulated. In doing so, my intention is to focus on work which foregrounds lived experience of landscape undergoing environmental change, largely negative change. I am in agreement with Tschakert et al. (2017, p. 7), arguing for the need to highlight the 'ways people "dwell" in places and landscapes and establish relationships through their daily encounters – intertwined with culture, history, and affective connections to the land, nonhuman species, and the weather and climate around them... [as] an alternative entry point to frequently detached scientific assessments of climate impact studies'. The overview and analysis provided here are not restricted to psychological and geographical analysis in which 'place' is a factor or variable in assessing health and well-being, instead taking in vital and animist perspectives on place which challenge straightforward distinctions between people as complex meaning processors and places as relatively inert. It outlines work centred on solastalgia as a prominent conceptualisation of 'environmentally induced place-based distress', before turning to critique and alternatives drawing on understandings of place developed in other disciplines. Filtered through the understanding of place reached at this point of the chapter, it closes with a discussion of the importance of recent, resurgent attempts to grant natural entities legal personhood and the importance of love and care for place to the Anthropocene stories to come. Before that, however, I want to follow the example set in other chapters of this book and ground our exploration in a specific and situated example that approaches the phenomenon in question.

Tonight I've said my goodbyes

> We wanted to protect something we loved,' she says. 'And our right to do that – our democratic right – was taken away, really, by state force. It was so horrible and disempowering.

These are the words of Jenny Hockey, arrested and detained by police in 2016 after protesting against a controversial tree-felling programme in Sheffield. In a pre-dawn manoeuvre, the construction company Amey, beneficiaries of a secretive £2.2 billion private finance initiative (PFI) contract with Sheffield council to improve its roads over 25 years, had erected 'protective barriers' around eight trees on Rustlings Road. South Yorkshire Police officers cordoned off the street and banged on residents' doors at 5 am, in the darkness, ordering them to move their vehicles. Jenny and two of her neighbours stepped past one of the barriers to stand under a tree as a protest and were arrested – they spent 8 hours in a police cell, before all charges were dropped.

Following a year or so of relatively minor objections and petitions, these arrests were a turning point in what has become a long-running protest, shaped by a sense amongst many locals that the definition of 'dying or damaging' trees – necessary to earmark them for destruction – was wilfully manipulated by Amey and the council to cut costs.[2] Chopping down trees and replanting saplings elsewhere is apparently a lot cheaper than looking after mature trees and working around them. Following a freedom of information request, it was revealed that the council had asked for up to 17,500 trees to be felled, almost half of the city's estimated 36,000 street trees (Behrens, 2016; Burn, 2018). Membership of the newly formed Sheffield Trees Action Groups (STAG) burgeoned, and protests and arrests followed through 2016–2019 across various Sheffield streets. Whilst some local people defended tree removal on grounds of safety and practicality, it is the voices of the many challengers that resonate with the focus of this chapter.

For some, the removal of trees tangibly contributes to an 'extinction of experience' – as each generation has less direct experience of the natural environment than the previous, the baseline of what is 'normal' shifts, and with it a gradual erosion of the felt benefits of a connection to nature, and a desire to value and protect it (Bird, 2007). Others have campaigned for trees as vital to public health, pointing to the evidence of the various health and well-being benefits of 'urban forests' and, conversely, lack of access to greenspace as marker of a range of individual and community problems (e.g. Beyer et al., 2014; Jonnes, 2017; Kuo and Sullivan, 2001).

Some also articulated a sense of powerlessness, intimately tied to disruption to what had been a taken-for-granted experience of place: 'People were going to work in the morning and coming home to entirely different-looking streets... It was ecological destruction carried out, in secret, by a multinational company with the explicit support of the local authority and the police' (local resident Paul Selby, cited in Drury, 2018). It turned out that many locals had long and deep attachments to their neighbourhood trees, and a sense of powerlessness was compounded by more personal and emotional feelings of loss. Local residents' 'tree stories', combined with photos, convey some of this depth of feeling. Here are two examples from the Sheffield Trees Action Groups website:

> Cherry, Wath Road, S7
> They're coming for this tomorrow (30/09/17) – it's not in a particularly fancy part of Nether Edge, but it's one of only two left on this not very green bit of S7, and we love it. 88% of residents voted to save it but it's down to be felled – mainly because the Tarmac machine would never get under it probably. Tonight I've said my goodbyes after 17 years of looking out into it, and listening to the owl who occasionally rests there at night and the to the bees who buzz around the blossom in spring. We tried.
>
> *(Helen Shipley)*
>
> Lime, Thornsett Road, S7
> I wanted to share this pic of the bottom of Thornsett [Road] with you; I took it on a crisp November morning in 2015 when my partner and I had just moved to the area and we were walking to work about 8am. The pic really sums up what the trees in this area mean to me and I guess, to so many other people – they're so enchanting in every season, so special to us, and I have never stopped feeling totally incensed about what is essentially environmental vandalism. I feel like if we can remember and record their beauty – well, that's something they can never take away from us, can they.
>
> *(Kate Elizabeth Mitchel)*

As long-time campaigner Joanna Dobson eloquently blogs, 'street trees are quotidian landmarks that punctuate both the space and the time in which we pass our everyday lives. To rip them out, as our council is doing, is to destroy not only the tree, but also something profoundly important to the identity of our city and to those of us who call Sheffield home' (Dobson, 2018). She makes clear how temporal and spatial dimensions of identity are anchored in our connections to place. In fact, 'place' can seem like an unwieldy and abstract term for what is being described here – it is the lively human and more-than-human entanglements that together constitute place as a phenomenally meaningful experience – even if we are 'only' talking about humans and trees in this example.

Our example of Sheffield's trees, and others like it, point to the extent to which place is integral to self, and attachment to place is imbued with an assemblage of attachments to others, broadly defined, including nonhuman. These trees offer only a small, specific example of 'ecological loss' – and not an especially profound form of social and environmental upheaval, perhaps – houses are still standing, livelihoods are not under threat. Nevertheless, although the focus here is Sheffield, similar tree-defence campaigns are being fought globally (BBC, 2018; Moore, 2014), as are protests to protect species through which together we constitute place as meaningful. Around the world, environmental degradation, both large and small scale, rapid and incremental, anticipated and ongoing, is emerging as a defining experience of the Anthropocene. And although, like climate change, it is a global phenomenon, it is experienced most intensely in specific places (Cunsolo Willox., 2012). In accounting for loss, we are not describing a static temporal and spatial configuration of what has been lost, but a process still underway and incomplete, revealing an entanglement that (still) runs deep, evident in protests on the urban fringes of a city in the north of the United Kingdom. But if we frame the significance of these experiences as 'sense of place', or 'place identity', we must take care to avoid a sterile, abstracted view of 'place' that is inert, external and distinct from human; nor to empty those places of the lively, animated, multi-species encounters that constitute them. If these kinds of localised, specific, nature- and place-based threats can engender such a response, what of the countless other examples of the degradation of familiar home-places already underway? Theory and research addressing intersections of loss, identity, a sense of belonging, place and more-than-human nature in the Anthropocene are the focus of this chapter.

But accounts of loss rarely tell the whole story, including the story of Sheffield's trees. At the time of writing, approximately 5,500 trees have been chopped down (STAG, 2019a, b), but the felling programme has now been 'paused' as a response to protests. Although the PFI contract remains in place and there are as yet no alternative plans, dialogue has begun; a compromise is apparently being sought. Collective resistance and articulation of loss and melancholy also appear to have revived localised, creative expressions of love of place and reminded residents of the value they place on trees and our more-than-human companions. It has long been known that threats to place identity – whereby, 'through personal attachment to geographically locatable places, a person acquires a sense of belonging and purpose which give meaning to his or her life' (Proshansky et al., 1983, p. 60) – can make it more salient; awareness of our positive attachment to place may increase (Breakwell, 1986; Cheng and Chou, 2015). Naturalist Robert Macfarlane wrote a poem for the Sheffield tree protestors called *Heartwood*, 'in defence of trees facing unjust felling anywhere in the world'. The poem was fashioned as a 'charm-against-harm' and hung round threatened trees by protestors, and an illustrated version strategically flyposted across the city. 'Blossom festivals', street parties and other celebrations of Sheffield's trees have also flourished, whilst networks have been formed with a global tree advocacy movement. In what follows, it is also considered vital, then, in the context of situated and specific places, to explore attempts to find solace, stay with the trouble and challenge disempowerment in the Anthropocene (Haraway, 2016).

Heartbreaking losses in real places

There can be no doubt that, for many of us, the negative impacts of Anthropocene realities are still experienced as fuzzy and remote. As I sit here writing this, I can access the latest news stories under the heading of nature and environment. Just today, I have read about the discovery that the second-largest emperor penguin colony in the world, somewhere between 15,000–24,000, was wiped out 'overnight' after an ice sheet in Antarctica collapsed – likely as a consequence of climate change. Meanwhile, satellite imagery and remote monitoring reveal that 12 million hectares (30 million acres) of tropical tree cover was lost globally in 2018 – equivalent to 30 football pitches every minute of every day of the year (Suliman, 2019), much of it in irreplaceable primary rainforest. One of the researchers responsible for the forestry data affirms that such figures 'represent heartbreaking losses in real places' – a point that applies to both of these stories, and countless more. And yet, as I return to the present moment, at my kitchen table, however troubling I might find this information, I can carry on with my life, relatively unperturbed. Of course, such knowledge might spur me to action of some kind, but it remains the case that my lived experience is relatively unaffected. Trees can be seen from my window, swaying in the breeze against a backdrop of shifting clouds; birdsong even makes itself heard through the rumble of traffic: 'The main obstacle that prevents us from confronting the ecological crisis at its most radical... resides in the unreliability of our common-sense itself which, habituated as it is to our ordinary life-world, finds it difficult to really accept that the flow of everyday reality can be perturbed' (Žižek, 2009, p. 445).

However, experience of place – in all its phenomenal, relational, sociocultural dimensions – is precisely where a reading of our relationship with the 'natural world' as both taken for granted and disconnected is complicated, especially in the context of the Anthropocene. This becomes clear when we ask: What happens when environmental change *does* begin to intrude upon lived realities, when a disrupted nature pierces the seeming imperturbableness of common-sense and everyday life, in the 'real places' which we inhabit? If we accept the invitation of the Anthropocene as a conceptual frame, it must be as a process, one which is underway, and one which is experienced in and through the entanglements of specific and situated places, including the temporal and spatial particularities of the cultural mediation of 'climate change', 'global warming', 'Anthropocene' and so on, and the ongoing impacts of colonialism, industrialism, state socialism and capitalism. At the very moment the Anthropocene draws us out as a species for special consideration, a version of human exceptionalism, if you like, it magnifies our human and more-than-human relational attachments and re-embeds the human species within a network of interdependency that is ongoing.

To adapt Schroder's claim that 'the language of CO_2 emissions and existential threat simply cannot convey the elemental truth to be witnessed in the material world' (2019, p. 52), we might say that however powerful the rhetoric of the Anthropocene narrative, its power to shape a profound response is rooted in first-order experiences of the changes it foretells – that is, direct and unmediated experience: 'the experiencing of *x,* in contrast to experiencing *x* through the intercession of *y* or *z*' (Heft, 2003, p. 151). We are differentially positioned in the maelstrom of encounters, of course. The distribution of threats and losses remains profoundly unequal and unjust, routinely mapping onto the residual fault lines of colonialism and capitalism, and is reflected in the tensions and alliances between 'full-stomach' and 'empty-belly' environmentalism

(Nixon, 2011, p. 5; Klein, 2015). If fall-out remains far from democratic, it is spreading, exceeding the boundaries of North–South, developed-developing – Schroder, cited above, is speaking specifically of wildfires in the United States. Noticing can have direct and immediate correlates, felt as corporeal, phenomenal associations – hunger, thirst, fear; experiencing precarious water supplies in a drought; fleeing for safety at a rapidly encroaching forest fire; mourning ill or dying companion species or migration from places made incrementally uninhabitable by climate change or pollution. But the individual and collective body can notice in many more ways the shock of the Anthropocene, such as in the experience of 'anticipatory loss' (Randall, 2009): the 'grief' associated with 'anticipated future ecological losses' (Cunsolo Willox and Ellis, 2018, p. 276), amplified by the discerning of increasingly ominous climate change scenarios – 'losses expected to come, but not yet arrived' (Cunsolo Willox, 2012, p. 140). The fact that historical and ongoing human activity – our (some of our) actions – are responsible for these losses laces these experiences for many with guilt, anxiety and all the defensive reactions they portend, conscious or otherwise.

Back in 2012, Ashlee Cunsolo Willox claimed that 'despite these intense feelings and experiences, the grief and mourning experienced by individuals and communities globally to anthropogenic climate change seems strangely silenced in public climate change discourse' (p. 141). Things are changing slowly, in terms of a steady stream of academic research developing typologies of loss and other shared emotional responses (e.g. Head, 2016; Lertzman, 2015; Mark, 2016) and more quickly as a wider cultural response.[3] Clearly, such phenomena are vital to any attempt to develop an Anthropocene psychology, and a number of summaries and overviews document the emerging terrain (Cunsolo and Ellis, 2018; Weintrobe, 2013). The intention in the rest of this chapter is more specifically to tie an analysis of 'intense feelings and experiences' that accompany noticing change to *place*. It looks to work in psychology, social science, anthropology and geography. It focuses on experiences of place that people hold explicitly dear, the sense of a home environment and one's felt sense of connection to it – *place attachment*, as it is referred to in some literature (Manzo and Devine-Wright, 2013). What follows is an exploration of place attachment under threat and attendant experiences, their framing in social science and humanities theory and research and a critical consideration of the contribution this work can make to Anthropocene stories.

Solastalgia: the home become suddenly unhomely

While there are numerous contenders for making conceptual sense of the disquiet provoked by the degradation of specific places and related feelings of actual and anticipatory, material and emotional-psychological loss – including nature-deficit disorder, eco-anxiety, ecological grief and existential outsideness (Mallett, 2012; Smith, 2018; Tschakert et al., 2013) – the chosen foil for exploring change, loss and identity in the context of the Anthropocene here is the concept of solastalgia. This concept is chosen because, in tandem with analogous conceptual developments, it explicitly focuses on place, and it offers a theoretical point of critical departure, whilst developed and critiqued in a range of empirical work. Solastalgia was offered as a new concept in health and identity by environmental philosopher Glenn Albrecht (2005). It is defined as 'the distress that is produced by environmental change impacting on people while they are directly connected to their home environment' (Albrecht et al., 2007, p. 95). Before exploring solastalgia in more detail, the network of existing theoretical and empirical traditions from which it emerges and depends upon is briefly outlined.

Whether explicit or not, the concept of solastalgia rests on claims about the importance of something approaching a 'sense of place' or attachment to place as fundamental to human experience, well-being and identity (Cresswell, 2004). The existence of such a bond has been subject to theory and research in numerous disciplines, and the range and variety of analogous ideas dashes the hope that a summary as brief as the one offered here can offer a coherent or comprehensive overview (Kaltenborn 1998; Lewicka, 2011; Low and Altman, 1992; Manzo and Devine-Wright, 2013). As a specific concept, place-attachment is based on the simple insight that 'places, like people or situations, evoke affective reactions' (Blaison and Hess, 2016) and are equally capable of being the object of strong attachments. Relatedly, the disruption of place attachments is capable of threatening one's sense of well-being, security and identity (Brown and Perkins, 1992; Fried, 2000; Fullilove, 1996; Speller and Twigger-Ross, 2009).

The study of place and its significance has been central to the development of human geography (Castree, 2009; Cresswell, 2004; Tuan, 1975) and to subsequent qualitative and phenomenological exploration of place attachment (Seamon, 2000). The study of place attachment and identity has taken a different, if related, theoretical and methodological direction in environmental psychology and psychometric studies – more quantitative in orientation with an emphasis on identifying individual differences in people's attachment to place (e.g. Scannell and Gifford, 2017). This has largely been at the expense of an understanding of human-place bonds as a dynamic experiential process, as involving meaning making and of the components of specific and situated places (Droseltis and Vignoles, 2010). As a result, the former tradition is more obviously the forbearer of solastalgia, though there are signs of psychologisation in attempts to develop 'environmental distress' scales aimed at measuring it quantitatively (e.g. Higginbotham et al., 2016). As with Lewicka's point about place attachment more generally, 'the best way to halt the development of a theory is to devise a personality scale' (2011, p. 226).

Whatever the tradition or orientation of research, work addressing place attachment and identity supports the established phenomenological claim 'that sense of place is a natural condition of human existence (dwelling = being)' (Lewicka, 2011, p. 209). Nature and the natural features of places have long featured as variables, physical assets that might encourage attachment, often conceptually distinguished from 'social' dimensions, or subsumed into them as social constructs (e.g. Alkon and Traugot, 2008), though the 'natural environment' is now becoming established as a dimension in its own right and/or in more complex interrelationship with 'social' factors (Hidalgo and Hernandez, 2001; Scannell and Gifford, 2010). In fact, outdoor and natural locations commonly emerge as preferred or favourite places in psychological studies (Korpela et al., 2009), including memories of childhood, and are therefore conceptually weighted as especially significant dimensions of place-attachment (Knez et al., 2018; Scannell and Gifford, 2010; Windhorst and Williams, 2015). More recently, experiential nature-relatedness, situated in place, is posited as a basic need (Baxter and Pelletier, 2019). We might add that there is a history of scholarship in anthropology and nature/ecology-oriented phenomenology, wherein the affordances of the natural world are integral to being-in-place (Abram, 2012; Chalquist, 2009; Ingold, 2002).

The concept of solastalgia pursues the depth of attachment to specific and situated natural places as they intersect with a broad concept of home, and with it people's sense of identity and belonging (Begg and Thompson, 2011). As will be explored below, it does so at the moment this attachment is disrupted or threatened. The development and application of the concept parallels and contributes to an emerging body of scholarship considering the relationship between climate change, place attachments and identities (e.g. Devine-Wright, 2013; Reser et al., 2011; Scannell and Gifford, 2013), but extends that focus to what would be more accurately referred to as Anthropocene places – those shaped and affected by anthropogenic impacts including but not limited to climate change.

Albrecht coined the term 'solastalgia' to make sense of the experiences of environmentally induced distress he had been encountering as a researcher whilst working with residents of the Upper Hunter region of New South Wales, Australia (Albrecht, 2005). Communities in the area have long been impacted by open-cut mining and other heavy industry. Albrecht's early definition of solastalgia is fuller than later summaries and soundbites, so it is reproduced in detail here:

> Solastalgia has its origins in the concepts of 'solace' and 'desolation'... literally, solastalgia is the pain or sickness caused by the loss or lack of solace and the sense of isolation connected to the present state of one's home and territory... It is the pain experienced when there is recognition that the place where one resides and that one loves is under immediate assault (physical desolation). It is manifest in an attack on one's sense of place, in the erosion of the sense of belonging (identity) to a particular place and a feeling of distress (psychological desolation) about its transformation. It is an intense desire for the place where one is a resident to be maintained in a state that continues to give comfort or solace
>
> *(Albrecht, 2005, p. 48)*

Albrecht and colleagues have operationalised the concept in studies of persistent drought and large-scale open-cut coal mining (e.g. Albrecht et al., 2007; Connor et al., 2008), and it has since been applied to range of places, people and contexts (e.g. Eisenman et al., 2015; Hendryx and Innes-Wimsatt, 2013; McNamara and Westoby, 2011; Smith, 2018; Tschakert and Tutu, 2010; Warsini et al., 2014). The notion of solastalgia has been developed and expanded to incorporate climatic and environmental changes across all continents and in many environments. Any attempt at a composite definition today cannot fully accommodate the variety of situations to which it has been applied and direction it has been taken conceptually. It extends, on the one hand, the forms taken by environmental change and ecosystem distress, and on the other, variations on the theme of how lived experience is affected by those changes. The term has become a focal point for what Seamon and Sowers assert to be a vital dimension of the study of a sense of place – the 'depth and complexity of place as it is experienced and fashioned by real people in real places' (2008, p. 43). Introducing critical voices is important at this juncture, as they help unsettle a tendency towards psychologising and instrumentalism in researching the psychosocial dimensions of climate change impacts on place. The case is made that constructive critique facilitates dialogue between the conceptualisation of solastalgia and insights offered by environmental humanities and Indigenous perspectives on the elements of a sense of place in the Anthropocene. In what follows, solastalgia is challenged and extended via a discussion of colonialism.

Colonialism and the imposed transformations of place

Albrecht and colleagues intended to use the concept of solastalgia to address 'the relationship between ecosystem health, human health, and powerlessness' (Connor et al., 2004). The latter is often overlooked in the rush to operationalise solastalgia as an indicator of 'place-based distress' and, relatedly, as a measurable mental health issue. Even if a sense of powerlessness is included in an instrument to detect the existence and extent of solastalgia, it misses the point that it is a relational configuration, one that includes relations of power; it is not reducible to, though it is likely to be reflected in, individual feelings of disempowerment. Powerlessness in the context of solastalgia is an individual and collective response to *imposed transformations* to place that are not, or at least not easily, remedied or resisted by inhabitants (Connor et al., 2004). Across the globe, relational power to shape place is asymmetrically divided between different individuals, groups and communities; this asymmetry is historically, socially and materially structured, such as is evident in colonialism and its legacies, the power of corporations, the state and the instruments of national and local government, but also community and campaign groups, protest and advocacy networks on various scales. Today this is most obvious in the extractivist activities of corporations, but these are often historical legacies of the countless acts of 'geographical violence' and 'traumatic dislocation' that accompanied colonialism (Said, 1995, p. 271). In Davis and Todd's words (2017, p. 762), for Indigenous peoples, 'the Anthropocene is not a new event, but only the continuation of practices of dispossession and genocide, coupled with a literal transformation of the environment, which have been under operation for the last five hundred years'. In the context of the more incremental impositions of the Anthropocene (extreme weather, persistent drought, rising sea levels, melting ice), experiences of powerlessness might become both more nebulous and widespread, but they are rooted in historical and political configurations of power that still shape opportunities for resistance, mitigation and adaptation.

Holding on to collective experiences of powerlessness and dispossession as central to experiences of solastalgia, the case has been made that the concept can be a useful tool for resisting colonial and corporate power. Kennedy (2016) reports on a singular success whereby a (non-Indigenous) community in Australia utilised the concept successfully in a court of law to appeal against government approval of coal-mine expansion: 'the Court held that the expansion of the mine would have had significant negative impacts upon the community and the environment, which would not have been outweighed by the projected economic benefits to be gained' (2016, p. 35). Such victories perhaps suggest the utility of conceptual tools for contributing to attempts to develop wider legal frameworks (e.g. Cullinan, 2011). In terms of colonial legacies and Indigenous dispossession, Pannell argues explicitly that the neologism potentially:

> [provides] anthropologists with a useful conceptual tool for understanding and framing the emotional experiences of many Indigenous people in Australia, who stand witness to the transformation and/or loss of their traditional homelands, or who find that they have been legally disenfranchised from their ancestral country by the stroke of a pen in a far-off capital city
>
> *(2018, p. 258)*

Her argument is premised on Albrecht's earlier emphasis on solastalgia as intimately linked to the dispossession of Indigenous people's culture and land, following colonialism and its impacts, and emphatically not an 'idealisation of a golden past, but a genuine grieving for the ongoing loss of "country" and all that entails' (Albrecht, 2005 p. 50). Albrecht notes a depth of connection to place in many Indigenous cultures that is distinct from European cultures, difficult even to comprehend. He cites Deborah Bird Rose to convey the vitalism and animism attached to 'country' in Indigenous cultures of Australia:

> Country is not a generalised or undifferentiated type of place, such as one might indicate with terms like 'spending a day in the country' or 'going up the country'. Rather, country is a living

entity with a yesterday, today and tomorrow, with a consciousness, and a will toward life. Because of this richness, country is home, and peace; nourishment for body, mind and spirit; heart's ease

(Rose, cited in Albrecht, 2005, p. 51)

It follows that imposed dispossession combined with a stronger attachment means culture and place are intimately intertwined, and the 'dis-ease' of solastalgia may well be felt more deeply by Indigenous people and reflected in a range of endemic social, psychological and physical problems. For Albrecht, the diagnosis of solastalgia is key to solving these problems, coupled with 'its negation by self-empowered Indigenous people being directly involved in the repair and restoration of their "home"' (2005, p. 51). Pannell suggests that such a diagnosis might help establish a basis for compensatory award of 'solatium' in Australian Law – relating to emotional harm arising from a loss of connection to land.

Whatever the pragmatic value of a diagnostic approach to solastalgia, the logic of utilising it as a conceptual frame for Indigenous experiences is problematic. If we accept that a loss of solace is more keenly and deeply felt by many Indigenous people as a result of their historical experiences and complex understandings of human and more-than-human relationality particularised through place (Nxumalo and Cedillo, 2017), would we not expect that the traditions and practices of different Indigenous cultures already have their own vocabulary and articulation of loss and mourning? Should we not consider that sense is being made of disconnection and displacement that have taken place against a backdrop of, and are implicated in, the unprecedented anthropogenic impacts of colonialism and globalisation – consolidated in the emerging Anthropocene? It is unfortunate that the eager application of solastalgia itself has the whiff of colonial imposition and missionary zeal. In academic terms, it seems to reflect the still prevalent tendency to ignore or marginalise Indigenous scholarship and understanding of pressing contemporary issues, and fix Indigenous culture as static 'tradition' (cf. Todd, 2016). To take just one brief example, in some forms of Māori culture, *tangi* refers to both a funeral rite, which is an important component of Māori cultural expression and identity in its own right (Nikora et al., 2012), and more simply, grieving. But also at a 'deeper, affective level' it is 'the weeping', which is described as:

a declaration about and a reference to the tragedy of land loss and cultural identity. *Tangi* flows from the remnants of land in which resides the wounded soul handed down by ancestors. Such weeping is not just for the immediate material loss, but also for the lost potential and the diminution of spiritual and cultural identity

(Henare, 2015, p. 84)

Perhaps Albrecht's solastalgia is a form of *tangi* for a non-Indigenous culture still struggling to develop conceptual and cultural frameworks to articulate that loss explicitly – the 'inchoate' form of mourning described by Lertzman (2015, p. 7), but less as a universal unconscious dynamic, and more as a culturally contingent one.

Similarly, it might be possible to develop a more explicitly *relational* consideration of solastalgia that more directly addresses processes of being and becoming as human and more-than-human entanglements in specific and situated places. From the perspective of a relational ontology, place is not just a 'place' with objects in it (parents, birds, trees, buildings, meadows) which we invest in, and mourn as they are defiled or degraded. Solastalgically saturated places are assemblages of multiple and multi-directional encounters through which we are constituted as humans – 'we become *through* the things we live amongst' (Askland and Bunn, 2018) – just as, if we adopt a thoroughgoing more-than-human and animist perspective, those 'things' become lively through us, anchoring in corporeal networks the 'placedness of the being of being human' (Benjamin, 2015, p. 15).

If we are to understand how 'the trauma of losing a sense of place lies within the ontological and rests somewhere in the connection between the actor and their realities' (p. 20), those 'realities' must be understood within a framework that grants them agency in encounters. However, whilst Durkalec et al. (2015) point to where a more relational view of place is being employed in a growing body of academic research (e.g. Cunsolo Willox, 2012; Tschakert et al., 2017), it is already a long-standing and often neglected conceptualisation in various forms of Indigenous knowledge; one that is being developed today by contemporary Indigenous scholarship and partnerships, evident, for example, in the 'co-becoming' spoken of by the Bawaka Research collective in attempting to represent a Yolŋu ontology – 'within which everything exists in a state of emergence and relationality' (Country et al., 2016, p. 456). This involves taking the step, with Haraway (2015; 2016), Tsing (2012; 2015), Neimanis et al. (2015) and others, towards an understanding of 'more-than-human others as social, agentic, and political participants in world-making with humans' (Nxumalo and Cedillo, 2017, p. 107), in accepting the Anthropocene as invitation.

Anthropocene as invitation

Whether solastalgia, *tangi* or an alternative, most theory and research speaks at the same time of enduring feelings of belonging invested in everyday landscapes, even if it owes its salience to experiencing it as under threat (Tschakert et al., 2013). And a sense of belonging, however forlorn or endangered, speaks of networks of attachment. In fact, the sociality that might emerge more explicitly from recognising experiences of threat and loss to 'place' is considered by some a basis for resistance and restoration – this was an essential component of Albrecht's original development of the term (2005; Connor et al., 2008). The realisation of the importance of connections to place, and its lively inhabitants, engenders a desire to hold on to it, defend and fight for it, perhaps even (re)affirms an ethical responsibility to nonhuman others. Accounts of place identity in environmental psychology and geography seem to support this sentiment, in that 'the more central a place is to identity, the more "we are willing to fight" for it when we feel that conditions are unsatisfactory' (Fresque-Baxter and Armitage, 2012, p. 260; Kaltenborn, 1998). This is evident in our opening example – in the creative collective reactions to the corporate felling of Sheffield's street trees described there. A love of trees, as cherished elements of place, persists.

A love of place – or *topophilia* (Tuan, 1974) – readily translates to natural environments and is residual in distress rooted in place – anguish and mourning only make sense in the context of love for what is lost (Ellis and Albrecht, 2017; West-Newman, 2008). Following Tuan, Ellis and Albrecht define topophilia as 'a positive emotional experience related to the health and vitality of place as expressed in feelings of joy, familiarity, and being "at home"' (Ellis and Albrecht, 2017, p. 162). There is as yet little research exploring the relationship between topophilia and solastalgia, love and mourning for place (Kingsley et al., 2013). What interests me, in closing this chapter, is how the persistence of topophilia is worth emphasising as a constructive and hopeful response to Anthropocene as invitation. The critical emphasis on solastalgia in this chapter helps us to recognise the importance of situated and specific relational ontology grounded, literally, in place. To further embrace the radical implications of this ontology, not least as it is manifest in various forms of Indigenous knowledge, means more than a recognition of the value of a 'human connection to place' or 'place-based distress'. It is to recognise the depth of interrelatedness between human and more-than-human worlds; and that 'more-than-human bodies, specific stories, ontologies, histories, as well as humans are all lively and entangled participants in the shaping of place' (Nxumalo and Cedillo, 2017 p. 102), even as they are created in specific and situated places through inequitable and asymmetrical relations (Tschakert et al., 2017).

In doing so, we must find ways to acknowledge and articulate loss, a familiar refrain in psychosocial engagements with the impacts of climate change (e.g. Randall, 2009), developing an open and 'critical stance toward real, anticipated, and generational loss that embraces both mourning and a shared feeling of vulnerability' (Tschakert et al., 2013, p. 23; Kelly, 2009). From here we might seek opportunities for deeper attachments with a more-than-human world (cf. Bennett, 2001). There is no guarantee that a collective sense of responsibility 'to live in ethical relationality with more-than-human others' (Nxumalo and Cedillo, 2017 p. 102) will follow. Nonetheless, there are plenty of signs of movements emerging that combine a fundamentally symbiotic view of life with a recognition of more-than-human agency, and a spirited defence of specific 'places'. These movements already stretch across the globe, such as in the spread of rewilding projects and the 'rise of the rights of nature', reflected in attempts, increasingly successful, to grant legal personhood to natural entities such as forests, mountains and rivers (Banda, 2018; Cullinan, 2011; Hutchinson, 2014; Kennedy, 2012; Maloney, 2018; O'Donnell, 2018; 2017; O'Donnell and Talbot-Jones, 2018; O'Donnell and Macpherson, 2019) – often with significant ownership of, or input from Indigenous communities (Gleeson-White, 2018).

I am the river, the river is me

Debates about ontology can seem obscure – what does it matter whether 'place' is related to as an external 'natural environment' containing objects that are important to us, or a lively conclave of 'reciprocal relations' (Diver et al., 2019)? But such distinctions are prescient in making a case for the rights of natural entities, exemplifying nothing less than an ontological shift: 'by granting the river legal standing the river is no longer an object, but has been transformed to a legal person which has rights and duties itself and which can enforce these rights against other legal persons' (Hutchinson, 2014, p. 179). In other words, following its framing within an ethical, reciprocal relationality, river becomes at least partially subjectivised (as opposed to objectified), rendered an 'actant' in the assemblage 'in that it is made to act by many others' (Latour, 2005, p. 46). A claim for rights here is still undeniably distinct from human rights, but on something closer to an equal ontological footing through new allegiances. Diver et al. define reciprocal relations as the 'underscoring of the mutual caretaking obligations held between nature and society, as intertwining entities that are co-constituted with one another' (2019, p. 1), and the translation into practice of 'our ethical obligations to care for, restore, and protect the land and resources that, in turn, support our existence' (p. 5).

A growth in the legal recognition of the 'rights of nature' has pursued an approach to place more explicitly attuned to how fundamental reciprocal relationality is to many forms of Indigenous knowledge. The defence of the rights of nature and natural entities has numerous historical precedents, in theory and practice. Roger Stone was an early academic proponent, offering an ethical, conceptual and practical orientation for recognising the legal rights of nature (Stone, 1972). We can go back further, if we acknowledge recognition of the rights of the more-than-human world as it is embedded and developed in Indigenous cosmologies, methodologies and practices. These have often jarred fundamentally with imposing colonialist and settler worldviews and attendant ontologies, suppressing any kind of formal power to enact or enforce any of these understandings in law, and further marginalising them in the process. As always, we should be mindful of specifics rather than lumping the experience of Indigenous communities together. In Aotearoa New Zealand, for example, the Treaty of Waitangi in 1840 set some principles for dialogue and partnership between the British Crown and the Māori, and the grounds for redress where the principles of the Treaty were breached. Following years of Māori protest concerning failures by the Crown to honour the Treaty, a process for redress and reconciliation was formally established in 1975 as an Act of Parliament to establish a permanent Waitangi Tribunal (Stokes, 1992). It took 10 more years before the Tribunal was extended historically to the signing of the Treaty in 1840. Although not legally binding, the Tribunal investigates claims brought by Māori against the Crown for breaches of Treaty promises. These include rights to 'natural resources' such as land, forests, rivers and oceans (Bess, 2001; De Alessi, 2012; Ruckstuhl et al., 2014; Te Aho, 2010).

A now well-known case in this context is the Whanganui River. The river runs 290 km from Mount Tongariro in the central North Island to the Tasman Sea on the island's west coast. The surrounding area has been occupied by Māori, particularly the Whanganui Iwi, for more than 800 years. Until recently, the riverbed was owned by the

Crown, and the river and catchment managed by local authorities (O'Donnell and Talbot Jones, 2018). Local Māori have long contested this arrangement, including the pursuit of change through the Waitangi Tribunal (Waitangi Tribunal, 1999; 2015). Following a lengthy 8-year negotiation, a landmark agreement was reached in 2017 as the Te Awa Tupua (Whanganui River Claims Settlement) Act.

There have been previous attempts to protect nature and natural entities through the judicial process. According to legal scholars O'Donnell and Talbot-Jones, the expansion of environmental law has tended to focus on the value of natural resources to the public and protection of the environment in terms of human benefit more or less exclusively, and so 'have often obscured the particular interests of "nature" behind the effects of environmental degradation on human interests' (O'Donnell and Talbot-Jones, 2018, p. 3). Ontologically, nonhumans remain fixed in the realm of objects, if ones that require protection, divided from natural and juridical persons (humans, corporations): the latter exercise rights over the former. As these authors also point out, although more explicit attempts have been made to enshrine the interests of nature constitutionally in the twenty-first century (in Bolivia, Ecuador and India for example), adequate representation, capacity to defend legally and power to enforce rights have all been lacking – in practice, 'they have no bite' (Daly, 2012; O'Donnell and Talbot-Jones, 2018; Whittemore 2011, p. 659).

The Te Awa Tupua Act is considered a landmark settlement in that it is one of the first to formally grant 'legal personhood' to a specific natural entity (Morris and Ruru, 2010; Rodgers, 2017). In fact, in the same year the Urewera Forest and Mount Taranaki in Aotearoa New Zealand (Maloney, 2018, p. 78), and the Ganges and Yamuna rivers in India, were also formally recognised as having legal personhood (see O'Donnell, 2017; O'Donnell and Talbot-Jones, 2018 for a comparative analysis). Legal personhood does not equate to having the same rights as a human; it is a legal fiction, historically extended to nonhuman entities such as corporations, charities and religious organisations, and in so doing attributing them certain legal rights, duties and responsibilities (O'Donnell and Talbot-Jones, 2018). The same applies in granting this status to a natural entity – a river and its catchment. What is unique about the Te Awa Tupua settlement is that the recognition of personhood arises from extensive negotiation between Māori and the Crown, and explicitly and formally incorporates a Māori approach to environmental management. There is already a great deal of emerging scholarship,

Indigenous, non-Indigenous and collaborative, exploring the implications of the Whanganui settlement (e.g. Cano Pecharroman, 2018; Hudson et al., 2016; Hutchison, 2014; Kennedy, 2012; Maloney, 2018; Rodgers, 2017). The key considerations here are what does it mean in practice, and what are its implications for losing and finding solace in Anthropocene places?

The Te Awa Tupua framework is a form of redress, enacting an earlier Waitangi Tribunal supporting Māori grievances relating to European settlement and a colonial history largely defined by oppression and dispossession (Hutchison, 2014; WT, 1999; 2015). But in explicitly stating that Māori values must be central to the settlement (Kennedy, 2012), it also identifies the river as a subject of reciprocal care, concerned with the interrelated health and flourishing of the river and its human and nonhuman inhabitants. The Act is effectively an attempt to negotiate very different ontological understandings of the river and, by extension, all inhabitants of Whanganui. Kennedy cites Niko Tangaroa, a Māori elder, who articulates this interdependent relationship: 'The river and the land and its people are inseparable. And so if one is affected the other is affected also. The river is the heartbeat, the pulse of our people.... . [If the river] dies, we die as a people. Ka mate te Awa, ka mate tatou te Iwi' (2012, p. 3). In conferring legal personality on the river system, the Tribunal accepts the human and more-than-human entanglement this worldview attests to. O'Donnell and Talbot-Jones go as far as to suggest that the settlement 'approximates the Whanganui Iwi worldview in law' (2018, p. 5), and for Hutchison, the granting of legal personhood demonstrates how enduring Māori relationships to nature and natural entities is now shifting wider society's values (2014).

The process set up to enact and enforce legal personhood – a vital limitation of past attempts to legislate for the rights of nature – is as follows. A guardian (Te Pou Tupua) is appointed – consisting of one representative of both the Crown and the Whanganui Iwi – as those permitted to speak, and stand, acting as one, for the river system (Maloney, 2018). The guardian is supported by a comprehensive institutional framework, consisting of advisory and strategy groups made up of community stakeholders, devised to be participatory and inclusive (Tschirhart et al., 2016). The framework is being supported by regular payments to the river, including 'a NZ$30 million contestable fund... which can be used for the purposes of giving the rights of the river and its catchment force and effect' (O'Donnell and Talbot-Jones, 2018, p. 5).

The guardian is required to defend the physical, ecological, spiritual and cultural rights of the river. Incorporating Māori cultural and spiritual values marks a distinctive approach 'unknown in environmental law in most Western legal systems' (Rodgers, 2017, p. 268). Māori spiritual and cultural interconnection with nature may be difficult to grasp from a non-Indigenous perspective. Hutchison offers an explanation by contrasting a Māori worldview with Western legal framings of property and personhood: 'Property ... refers to something in the outside world, separate from oneself ... the idea of property ... requires the notion of thing, and the notion of thing requires separation from self. This intuition makes it seem appropriate to call parts of the body property only after they have been removed from the system' (Radin, cited in Hutchison, 2014, p. 181).

By contrast, to Whanganui Iwi, reflecting the broader Māori worldview, the river is not a 'thing', but part of the interconnected 'body', part of oneself: 'because the river is not separate but rather part of the people, it cannot be viewed as property' (Hutchinson, 2014, p, 181). Instead, the Iwi contend that the river 'owns' the Iwi, meaning that the Iwi have obligations and responsibilities toward the river. Hutchison goes on to spell out the reciprocal relationality embedded in Māori cultural and spiritual understanding of the Whanganui river: 'the use of the river's resources was always conditional on satisfying obligations to ancestral values and future generations' (2014, p. 181). In becoming a legal person within this specific context, the ontological framing of the river is shifted, from a 'thing' existing primarily for human use, to a figure of co-becoming, a matter of care, an entangled extension of revered being-in-place. As the Te Awa Tupua settlement comes into force, O'Donnell and Talbot-Jones follow earlier commentators in striking a note of cautious optimism – 'legal rights are only worth having if they can be enforced' (p. 7). Nonetheless, efforts have been made to ensure duties and responsibilities to observe the rights of the river and the capacity to defend it legally are identified and in place, issues which have hindered past attempts.

I have only offered a brief exploration of reciprocal relationality and a love of place as it is manifest in the rights of nature movement – there is not the space here to offer a detailed engagement with the latter (see O'Donnell and Talbot-Jones, 2018, for a thorough account of legal process and attendant challenges). What can be said in light of this short discussion is that the Te Awa Tupua Act is about something more than a recognition of the importance of place for well-being, an innovative resource management solution, more even than an example of the ongoing spirited defence of place imbued with animism and vitality; though it is arguably all these things. It is an attempt to enact a form of reciprocal relationality deeply rooted in a relational ontology of place, all the more compelling in the context of Aotearoa New Zealand, precisely, as Kennedy reminds us, 'because it is an agreement to define a natural resource according to the worldview of Māori, the Indigenous people of Aotearoa' (2012, p. 11). By enshrining that worldview in law, the river also becomes a bridge, connecting Crown and Māori through institutional arrangements acceptable to both (Hutchison, 2014).

Nonetheless, reciprocal relationality and topophilia are not restricted to contexts where longstanding Indigenous knowledge has a historical precedent, nor to the formal pursuit of governance and legal rights. In their overview of where such practices are being successfully mobilised, Diver et al. (2019) note a combination of formal and informal practices, across a range of Indigenous and non-Indigenous community case studies. These are contexts akin to the place-based distress described earlier in this chapter – people responding to upheavals in the local landscape including 'intense pressures from global real estate markets, industrial forestry, commercial fishing interests, coal mining, and other extractive industries' (Diver et al., 2019, p. 7) whilst remaining in place. However, their avowed focus is 'community resurgence', as specifically evident in attempts to restore and protect reciprocal relations. The example most obviously aligned with the study of solastalgia is the Appalachian mountain region communities (non-Indigenous) in the United States. The region has been a site of industrial coal mining for generations, including surface mining, and remains one of the few remaining major coal-producing areas in the United States. As the authors summarise, 'even as coal miners have suffered from black lung disease, injuries, and other debilitating health issues, large economic and political forces push for continued fossil fuel extraction in Appalachia, while lessening regulation' (p. 17). Mining has significantly impacted on people, landscape and natural entities, including the watershed: thousands of miles of waterway have been polluted by acid mine drainage, many species have been killed off and the landscape degraded. Nonetheless, Diver et al. recount a narrative of recovery and resurgence via existing research into watershed (Lukacs and Ardoin, 2013). Over time, local residents have come together to care for the watershed, through forms of reciprocity that enmesh 'social' and 'natural' connections. The practicalities involved are worth recounting in detail:

> Some watershed residents reported that they, at first, did not believe change was possible. It took actually seeing a fish swimming in the stream to demonstrate that the watershed group was effective. Some residents watched the local group's efforts for years before joining as a group member themselves. Other non-member residents supported the group in many, often invisible ways, such as cooking for watershed events or reporting sudden stream changes to a watershed group leader... Visible results of watershed group success – projects, events, meetings, and environmental outcomes – motivated the initial and ongoing participation of local residents in watershed groups. Through many forms of participating in caring for impacted watersheds, group member perceptions of these places, and of their own ability to clean them up, changed. Thus, the restoration process, and increased watershed health resulting from restoration activities, motivated caretaking actions, thereby generating a positive feedback loop between watershed group participation and place re-making
>
> *(Diver et al., 2019, p. 19)*

Interestingly the term 'watershed' is now used by many volunteers to refer both to themselves as a group and the place – a recognition of interconnection, and an emergence of 'Place-thought' (Watts, 2013) through reciprocal relations of community resurgence more readily recognisable in examples of Indigenous responses (Diver et al., 2019).

Developments such as this clearly relate to a 'presence of place', a love for and a willingness to protect and defend it. In the course of this discussion, we have become wary of inert, abstract and unidirectional framings of 'place'; which inadvertently binarise 'people' and their 'environment'. Vitally, it might also be alien to many of the Indigenous people bearing the experiential brunt of the Anthropocene's ecological crisis, which, although heterogeneous, often share an already existing understanding of reciprocal relationality which animates the human and more-than-human relations that constitute 'place' (e.g. Arsenault et al., 2018; Kovach, 2009; Littlebear, 2009; McGregor 2014), and provides a significant head start in articulating an accompanying protest and political imaginary. To accept the Anthropocene as invitation, we must recognise and help articulate deeply felt losses as a starting point for action, but we can also strive, however awkwardly and imperfectly, to break out of the explanatory models that have for so long held 'nature' as an inert and malleable backdrop to a human drama, and embrace and develop a more lively, animated narrative of reciprocal relationality. This requires 'two-eyed seeing': 'to learn from one eye with the strengths of Indigenous knowledges and ways of knowing, and from the other eye with the strengths of western knowledges and ways of knowing' (Arsenault et al., 2018, p. 4); 'not integrating, but weaving knowledges so that each way of seeing maintains its own integrity, while enhancing perspective and broadening understanding' (Diver et al., 2019, p. 4).

Finally: on finding solace

Finally, a reminder that a primary form of attachment, though often neglected in academic work, is that a meaningful connection to place and is about care, love, pleasure and delight (de la Bellacasa, 2011; Bennett, 2001). Finding solace in place is also about recognising moments of 'unconditional allegiance' with existence, an attachment to life that is embodied in the reality of being in place. Enchantment is not simple, but an only partially knowable and controllable basis for ethics, for making others matters of care – 'the unknowability and manufacturability of this ethical ground find their parallels in the way that enchantment hits one as if from out of the blue, without warning' (Bennett, 2001, p. 169). Just as for Bennett, the 'story of disenchantment leaves out important things', a solastalgic frame should not blind us to the enduring power of our attachment to the natural world. For Bennett, new scientific instruments and practices are windows to a further capacity for enchantment. Seeing with two eyes, we strive to add Indigenous epistemologies, alive to heterogeneity, boundaries and limits, and not as fixed traditions, but as emerging and collaborative forms that remain distinct (Hunt, 2014; Todd, 2016). Posthuman and more-than-human scholarship enters our vision, too, not as a pre-established perspective which incorporates and legitimises Indigenous voices, but as also heterogeneous (Åsberg, 2018). In all, we see modes of enchantment, without which 'we might not have the energy and inspiration to enact ecological projects, or to contest ugly and unjust modes of commercialisation, or to respond generously to humans and nonhumans that challenge our settled identities' (Bennett, 2001, p. 174).

Summarising the research into climate change and place-based health and well-being, Cunsolo-Willox et al. highlight evidence of how 'place-specific climatic and environmental changes impact physical, bodily, social, economic, cultural, emotional, and psychological connections with the land, and, as a result, negatively affect the physical, mental, and emotional health and well-being of individuals and communities' (2012, p. 544). This particular framing of 'climatic and environmental changes' affecting place, affecting us (humans), tells a very particular story about who and what count as entities and agents, who and what are meaningfully encountered and entangled. It lends itself to particular framings of solutions. What is significant about this body of research for Cunsolo Willox et al. is that it 'indicates that climate-health research and adaptation strategies can be enhanced by considering the importance of local connections to and sense of place' (ibid.). While enhancing 'adaptation' can mean many things, it is easily appropriated within state-sponsored deferrals of deeper collective social change. The range of *reciprocal* connections involved in 'place' and their affective impacts on humans and others are more varied and complex.

This chapter has developed Anthropocene psychology as fundamentally grounded in experiences of *place*. Anthropocene psychology is a terrapsychology, in that it begins with the premise that 'we put the presence of world at the centre of psychology' and 'that we are not really separate from the sites where we live and work' (Chalquist, 2009). Distinguishing between a more or less relational ontology of place might not always matter on the ground (!), but it creates a space for different traditions and points of emphasis that can encourage us to tell very different Anthropocene stories, with different priorities and permutations. Whilst Albrecht's work, in particular, incorporates concepts from multiple disciplines and knowledge bases, insights from sources including Indigenous knowledge, anthropology and ecopsychology offer livelier and more relational definitions of place, which have been approached from various starting points already in previous chapters (e.g. Abram, 2012; Bennett, 2001; Country et al., 2016). Although varied, they emphasise how human existence *is* an element of the reality of a 'presence of place' – an important distinction from 'sense of place' – along with 'its ecology, its geology, its plants and animals, its history and architecture, politics and artwork' (Chalquist, 2009). These perspectives more explicitly challenge dominant Western ontologies and epistemologies of people and place. Beyond extending an ontology of place, this chapter has considered how, to echo Haraway's call, 'staying with the trouble' is integral to the experiences of many communities who remain in place, and here we retain an emphasis on the creative and collective resistance of imposition present in Albrecht's perspective, but often overlooked in applications. Heartbreaking loss is being experienced in specific places, but out of the ruins, care and love endure and may yet emerge in new forms, more 'symbiotically alive to a multiplicity of nonhuman critters and things' (Haraway, 2015, p. 164). In what remains of profound human and more-than-human entanglements, 'we might look around to notice this strange new world, and we might stretch our imaginations to grasp its contours' (Tsing, 2015, p. 3).

Notes

1. It is worth noting Devine-Wright's critical assertion that research to date into a 'sense of place' in the context of climatic disruption has neglected 'the interrelations between multiple place attachments and identities that are polylocal and polyscalar' (2013, p. 64). Anthropocene stories likely speak, at least for some, of simultaneous attachments to more than one place (polylocal) and to places at different scales (polyscalar).
2. For a timeline of protest, see https://www.yorkshirepost.co.uk/our-region/south-yorkshire/sheffield/the-battle-to-save-sheffield-s-trees-six-years-on-and-the-fight-continues-here-s-what-you-need-to-know-1-9054259.
3. See, for example, the establishment of November 30 as a 'Remembrance Day for Lost Species' (RDLS). See https://www.lostspeciesday.org and https://undark.org/article/new-mourning-species-extinction/.

References

Abram, D. 2012. *The Spell of the Sensuous: Perception and Language in a More-Than-Human World*. Vintage.

Adger, W. N. 2016. Place, well-being, and fairness shape priorities for adaptation to climate change. *Global Environmental Change*, 100(38), A1–A3.

Albrecht, G. 2005. 'Solastalgia'. A New Concept in Health and Identity. *PAN: Philosophy Activism Nature*, (3), 41–55.

Albrecht, G. 2011. Chronic environmental change: Emerging 'psychoterratic' syndromes. In *Climate Change and Human Well-Being*. New York, NY: Springer, pp. 43–56.

Albrecht, G., Sartore, G. M., Connor, L., Higginbotham, N., Freeman, S., Kelly, B., Stain, H., Tonna, A. and Pollard, G. 2007. Solastalgia: the distress caused by environmental change. *Australasian Psychiatry*, 15(sup1), S95–S98.

Alkon, A. H. and Traugot, M. 2008. Place matters, but how? Rural identity, environmental decision making, and the social construction of place. *City and Community*, 7, 97e112.

Arsenault, R., Diver S., McGregor D., Witham A. and Bourassa C. 2018. Shifting the framework of Canadian water governance through Indigenous research methods: Acknowledging the past with an eye on the future. *Water*, 10(1):49.

Åsberg, C. 2018. Feminist posthumanities in the Anthropocene: Forays into the postnatural. *Journal of Posthuman Studies*, 1(2), 185–204.

Askland, H. H. and Bunn, M. 2018. Lived experiences of environmental change: Solastalgia, power and place. *Emotion, Space and Society*, 27, 16–22.

Banda, M. 2018. Why should trees have legal rights? It's second nature. The Globe and Mail 1 June 2018 https://www.theglobeandmail.com/opinion/article-why-should-trees-have-legal-rights-its-second-nature/.

Baxter, D. E. and Pelletier, L. G. 2019. Is nature relatedness a basic human psychological need? A critical examination of the extant literature. *Canadian Psychology*, 60(1), 21–34.

BBC 2018. How the people of Delhi saved 16,000 trees from the axe. *BBC News*. July 9 2018. Accessed https://www.bbc.co.uk/news/world-asia-india-44678680

Begg, P. and Thompson, S. 2011. *Tackling Solastalgia: Improving Pathways to Care for Farming Families. Clinical Data Mining in an Allied Health Organization: A Real World Experience.* Sydney: Sydney University Press, pp. 83–100.

Behrens, D. 2016. 'Inexcusable': Three arrested after 'pig-headed' Sheffield Council mounts dawn chainsaw raid on trees. *Yorkshire Post*, 17 November 2016. Accessed https://www.yorkshirepost.co.uk/news/environment/inexcusable-three-arrested-after-pig-headed-sheffield-council-mounts-dawn-chainsaw-raid-on-trees-1-8243221

de La Bellacasa, M. 2011. Matters of care in technoscience: Assembling neglected things. *Social Studies of Science*, 41(1), 85–106.

Benjamin, A. 2015. *Towards a Relational Ontology: Philosophy's Other Possibility.* New York: Suny Press.

Bennett, J. 2001. *The Enchantment of Modern Life: Attachments, Crossings, and Ethics.* Princeton University Press.

Berry, H. L., Hogan, A., Owen, J., Rickwood, D. and Fragar, L. 2011. Climate change and farmer's mental health: Risks and responses. *Asia-Pacific Journal of Public Health*, 23(2), 1295e1325.

Bess, R. 2001. New Zealand's Indigenous people and their claims to fisheries resources. *Marine Policy*, 25(1), 23–32.

Beyer, K., Kaltenbach, A., Szabo, A., Bogar, S., Nieto, F. and Malecki, K. 2014. Exposure to neighborhood green space and mental health: Evidence from the survey of the health of Wisconsin. *International Journal of Environmental Research and Public Health*, 11(3), 3453–3472.

Bird, W. 2007. Natural Thinking: A report for the RSPB: Investigating the Links between the Natural Environment, Biodiversity and Mental Health. Sandy: RSPB. Accessed 27/08/19 http://ww2.rspb.org.uk/Images/naturalthinking_tcm9-161856.pdf.

Blaison, C. and Hess, U. 2016. Affective judgment in spatial context: How places derive affective meaning from the surroundings. *Journal of Environmental Psychology*, 47, 53–65.

Breakwell, G. M. 1986. *Coping With Threatened Identities*. Hove: Psychology Press.

Brown, B. B. and Perkins, D. D. 1992. Disruptions in place attachment. In *Place Attachment*. Boston, MA: Springer, pp. 279–304.

Burn, C. 2018. The battle to save Sheffield's trees: Six years on and the fight continues… here's what you need to know. *Yorkshire Post* March 12 2018. Accessed https://www.yorkshirepost.co.uk/our-region/south-yorkshire/sheffield/the-battle-to-save-sheffield-s-trees-six-years-on-and-the-fight-continues-here-s-what-you-need-to-know-1-9054259

Cano Pecharroman, L. 2018. Rights of nature: Rivers that can stand in court. *Resources*, 7(1), 13.

Campbell, N., Du Cann, C., Hunt, N. and Hill, T. (eds). 2018. *Dark Mountain Issue 14 Terra*. Dark Mountain Project.

Castree, N. 2009. Place: Connections and boundaries in an interdependent world. In Clifford, Holloway, Rice, Valentine (Eds.), *Key Concepts in Geography*, 2nd ed. London: Sage, pp. 153–172.

Chalquist, C. 2009. A look at the ecotherapy research evidence. *Ecopsychology*, 1(1), 1–11.

Cheng, C.-K. and Chou, S.-F. 2015. The influence of place change on place bonding: A longitudinal panel study of renovated park users. *Leisure Sciences*, 37(5), 391e414.

Connor, L., Higginbotham, N., Freeman, S. and Albrecht, G. 2008. Watercourses and discourses: Coalmining in the Upper Hunter Valley, New South Wales. *Oceania*, 78(1), 76–90.

Connor, L., Albrecht, G., Higginbotham, N., Freeman, S. and Smith, W. 2004. Environmental change and human health in Upper Hunter communities of New South Wales, Australia. *EcoHealth*, 1(2), 47–58.

Country, B., Wright, S., Suchet-Pearson, S., Lloyd, K., Burarrwanga, L., Ganambarr, R., Ganambarr Stubbs, M., Ganambarr, B., Maymuru, D. and Sweeney, J., 2016. Co-becoming Bawaka: Towards a relational understanding of place/space. *Progress in Human Geography*, 40(4), 455–475.

Cresswell, T. 2004. *Place: A Short Introduction*. Black.

Cullinan, C. 2011. *Wild Law: A Manifesto for Earth Justice*. Cape Town, South Africa: Syber Ink.

Cummins, S., Curtis, S., Diez-Roux, A. V. and Macintyre, S. 2007. Understanding and representing 'place' in health research: a relational approach. *Social Science and Medicine*, 65(9), 1825–1838.

Cunsolo, A. and Ellis, N. R. 2018. Ecological grief as a mental health response to climate change- related loss. *Nature Climate Change*, 8(4), 275.

Cunsolo Willox, A. 2012. Climate change as the work of mourning. *Ethics and the Environment*, 17(2), 137–164.

Daly, E. 2012. The Ecuadorian exemplar: the first ever vindications of constitutional rights of nature. *Review of European, Comparative and International Environmental Law*, 21(1), 63–66.

Davis, H. and Todd, Z. 2017. On the importance of a date, or decolonizing the Anthropocene. *ACME: An International E-Journal for Critical Geographies*, 16(4).

De Alessi, M. 2012. The political economy of fishing rights and claims: The Maori experience in New Zealand. *Journal of Agrarian Change*, 12(2–3), 390–412.

Devine-Wright, P. 2013. Think global, act local? The relevance of place attachments and place identities in a climate changed world. *Global Environmental Change*, 23(1), 61–69.

Diver, S., Vaughan, M., Baker-Médard, M. and Lukacs, H. 2019. Recognizing 'reciprocal relations' to restore community access to land and water. *International Journal of the Commons*, 13(1).

Dobson, J. 2018. Of street trees and solastalgia. Accessed April 15 2018 https://joannadobson.com/2018/04/13/of-street-trees-and-solastalgia/.

Droseltis, O. and Vignoles, V. L. 2010. Towards an integrative model of place identification: Dimensionality and predictors of intrapersonal-level place preferences. *Journal of Environmental Psychology*, 30(1), 23–34.

Drury, C. 2018. Sheffield's tree massacre: How locals battled to protect Europe's greenest city. Accessed Thursday 12 April 2018 The Independent. https://www.independent.co.uk/news/long_reads/sheffield-tree-massacre-parks-green-city-spaces-felling-street-council-yorkshire-a8286581.html.

Durkalec, A., Furgal, C., Skinner, M. W. and Sheldon, T. 2015. Climate change influences on environment as a determinant of Indigenous health: Relationships to place, sea ice, and health in an Inuit community. *Social Science and Medicine*, 136, 17–26.

Eisenman, D., McCaffrey, S., Donatello, I. and Marshal, G. 2015. An ecosystems and vulnerable populations perspective on solastalgia and psychological distress after a wildfire. *EcoHealth*, 12(4), 602–610.

Ellis, N. R. and Albrecht, G. A. 2017. Climate change threats to family farmers' sense of place and mental wellbeing: A case study from the Western Australian Wheatbelt. *Social Science and Medicine*, 175, 161–168.

Fresque-Baxter, J. A. and Armitage, D. 2012. Place identity and climate change adaptation: a synthesis and framework for understanding. *WIREs Climate Change*, 3, 251–266.

Fried, M. 2000. Continuities and discontinuities of place. *Journal of Environmental Psychology*, 20(3), 193–205.

Fullilove, M. T. 1996. Psychiatric implications of displacement: Contributions from the psychology of place. *American Journal of Psychiatry*, 153, 12.

Gleeson-White, J. 2018. It's only natural: the push to give rivers, mountains and forests legal rights, The Guardian, Accessed April 1 2018. https://www.theguardian.com/australia-news/2018/apr/01/its-only-natural-the-push-to-give-rivers-mountains-and-forests-legal-rights.

Haraway, D. 2015. Anthropocene, Capitalocene, Plantationocene, Chthulucene: Making kin. *Environmental Humanities*, 6(1), 159-165.

Haraway, D. 2016. *Staying With the Trouble: Making Kin in the Chthulucene.* Durham, NC: Duke University Press.

Head, L. 2016. *Hope and Grief in the Anthropocene: Re-conceptualising Human–Nature Relations.* London: Routledge.

Heft, H. 2003. Affordances, dynamic experience, and the challenge of reification. *Ecological Psychology*, 15(2), 149–180.

Henare, M. 2015. Tapu, mana, mauri, hau, wairua: A Maori philosophy of vitalism and cosmos.

Hendryx, M. and Innes-Wimsatt, K. A. 2013. Increased risk of depression for people living in coal mining areas of central Appalachia. *Ecopsychology*, 5(3), 179–187.

Hess, J. J., Malilay, J. N. and Parkinson, A. J. 2008. Climate change: the importance of place. *American journal of preventive medicine*, 35(5), 468–478.

Hidalgo, M. C. and Hernandez, B. 2001. Place attachment: Conceptual and empirical questions. *Journal of Environmental Psychology*, 21(3), 273–281.

Higginbotham, N., Connor, L., Albrecht, G., Freeman, S. and Agho, K. 2016. Validation of an environmental distress scale. *EcoHealth*, 3(4), 245–254.

Hudson, M., Collier, K., Awatere, S., Harmsworth, G., Henry, J., Quinn, J., ... Robb, M. 2016. Integrating Indigenous knowledge into freshwater management. *Science in Society*, 8, 1–14.

Hunt, S. 2014. Ontologies of Indigeneity: The politics of embodying a concept. *Cultural Geographies*, 21(1), 27–32.

Hutchison, A. 2014. The Whanganui river as a legal person. *Alternative Law Journal*, 39(3), 179–182.

Ingold, T. 2002. *The Perception of the Environment: Essays on Livelihood, Dwelling and Skill*. Routledge.

Jonnes, J. 2017. *Urban Forests: A Natural History of Trees and People in the American Cityscape*. Penguin.

Kaltenborn, B. P. 1998. Effects of sense of place on responses to environmental impacts. *Applied Geography* 18(2):169–189.

Kelly, U.A. 2009. Learning to lose: Rurality, transience, and belonging (a companion to Michael Corbett). *Journal of Research in Rural Education*, 21(11), 1e4.

Kennedy, B. 2012. I Am the River and the River Is Me: The Implications of a River Receiving Personhood Status. Cultural Survival Quarterly Magazine. December 2012. Accessed 24/08/19 https://www.culturalsurvival.org/publications/cultural-survival-quarterly/i-am-river-and-river-me-implications-river-receiving.

Kennedy, A. 2016. A case of place: Solastalgia comes before the court. *PAN: Philosophy Activism Nature*, 12, 23–33.

Kingsley, J. Y., Townsend, M. and Henderson-Wilson, C. 2013. Exploring Aboriginal people's connection to country to strengthen human-nature theoretical perspectives. In *Advances in Medical Sociology, Volume 15, Ecological Health: Society, Ecology and Health*. Bingley: Emerald Group Publishing, pp. 45–64.

Klein, N. 2015. *This Changes Everything: Capitalism vs. the Climate*. New York: Simon and Schuster.

Knez, I., Butler, A., Sang, Å. O., Ångman, E., Sarlöv-Herlin, I. and Åkerskog, A. 2018. Before and after a natural disaster: Disruption in emotion component of place-identity and wellbeing. *Journal of Environmental Psychology*, 55, 11–17.

Korpela, K. M., Ylén, M., Tyrväinen, L. and Silvennoinen, H. 2009. Stability of self-reported favourite places and place attachment over a 10-month period. *Journal of Environmental Psychology*, 29(1), 95–100.

Kovach, M. 2009. *Indigenous Methodologies: Characteristics, Conversations and Contexts.* Toronto, Canada: University of Toronto Press.

Kuo, F. E. and Sullivan, W. C. 2001. Aggression and violence in the inner city: Effects of environment via mental fatigue. *Environment and Behavior*, 33(4), 543–571.

Latour, B. 2005. *Reassembling the Social: An Introduction to Actor-Network-Theory.* Oxford/New York: Oxford University Press.

Lertzman, R. 2015. *Environmental Melancholia.* London: Routledge.

Lewicka, M. 2011. Place attachment: How far have we come in the last 40 years?. *Journal of Environmental Psychology*, 31(3), 207–230.

Littlebear, L. 2009. Naturalizing Indigenous Knowledge, Synthesis Paper. University of Saskatchewan, Aboriginal Education Research Centre, Saskatoon, Sask. and First Nations and Adult Higher Education Consortium, Calgary, Alta. Retrieved from http://www.aerc.usask.ca/.

Low, S. M. and Altman, I. 1992. Place attachment: A conceptual inquiry. In Altman I. and Low S. M. (Eds.), *Place Attachment.* New York: Plenum Press, pp. 1–12.

Lukacs, H. and N. M. Ardoin. 2013. The relationship of place re-making and watershed group participation in Appalachia. *Society and Natural Resources*, 27(1):55–69.

Mallett, R. K. 2012. Eco-guilt motivates eco-friendly behavior. *Ecopsychology*, 4(3), 223–231.

Maloney, M. 2018. Environmental law: Changing the legal status of nature: Recent developments and future possibilities. *LSJ: Law Society of NSW Journal*, Issue 49, 78–79.

Manzo, L. C. and Devine-Wright, P. 2013. *Place Attachment: Advances in Theory, Methods and Applications.* Routledge.

Mark, A. 2016. Don't organize, mourn: Environmental loss and musicking. *Ethics and the Environment*, 21(2), 51–77.

McGregor, D. 2014. Traditional knowledge and water governance: The ethic of responsibility. *AlterNative: An International Journal of Indigenous Peoples*, 10(5):493–507.

McNamara, K. E. and Westoby, R. 2011. Solastalgia and the gendered nature of climate change: An example from Erub Island, Torres Strait. *EcoHealth*, 8(2), 233–236.

Moore, D. 2014. Defending and Expanding the Urban Forest: Opposing Unnecessary Tree Removal Requests. Treenet. Accessed https://treenet.org/resources/defending-and-expanding-the-urban-forest-opposing-unnecessary-tree-removal-requests/.

Morris, J. D. and Ruru, J. 2010. Giving voice to rivers: legal personality as a vehicle for recognising Indigenous peoples' relationships to water? *Australian Indigenous Law Review*, 14(2), 49–62.

Neimanis, A., Åsberg, C. and Hedrén, J. 2015. Four problems, four directions for environmental humanities: Toward critical posthumanities for the Anthropocene. *Ethics and the Environment*, 20(1), 67–97.

Nikora, L. W., Masters-Awatere, B. and Awekotuku, N. T. 2012. Final arrangements following death: Maori indigenous decision making and tangi. *Journal of Community & Applied Social Psychology*, 22(5), 400–413.

Nixon, R. 2011. *Slow Violence and the Environmentalism of the Poor.* Harvard University Press.

Nxumalo, F. and Cedillo, S. 2017. Decolonizing place in early childhood studies: Thinking with Indigenous onto-epistemologies and Black feminist geographies. *Global Studies of Childhood*, 7(2), 99–112.

O'Donnell, E. 2017. At the intersection of the sacred and the legal: Rights for nature in Uttarakhand, India. *Journal of Environmental Law*, 30(1), 135–144.

O'Donnell, E. 2018. *Legal Rights for Rivers: Competition, Collaboration and Water Governance.* Routledge.

O'Donnell, E. L. and Talbot-Jones J. 2018. Creating legal rights for rivers: lessons from Australia, New Zealand, and India. *Ecology and Society*, 23(1), 7-17.

O'Donnell, E. and Macpherson, E. 2019. Voice, power and legitimacy: the role of the legal person in river management in New Zealand, Chile and Australia. *Australasian Journal of Water Resources*, 23(1), 35–44.

Pannell, S. 2018. Framing the loss of solace: Issues and challenges in researching Indigenous compensation claims. *Anthropological Forum*, 2(3), 255–274.

Proshansky, H. M., Fabian, A. K. and Kaminoff, R. 1983. Place-identity: Physical world socialization of the self. *Journal of Environmental Psychology*, 3(1), 57–83.

Randall, R. 2009. Loss and climate change: The cost of parallel narratives. *Ecopsychology*, 1(3), 118–129.

Reser, J. P., Morrissey, S. A., Ellul, M., 2011. The threat of climate change: psychological response, adaptations, and impacts. In Weisbecker, I. (Ed.), *Climate Change and Human Well Being.* Springer Publications, pp. 19–42.

Rodgers, C. 2017. A new approach to protecting ecosystems: The Te Awa Tupua (Whanganui River Claims Settlement) Act 2017. *Environmental Law Review*, 19(4), 266–279.

Ruckstuhl, K., Thompson-Fawcett, M. and Rae, H. 2014. Māori and mining: Indigenous perspectives on reconceptualising and contextualising the social licence to operate. *Impact Assessment and Project Appraisal*, 32(4), 304–314.

Said, E. W. 1995. *Culture and Imperialism.* New York: Vintage Books.

Scannell, L. and Gifford, R. 2010. The relations between natural and civic place attachment and pro-environmental behavior. *Journal of Environmental Psychology*, 30, 289e297.

Scannell, L. and Gifford, R. 2013. Personally relevant climate change: The role of place attachment and local versus global message framing in engagement. *Environment and Behavior*, 45(1), 60–85.

Scannell, L. and Gifford, R. 2017. Place attachment enhances psychological need satisfaction. *Environment and Behavior*, 49(4), 359–389.

Seamon, D. 2000. A way of seeing people and place. In Wapner S., Demick J., Yamamoto T., Minami H. (Eds.), *Theoretical Perspective in Environment-Behavior Research: Underlying Assumptions, Research Problems, and Methodologies.* Boston, MA: Kluver Academic/Plenum Publishers, New York, pp. 157–178.

Seamon, D. and Sowers, J. 2008. Place and placelessness (1976): Edward Relph. In P. Hubbard, R. Kitchin and G. Valentine (Eds.), *Key Texts in Human Geography.* London: Sage, pp. 43–52.

Smith, R. 2018. Solastalgia in Istria, Croatia. *Utopia and Neoliberalism: Ethnographies of Rural Spaces*, 46, 149.

Speller, G. M. and Twigger-Ross, C. L. 2009. Cultural and social disconnection in the context of a changed physical environment. *Geografiska Annaler: Series B, Human Geography*, 91(4), 355–369.

STAG (Sheffield Trees Action Group). 2019a. https://savesheffieldtrees.org.uk/key-facts/.

STAG (Sheffield Trees Action Group). 2019b. Tree stories https://savesheffieldtrees.org.uk/your-tree-stories/.

Stone, C. D. 1972. Should trees have standing—toward legal rights for natural objects. *Southern California Law Review*, Issue 45, 450–502.

Stokes, E. 1992. The treaty of Waitangi and the Waitangi tribunal: Maori claims in New Zealand. *Applied Geography*, 12(2), 176–191.

Suliman, A. 2019. World's forests in 'emergency room after big losses'. *The i*, 26 April 2019.

Te Aho, L. 2010. Indigenous challenges to enhance freshwater governance and management in Aotearoa New Zealand-the Waikato river settlement. In Spiller, C. and Wolfgramm, R. (Eds.). *Indigenous Spiritualities at Work: Transforming the Spirit of Enterprise.* IAP, pp. 77–98.

Todd, Z. 2016. An Indigenous feminist's take on the ontological turn: 'Ontology' is just another word for colonialism. *Journal of Historical Sociology*, 29(1), 4–22.

Tribunal, W. 1999. The Whanganui River Report. Wai 167. Accessed https://forms.justice.govt.nz/search/Documents/WT/wt_DOC_68450539/Whanganui%20River%20Report%201999.pdf.

Tribunal, W. 2015. He Whiritaunoka: The Whanganui Land Report. WAI, 903, 2015. Accessed https://forms.justice.govt.nz/search/Documents/WT/wt_DOC_135650183/He%20Whiritaunoka%20Vol%203%20W.pdf.

Tschakert, P. and Tutu, R. 2010. Solastalgia: Environmentally induced distress and migration among Africa's poor due to climate change. In *Environment, Forced Migration and Social Vulnerability.* Berlin, Heidelberg: Springer, pp. 57–69.

Tschakert, P., Barnett, J., Ellis, N., Lawrence, C., Tuana, N., New, M., Elrick-Barr, C., Pandit, R. and Pannell, D., 2017. Climate change and loss, as if people mattered: values, places, and experiences. *Wiley Interdisciplinary Reviews: Climate Change*, 8(5), p.e476.

Tschakert, P., Tutu, R. and Alcaro, A. 2013. Embodied experiences of environmental and climatic changes in landscapes of everyday life in Ghana. *Emotion, Space and Society*, 7, 13–25.

Tschirhart, C., Mistry J., Berardi A. et al. 2016. Learning from one another: evaluating the impact of horizontal knowledge exchange for environmental management and governance. *Ecology and Society*, 21(2), 1-14.

Tsing, A. L. 2015. *The Mushroom at the End of the World: On the Possibility of Life in Capitalist Ruins.* Princeton University Press.

Tsing, A. 2012. Unruly Edges: Mushrooms as Companion Species For Donna Haraway. *Environmental Humanities*, 1(1), 141–154.

Tuan, Y.-F. 1974. *Topophilia: A Study of Environmental Perception, Attitudes, and Values.* Englewood Cliffs, NJ: Prentice Hall.

Tuan, Y. F. 1975. Place: An experiential perspective. *Geographical Review*, 65(2): 151–165.

Warsini, S., Mills, J. and Usher, K. 2014. Solastalgia: living with the environmental damage caused by natural disasters. *Prehospital and Disaster Medicine*, 29(1), 87–90.

Watts, V. 2013. Indigenous place-thought and agency amongst humans and non humans (First Woman and Sky Woman go on a European world tour!). *Decolonization: Indigeneity, Education and Society*, 2(1), 20–34.

Weintrobe, S. (Ed.). 2013. *Engaging with Climate Change: Psychoanalytic and Interdisciplinary Perspectives.* Routledge.

West-Newman, C. L. 2008. Beach crisis: Law and love of place. *Space and Culture*, 11(2), 160–175.

Whittemore, M. E. 2011. The problem of enforcing nature's rights under Ecuador's constitution: Why the 2008 environmental amendments have no bite. *Pacific Rim Law and Policy Journal*, 20, 659–691.

Windhorst, E. and Williams, A. 2015. Growing up, naturally: The mental health legacy of early nature affiliation. *Ecopsychology*, 7(3), 115–125.

Žižek, S. 2009. *In Defense of Lost Causes.* London: Verso.

6

BETWEEN THE WHALE AND THE KĀURI TREE

Multi-species encounters, indigenous knowledge and ethical relationality in the Anthropocene

> *at a time when human activities have become so deeply embedded in earth surface processes that even the molecular composition of the atmosphere bears our signature, the most urgent task for all fields of human endeavour is to reframe our relations to the more-than-human world.*
>
> (Head, 2016, p. 55)

> *When anthropologists and other assembled social scientists sashay in and start cherry-picking parts of Indigenous thought that appeal to them without engaging directly in (or unambiguously acknowledging) the political situation, agency, legal orders and relationality of both Indigenous people and scholars, we immediately become complicit in colonial violence. When we cite European thinkers who discuss the 'more-than-human' but do not discuss their Indigenous contemporaries who are writing on the exact same topics, we perpetuate the white supremacy of the academy.*
>
> (Todd, 2016a, p. 18)

> *Ko ahau te tohorā, te tohorā ko ahau (I am the whale, and the whale is me).*

Introduction

The explosion of multi-species, posthuman and transspecies theory and research invites us to extend what we consider a meaningful encounter across the species barrier. In this chapter I take up that invitation, to further flesh out an Anthropocene psychology. I am concerned with relationships between human and more-than-human, without any recourse to established and accepted 'topics of interest' in psychology. I am also keen to engage with approaches that enrich and challenge established academic perspectives. To that end, this chapter engages numerous recent calls to 'indigenize' and 'decolonize' the Anthropocene, via the figure of the whale. In doing so, I adopt the tools Zoe Todd suggests for employing Indigenous ontologies with care and respect: accounting for one's own location, engaging with *specific* Indigenous ontologies, focusing on locally informed responses to *in situ* challenges and, finally, reading and citing Indigenous scholarship (Todd, 2016a).

In so doing, my own commitment to particularity in this book is also maintained. In this chapter I consider human–whale encounters in the Anthropocene era and how they might be framed within a posthuman or more-than-human ontology before making the case for a more thorough indigenising of the Anthropocene. I engage with a Māori perspective, especially as it pertains to multi-species relationality, and specifically to the phenomena of mass whale stranding as it is understood within a Māori ontology – as a localised response to *in situ* challenges. To address the challenge of a Māori articulation of holism, the chapter is then extended to consider the forests of Aotearoa New Zealand and the plight of the kāuri tree, following the anthropogenic spread of a deadly pathogen in recent years. I consider how Māori have approached this 'biosecurity' threat and how their tradition and knowledge practices open up surprising connections between humans, trees and whales, extended further here via a discussion of mycorrhizal networks. I argue that in approaching specific and situated applications of Indigenous ontologies in some of its grounded everyday complexity, there is the potential to open up psychology to a more radical and ethical biocentric relationality.

Beaching whales

As an important migration route for whales, the Aotearoa New Zealand coastline has seen its fair share of strandings, but in recent years, here, as elsewhere, there appears to be an unprecedented number.[1] In November

2018, 140 pilot whales mass beached (Project Jonah, n.d.). In the same year, rare pygmy whales stranded in numbers on the shores of the same country for the first time; the largest whale stranding in New Zealand's history occurred in 2017, when 400 pilot whales stranded in Golden Bay.[2] Rachel Giggs's essay tells of the day she found herself in the presence of a stranded whale on the Australian coast (2015). After various failed attempts by the public and attendant wildlife officers to save the whale, it is left to its fate. She and others remained close by, as it slips to its death. In this passage, she conveys the experience:

> Towards the end, low tide and a small group persisting, I shuffled in close to hear its irregular gasps. The whale's eye – midnight, mid-ocean – had no eyelashes and, according to another wildlife officer, no tear ducts (for what would be the point of crying in the sea?). I hovered as near as I was able to, speaking sometimes to the whale's blowhole. What felt important in that moment was the act of seeing this through to the end, of agreeing not to leave the whale alone. Kinship, I guess, was what we proffered. Who could say if it was more or less welcome than the barbiturate injection still packed up in the van? No one clicked a cartridge into a rifle or brandished the merciful stick of explosive. Nature, as they say, would run its course. That was a phrase we trusted. We repeated it.
>
> Inside the whale it grew hotter and hotter, though that proved difficult to imagine. We humans, I think, devise death as a gradual loss of fire; the gleam retracted from every corner, pulled to a wick within, guttering out. The whale's descent was different. I had an idea of each sentence as I spoke it, cool and round as a stone, dropping for five minutes or longer down into the whale's head. But what did the whale understand by my speech? A germane sound, inlaid with information, or just noise, background babble as the wind speaks in the trees, as dogs bark, being dragged off by their owners on leashes. Do human voices sound as ethereal to the whale as whale voices sound to us? Or do we scratch and irritate the whale, a pin in the ear?

Griggs describes the experience as one of *encounter*, wrought with a corporeality that is both connective and incongruous. People commonly describe witnessing a stranding whale as a mysterious, and often harrowing, experience. Re-floating in time to survive is a difficult and uncertain process, even with willing help at hand, so once stranded, whales will often die of dehydration, collapse under their own weight or drown in a subsequent high tide (Tipa, 2014). Human accounts of encounters with whales in these situations speak of a deeply felt horror, compounded in sensing the fear and desperation conveyed by the whales they are trying to help, usually futilely (BBC, 2018a). Pilot whales, the species that beached in their hundreds on Aotearoa New Zealand's shores in 2018, can measure up to 20 feet (6.1 m) and weigh up to 3 tons (2,700 kg). The physical presence, the sheer bodily mass of such a phenomenon, is both an obstacle and a conduit to its human comprehensibility, a profoundly uncanny multi-species encounter – 'life on that scale – *mammalian* life on that scale – so unfamiliar and familiar simultaneously' (Giggs, 2015). As a meeting, it jars with the more accustomed and comfortable 'zoological gaze' (Franklin, 1999), in which the spectacle of nonhuman animal performance is integral to leisure and tourism practices of zoos, aquariums and wildlife parks (Cloke and Perkins, 2005, p. 907). Going further, as a situated, mutually embodied encounter, it is a tangible example of Alaimo's concept of *trans*-corporeality,

> in which the human is always intermeshed with the more-than-human world, [and in] which the substance of the human is ultimately inseparable from 'the environment'. It makes it difficult to pose nature as mere background […] for the exploits of the human since 'nature' is always as close as one's own skin– perhaps even closer. Indeed, thinking across bodies may catalyze the recognition that the environment, which is too often imagined as inert, empty space or as a resource for human use, is, in fact, a world of fleshy beings with their own needs, claims, and actions
> *(2012, p. 2)*

This story, and this moment of recognition, as a real, specific, situated embodied encounter, opens up, represents an Anthropocene story, in Lidskog and Waterton's specific sense:

> Anthropocene stories continuously highlight the multiple, interdependent relations within nature, within different forms of materiality, within technologies and within social systems, but they also stress the interconnections between these domains. Thus, the narrative deepens our sense of the interrelatedness between nature and society.
> *(Lidskog and Waterton, 2018 p. 9)*

In this account, lots of threads intertwine, ones that constitute multiple versions of an Anthropocene narrative – sometimes at odds, perhaps incommensurable, but worth taking heed of.

Indigenising the Anthropocene

Part of the posthuman or more-than-human turn has been a belated recognition that Indigenous knowledge offers an understanding of multi-species interdependency and emergent co-becoming of human and more-than-human life – 'the always-already existence of some forms of posthumanities' (Åsberg, 2018, p. 192). Despite enormous variety, Indigenous knowledge (IK) shares an understanding of human life as being an embodiment of, and embedded in, the natural world, shaped by generations of connection with place (Kawagley, 1995). An Indigenous commitment to environmental protection of and for 'future generations' is well established (Kawagley, 1995; McGregor, 2014) and long understood to be a multi-species affair, incorporating 'plants, animals, water, and all living things' (Mankiller, 2009). There is growing attention paid to the knowledge and experience of Indigenous people in relation to climate change and associated harms (King, Skipper, & Tāwhai, 2008; Newton, Paci, & Ogden, 2005; Smith, 2015), whilst a resurgent interest in animist logic amongst anthropologists marks a 'growing affective, intellectual, and political investment in Indigenous knowledges' (Harvey, 2013, p. ii) and more attempts to learn with and from Indigenous perspectives and scholars (Country et al., 2016; Kohn, 2013; Wright et al. 2012).

Attention to animism as an organising principle is echoed in Bronislaw Szerszynski's assertion of the need to expand Anthropocene imaginaries to include the 'multiple narratives of indigenous and colonized peoples' (2017, p. 254). Such perspectives have been neglected and marginalised in the rapid ascendancy of Western scientific conceptualisations of the Anthropocene, which tend to denote 'a singular geochronological story of a singular planet', a 'falsely unified' and Eurocentric story of the Earth's transformation (ibid.). Accordingly, he champions any move to 'decolonize', 'descularize' or 'indigenize' the Anthropocene. Presumably, the hope here is that such a move can further enliven what is being laid out as an increasingly apparent Anthropocene reality – human entanglement in 'co-constitutive relationships with nature and the environment, with science and technology, and with vulnerable embodiments of both human and nonhuman kinds' (Åsberg, 2018, p. 192). What this might mean in practice, and how a 'desecularized' or 'indigenized' Anthropocene imaginary can help us make better sense of processes underway, are much more difficult questions to answer – and not addressed in any detail by Szerszynski.

Indigenous feminist Red River Métis and Otipemisiwak scholar Zoe Todd *does* explicitly consider what it might mean to more actively and practically 'indigenize' the Anthropocene (Todd, 2015). For Todd, 'Indigenous thought, praxis, and art is necessary in order to bring Indigenous epistemologies, ontologies, and practices to the fore in a meaningful and ethical way' (2015, p. 243). Meaning and ethics are derived from the ways in which 'contemporary Indigenous (more-than-human) relations continue to draw on ancient cosmologies and sustain understandings of reciprocity and responsibility' (Panelli, 2010, p. 84). Here, we see deeper knowledge traditions making sense of the interdependence of planetary life, blindness to which, not least in the flurry of posthumanisms, becomes a form of what Sami scholar Rauna Kuokkanan calls 'epistemic ignorance' (2007). Following Todd, then, there is a need to move beyond merely *asserting* the value of an Indigenous approach in general and explore what it has to say in detail. This is not to advocate some kind of 'discovery' of the relevance of Indigenous perspectives to the Anthropocene. They are contemporaneous, and Indigenous understanding and activism has been, remains and no doubt will continue to be, integral to bringing environmental issues and the 'dreaming of an otherwise' to the fore internationally (Todd, 2016a, p. 5; Mankiller, 2009).

It can be further wrongly implied that these are 'simpler' or dormant perspectives, to be fed into the machine of Western social science or humanities theory building to have purchase – grist to the mill of the organising concepts of 'common cosmopolitan concern', always emergent, human and more-than-human, Chthulucene.[3] In this chapter, I consider how Indigenous knowledge, on its own terms, can advance beyond the assertion and re-assertion of a relational ontology that incorporates human and more-than-human worlds. My intention is decidedly *not* to appropriate these perspectives at 'a level of abstracted engagement once again' whereby 'Indigenous histories are still regarded as story and process—an abstracted tool of the West' (Watts, 2013, p. 28). Neither is it to speak *for* Indigenous actors – why would this be necessary? Instead, I attempt to understand and describe how the organising concepts of a *specific* Indigenous approach – Māori – help us make *situated* sense of human-environmental crisis in the context of multispecies, human and more-than-human relations in ways that we – non-Indigenous and Indigenous alike – might be able to meaningfully further extrapolate from, to enrich a fledgling Anthropocene psychology.

Tools for employing Indigenous ontologies

To speak of Indigenous understandings of multispecies relations legitimately, Todd offers three 'practical tools for employing indigenous ontologies…with care and respect' (2016a), crafted with the assistance of Vanessa Watts (2013) and Juanita Sundberg (2014). These are: accounting for location (Sundberg 2014), for Indigenous Place-Thought (Watts, 2013) and consideration of 'the ongoing colonial imperatives of the academy' (Todd, 2016a, p. 9). The first, 'location', can be considered in at least three aspects. One is to account for one's *own* location – 'by telling you who I am and where I am from so that you can situate how and why I know what I know' (Todd, 2016b); another is to locate accounts within *specific* Indigenous ontologies, rather than abstracting or homogenising them as 'indigenous perspectives'; a third aspect is to account for 'locally informed responses to in situ challenges' (Todd, 2015, p. 251). In terms of the first aspect, in locating myself as a non-Indigenous scholar employed by a British university, embedded in Euro-American traditions of academic discourse, I am no doubt pointing to limits of the extent to which I can avoid, to paraphrase Todd, being just another white voice speaking an Indigenous story (2015, p. 251). I fully accept this limitation, but it seems nonetheless a worthwhile endeavour to do more than pay lip-service to 'Indigenous perspectives' in general and instead to attempt to pay attention to Indigenous cosmologies, as they are specifically, situationally located (Sundberg, 2014), and as they try to make sense of ecologically beleaguered ecosystems and their inhabitants, citing Māori and Indigenous scholarship. As well as accounting for my own location, this chapter will engage with a specific Indigenous ontology – Māori – and consider it as a response to the situated challenges of stranded whales and diseased trees in the context of anthropogenic impacts, thus addressing the second two aspects of 'location' as Todd presents them.

The second of Todd's tools is to account for what Anishinaabe/Haudenosaunee scholar Vanessa Watts refers to as 'Indigenous Place-Thought', which is 'based upon the premise that land is alive and thinking and that humans and non-humans derive agency through the extensions of these thoughts' (Watts, 2013, p. 21). This entails taking seriously 'a theoretical understanding of the world via a physical embodiment'. Place-Thought is not a 'mythic' alternative interpretation of interdependence, it is human thought and action as 'derived from a *literal* expression of particular places and historical events' (emphasis added) that must be read through an accounting of location. As a non-Indigenous scholar, raised on an ontology whereby nature is commonly understood as external and inert, this is a difficult position to embody.[4] Nonetheless, as a relative 'outsider' in terms of class background, whilst harbouring animist inclinations nurtured by similarly 'outsider' cultural narratives and conventions for many years, it is at least not an inimical task, however far short one falls. Place-Thought is here recognised, and approached, as an articulation of Māori recognition of our embeddedness in place – *tangata whenua* ('people of the land') – 'biocentric relationality' as expressed through knowledge and practices described in what follows (Ritchie, 2013). Multiple and varied Māori values are expressed through and in connections with the physical environment – 'in tangible geographical locations and in plants, animals, and associated habitats' (Awatere, Harmsworth and Robb, 2017 P. 152; see p. 152 for detailed examples).

Todd's third practical tool, at its simplest, is about reading and citing Indigenous scholarship, rather than defaulting to Euro-Western traditions of abstract and appropriation. If we accept, along with Todd, that 'rather than engage with the Anthropocene as a teleological fact implicating all humans as equally culpable for the current socio-economic, ecological, and political state of the world... we should turn to examining how other peoples are describing our "ecological imagination"' (Todd, 2015, p. 252), there is much ground to be made up. She points us towards 'Indigenous thinkers who have been writing about Indigenous legal theory, human-animal relations and multiple epistemologies/ontologies for decades' (2016, p. 14). A number of the thinkers she highlights are cited here, such as Donald, Watts and TallBear. Considering the specific and situated focus mentioned above, much of the discussion homes in on Māori scholarship – as a localised exemplar of 'a twenty- first-century indigenous knowledge articulation' (TallBear, 2015, p. 230) – and attendant language, terminology and methods in particular, rather than Indigenous knowledge in general, and some, purposefully limited, reference across to cognisant research and debate in posthuman and more-than-human literature. It should be noted that these are not mutually exclusive fields – there is, in fact, an increasing amount of cross-fertilisation and collaboration underway.

In sum, the situated and the specific of human and more-than-human worlds and multi-species relations in the Anthropocene are here tackled, in part, through the Indigenous perspective of Māori. In doing so, all of Todd's suggested tools as described above are utilised, however clumsily. If nothing else, this can be a modest contribution both to attempts to challenge the erasure of non-European ontologies from the Anthropocene narrative to date (Sundberg, 2014) and to redress the non-citation of Indigenous scholarship (Todd, 2015). What follows is a narrative about how human activity reverberates through human and more-than-human worlds, and offered as an invitation, it is about constituting Anthropocene psychology as thinking in new and old ways about our interdependency. Such proclamations can tend towards the abstract, the opaque and the always emerging, and whilst abstraction is not wholly avoided here, our case allows us to meet the call for greater specificity and situatedness in more-than-human scholarship (Lorimer, 2019), to ground it in messy particulars. So, with these tools in mind, let us move beyond exhorting the value of adopting a more-than-human perspective and start exploring 'the complexity that exists within the situated and the specific' (Lorimer, 2019).

The porosity of boundaries: whales and Māori

> So we are talking about enlightenment. I heard a teacher say – 'But you Māori boys here have to learn Pākehā [New Zealanders who are of European descent] skills at school. That is why you have come to school'. And I said to him on the quiet – 'What arrogance. Enlightenment belongs to humanity. Pākehā do not have the monopoly over enlightenment'
>
> *Rangimarie Rose Pere*

A Māori worldview rests on 'an intricate, connected and holistic relationship with the natural world... an interconnected relationship which has developed over thousands of years into an in depth knowledge base' (Harmsworth and Awatere, 2013; Rodgers, 2017, p. 3). At the root of Māori cosmology, in particular, is the understanding that 'humanity and all things of the natural world are always emerging, always unfolding' (Hunsane, 2001, p. 198). At the heart of a Māori view of life is a philosophy of vitalism and animism (Henare, 2001). Māori vitalism is evident as a 'belief in an original singular source of life in which that life continues as a force that imbues and animates all forms and things of the cosmos' (Henare, 2001, p. 204). The connections between all forms of life, human and other-than-human, tangible and intangible alike (Hindle and Matthewman, 2017), are articulated though *whakapapa* – literally meaning 'genealogy' – a taxonomic and historical framework that includes and links 'all animate and inanimate, known and unknown phenomena in the terrestrial and spiritual worlds' (Taonui, 2011, p. 1) and traces 'the origin of the universe and the world... through a series of ordered genealogical webs that go back hundreds of generations to the beginning' (Harmsworth and Awatere, 2013, p. 274).[5]

Whakapapa 'maps relationships', whereby those relations are extended through time, place and spiritual realms (Taonui, 2011, p. 1). The centrality of *whakapapa* within Māori culture 'cannot be overstated', and it is a fundamental articulation of the Māori relationship to land as living: 'To "know" oneself is to know one's *whakapapa*. To "know" about a tree, a rock, the wind, or the fishes in the sea is to know their *whakapapa*' (Robert and Wills, cited in Whitt et al., 2001, p. 708). Māori have developed a rich and complex religion, metaphysics and philosophy that rest upon an understanding of the 'symbiotic relations between humanity, the physical world of nature, and the spiritual world' (Harmsworth and Awatere, 2013; Henare, 2001, p. 207). Within a Māori epistemology, 'spiritual' articulates something very different from meanings we might associate with it in English. Meyer's definition captures this in a way that helps me, as a non-Indigenous scholar, grasp something of its Māori meaning: 'Knowledge that endures is a spiritual act that animates and educates' (Meyer, 2014, p. 156). Through *whakapapa* and other intersecting knowledge practices, it has been explicitly articulated and clarified by Māori as a core set of values, an ethics inseparable from ecological and environmental sustainability, summarised by Henare (2001, p. 212) as:

> A reverence for the total creation as one whole; a sense of kinship with other beings; a sacred regard for the whole of nature and its resources as being gifts from the spiritual powers; a sense of responsibility for these gifts (*taonga*) as the appointed stewards and guardians; a distinctive economic ethic of reciprocity; and a sense of commitment to safeguard natural resources for future generations.

Though only briefly introduced here, *whakapapa* is a constituent part of a rich Māori worldview and a conceptual framework that is already rooted in relationality and co-becoming, whereby 'the identity of things in the world is not understood as discrete or independent, but emerges through, and as, relations with everything else' (Jones and Hoskins, 2016, p. 25). Like many other forms of Indigenous knowledge, it already incorporates multi-species relations within an ethics of care and responsibility, one that includes human–whale entanglements (Rodgers, 2017).

A sign from the sea?

A few months after the Aotearoa New Zealand strandings described at the beginning of this chapter, a half-page story in British newspaper *The Guardian* caught my eye.[6] What drew my attention first of all was the space granted to a Māori perspective on whale strandings in this particular context. Though brief, it offered me, as an environmental and human–animal studies scholar rooted in Western (social) scientific traditions, a glimpse of an *alternative* understanding of the Anthropocene, and of human–animal entanglement, as applied to the specific and situated phenomenon of mass strandings. The story focused in on Hori Parata, an elder of the Ngatiwai *Iwi* whose home is on the eastern Northland of Aotearoa New Zealand. He is an environmental resource manager, working in collaboration with the New Zealand Department of Conservation, and recognised as a leading Māori whale expert. Like others occupying a similar role, Parata is formally responsible for overseeing the treatment of stranded whales in line with Ngatiwai principles and traditions.[7]

A Māori emphasis on interconnection means that whales are always already embedded in a network of lively relations that have personal and cultural meaning. Going further, *tikanga* – 'the customary system of values and practices that have developed over time and are deeply embedded in the social context' – works within the taxonomic framework of *whakapapa* to incorporate ethical, reciprocal obligations and responsibilities as they reverberate through these material and spiritual understandings, and specific ideas concerning how 'relations between people and between people, earth and sea must be conducted' (Henare, 2001, p. 198). This sense of reciprocity is further embedded through localised affective place and kinship bonds. These bonds can be transspecies – whereby whales (tohorā) become *whānau* – members of an extended family or community of related families who live together in the same area (Tipa, 2014).

In recognising that more whales are beaching and dying, 'an acute sense of grief' is reported to have been growing for some time among Māori – intimately related to the sacred significance of whales in Māori culture and history (Marris, 2018). Simply stated, 'their whale kin are sick, and trying to escape an increasingly polluted and unpredictable ocean'; they are 'fleeing' the ocean. To cite Parata once more: 'Our ancestors tell us the strandings are a sign from the sea. So what is the sea telling us? We need to listen' (Roy, 2019). If established marine science is reticent about reading strandings as 'a sign from the sea', there is nonetheless rapidly growing recognition that their ocean home is an increasingly contaminated and capricious environment, and serious scientific debate about whether recent mass stranding 'spikes' across the world are correlated with anthropogenic impacts on ocean health (Parsons et al., 2015; Parsons, 2017).[8] So we reach an impasse. Māori elders urge us to listen, posthuman scholars to develop our modes of attention; marine biologists continue their research and debate their findings. Different methods sympathetic to this insistence, Māori approaches to research (Royal, 2012; Smith, 2015; Walker et al., 2006), collaborative ethnography and interdisciplinary field work might help us understand and address whale stranding, but until then the returns on a Māori-inflected Anthropocene narrative might appear slim. Where do we go from here in the meantime? For a worldview premised on relational holism, part of the problem is considering a phenomenon in isolation. Making further lively connections opens up the story, and now we move inland to the forest, before returning to the oceans once more.

Kāuri dieback

Sticking with the Māori, and with localised responses to *in situ* challenges, we turn to the forests of Aotearoa New Zealand's North Island. The kāuri (*Agathis australis*) is a giant native conifer of the North Island. They can reach up to 50 m tall and live for over 2,000 years. The kāuri forests are among the oldest woodlands in the world, and the kāuri is significant in Māori culture and history, featuring centrally in their cosmology and origin myths (Te Ao Mārama) – in some versions of which the kāuri tree emerged from a divine battle as the link between heaven and earth (Shortland, 2011, p. 14). It is now considered a *taonga* (treasured, sacred) plant for all New Zealanders, and for many Māori, 'the [kāuri] tree is the centrepiece of cultural and spiritual beliefs'

(Lambert et al., 2018, p. 112). The kāuri also reflects a more general but vital connection between people and forests in Māori *whakapapa* tradition – both were created by the god Tāne, and the forest is established in Māori traditions for its abundance of life and provision of necessities (Taonui, 2007).

Kāuri forests have been substantially depleted by logging, beginning with the arrival of European settlers in the 1700s, and rapidly escalating following colonisation – settlers used the timber for building properties, and the British Navy exported boatloads of kāuri-wood spars in the 1800s (King, 2003). Increased demand for farmland and timber in the twentieth century means that today, approximately 4% of uncut forest remains.[9] These vestiges of ancient kāuri forest are now exposed to another anthropogenic impact – the spread of a water and soil-borne pathogen, *Phytophthora taxon Agathis* (PTA), commonly known as kāuri dieback, which threatens their extinction (Bellgard et al., 2016; Weir et al., 2015).[10] Dieback was only formally identified in 2008, but has likely been present in Aotearoa New Zealand for at least 40 years (Chetham and Shortland, 2013, p. 5). The pathogen first infects kāuri roots, then aggressively works its way through trunk, branches and canopy, eventually causing death (Bellgard et al., 2016).[11] Its origins are uncertain, but the incidence and spread of dieback strongly correlates with human activity, particularly in transferring contaminated soils from between places, and with movement from infected to non-infected plants via spoors (Horner, Hough and Zydenbos, 2014).

Since 2008, kāuri dieback has been formally designated an 'unwanted organism' – a pest of national priority, triggering a national biosecurity response (Lambert et al., 2018, p. 213). That response was initially defined by a focus on the pathogen itself, in attempts to curtail and contain its movement – footwash stations, eradicating possible vectors (feral pigs and goats), new recreational paths and restricting access. This response echoes the conservation and biosecurity regimes of countless 'developed' nations, including Aotearoa New Zealand, and the familiar claims made about 'nature': 'that it is complex, but knowable; non-linear, but manageable; outside culture, but endangered by culture; and that Western rationality can save it' (Ginn, 2008, p. 339). It was unsuccessful – the rate of kāuri dieback initially increased. However, a joint Māori–government agency programme was established in 2009 to monitor and manage the spread of the pathogen (Lambert et al., 2018), reflecting growing acknowledgement of the value of other forms of Indigenous knowledge in relation to forest conservation (Singh et al.,

2015; Souto et al., 2014) and Māori knowledge applied to other habitats such as rivers and waterways (Harmsworth et al., 2016; Tipa and Tierney, 2006).

Anthropocene psychology: thinking with the forest?

The joint programme provided Māori researchers with some funding to monitor kāuri dieback (Chetham and Shortland, 2013; Lambert et al., 2018; Ngakuru, Marsden and Nuttall, 2010; Shortland, 2011). Their approach is defined by attending to both environmental and cultural indicators of ecological health, and rooted in programmes that are organised and managed by local communities (Harmsworth and Jollands, 2007; Reed, 2008), a point forcibly made in Indigenous scholarship (Harmsworth et al., 2011; Harmsworth and Awatere, 2013; Necefer et al., 2015). At their simplest, cultural indicators of environmental health are those derived from the understandings of those people who have had close contact with the issue, place or environment in question, as communities, over time – 'because there's that generational knowledge of knowing their environment and their backyard, so they do see trends of change, then those trends act as their cultural indicators of change' (Dixon, 2014). For *tangata whenua*, cultural indicators reflect generations of 'spiritual and survival patterns that were based on observation and obligation' (Shortland, 2011, p. 10).

The approach taken to kāuri dieback in the work cited here explicitly advocates the application of mātauranga Māori. Whilst it is broadly used to refer to a Māori knowledge-base, mātauranga Māori is more specifically defined as 'the pursuit and application of knowledge and understanding of Te Taiao [the natural world], following a systematic methodology based on evidence, incorporating culture, values and world view' (Hikuroa, 2016, p.1), integral to which is the specific form of holistic animism at the heart of Māori Indigenous knowledge (Mark-Shadbolt et al., 2018). The health of the kāuri is inseparable from the health of the Waipoua forests in which they dwell, the health of which, in turn, 'is inextricably linked by Te Roroa Māori [the people of the region] to the mauri (spirit, essence) and mana (respect, authority, status, spiritual power) of their communities, elders and succeeding generations' (p. 118). Kāuri health is approached through its connections to other species (including human), places, histories, as understood through the relationships and practices that have endured between Māori, as

Aotearoa New Zealand's *tāngata whenua* [people of the land] and kāuri (Shortland, 2011).

In practice, a Māori approach to monitoring dieback is a form of 'attentive relationality'. First, it exemplifies how Indigenous knowledge 'extend[s] the range of nonhuman beings with which we can be in relation' – including trees (TallBear, 2015). The Māori common word for forest is *ngahere*, which means 'the binding of diverse species living together' (Shortland, 2011, p. 14), whereby each is dependent on the other to survive and flourish. 'The individual species within the ngahere rely upon one another to thrive, each is as important as the other no matter how tall, small, or large. Indicators for kāuri health must therefore be derived from other species within the forest in addition to the kāuri' (ibid.). It follows that an initial step in approaching the monitoring of kāuri dieback is to widen the scope of enquiry, taking in other species which coexist with kāuri. To establish *which* species coexist and therefore can be included as 'indicators', a number of steps are followed. The first is to identify species living on kāuri, then those living close by, then to identify other forest species already known to be especially susceptible to environmental change and, finally, the examination of all the species identified in these first three steps 'for knowledge of their cultural value and their value as a cultural health indicator' (Shortland, 2011, p. 7). The kāuri itself is well known as a 'host tree' (Harrison-Smith, 1938), hence the 60 or so species identified in the first stage as living on and with the kāuri, whilst over 30 more were identified in subsequent stages.

The framework for ascertaining health within and amongst species was derived from mātauranga Māori understandings of the domains of *atua* – spiritual guardians (Chetham and Shortland, 2013; Shortland, 2011). Species identified are framed within different domains, which together constitute a holistic approach to health, and accounting for their whakapapa deepens and animates this holistic understanding. As we might expect, as many as 90 species of tree, minor flora, reptile and insect are identified within the realm of Tane Mahuta, atua of the Forest, as the main focus and key elements of ngahere. However, there are more realms, all of which help frame the relational importance of additional species. Two of especial significance are Papatuanuku (earth mother) and Tangaroa (god of seas, rivers and lakes). The former realm draws attention to leaf litter, dead wood, soil and rock, the latter to the importance of access to water and moisture to grow for kāuri but also for companion species, and the quality of that water, as measured through Māori perceptions of water (see Morgan, 2007, p. 27), and both soil and water as potential vectors of the kāuri dieback pathogen. Other domains and related values frame the role of air quality and currents, heat and light, human influence, variation in life and reproductive stages. These are all operationalised as indicators, observable by researchers in the field, and often combine with established environmental science observations and measurements where considered appropriate.

Recognising their own active role as species within the ngahere, the researchers must also prepare *themselves* by practicing self-examination – *wairua* (Chetham and Shortland, 2013, p. 66). This is described by a *kaumatua* (Māori elder) as recognising one's own inseparableness from ngahere, and another as 'doing a personal check on your own spiritual health before doing one on the forest... and ensuring that you come informed' (Shortland, 2011). Karakia, an aspect of wairua, is literally translated as the offer of prayer or incantation, but within this context is described more as ensuring one is spiritually prepared – in the right mind, exercising one's potential, committed to a duty of care (Shortland, 2011, p. 48), again, understanding one's self as a constituent part of ngahere.

As with parallel ecological challenges, the utilisation of Māori knowledge to understand, manage and prevent kāuri dieback is far from a simple story of open collaboration and success (Coombes, Johnson and Howitt, 2013). According to social scientist Melanie Shadbolt from Māori biosecurity network Te Tira Whakamātaki (cited in Hurihanganui, 2017), 'our frustration is that Māori not only are excluded from the system, but we're excluded from solutions as well and we're not funded equitably or even included in the conversations about how we make decisions about what is funded', echoing Kennedy and Jefferies's concerns 10 years earlier. Lambert et al., specifically acknowledge resistance and a lack of recognition from forestry managers and government agencies, and that the programme 'is yet to realise the potential of Māori knowledge and customs to manage successfully kāuri dieback' (Lambert et al., 2018, p. 111). It seems a colonial temporal discourse still frames approaches to the assessment of ecological impacts. Against this backdrop, it is something of an understatement to say that a meaningful integration of culture and spirituality is beyond the range of convenience for a Western conservation science assessment of ecological impact, but for Māori, 'such an approach is essential to capture the wider well-being of their forest systems' (Lambert et al., 2018, p. 119).[12]

Whatever the potential of a Māori approach to reversing the decline of kāuri and health of ngahere, it also offers, through this application, a practical embodiment of the kind of methodological approach often called for by posthuman and more-than-human scholarship, as a 'holism without boundaries' (Smart and Smart, 2017, p. 8). In these emerging fields, much emphasis is placed on overlapping ethical and epistemological orientations that cultivate 'arts of attentiveness' (Kirksey and Helmreich, 2010) and 'becoming-witness' to other forms of life (van Doreen and Rose, 2016), 'attending deeply' (Head, 2016, p. 69; Wright, 2015, p. 392), 'crafting new tools for noticing' (Tsing, 2015, p. 25), and 'a methodology of attending' that attempts to 'become less hard of hearing in the context of a communicative and vibrant more-than-human world' (Country et al., 2015, p. 278). It might be tempting to think of environmental health monitoring of biosecurity and ecosystem concerns as irrelevant to the specifics of a more-than-human ethnography which 'must pay attention to entanglements between non-humans and humans, as well as between people in different locations' (Smart & Smart, 2017, p. 7). However, I think it offers a template for the practice of what van Doreen and Rose champion as 'ecological animism', which 'responds to a world in which all life—from the smallest cell to the largest redwood—is involved in diverse forms of adaptive, generative responsiveness' (2016, p. 82; see also Bird-David, 2000). Again, I am wary here of assuming Indigenous knowledge must be subsumed to a more articulate or authoritative conceptualisation elsewhere, when, in fact, it is more likely that 'multispecies ethnography has starting points that only partially contain indigenous standpoints' (TallBear, 2015).

A Māori approach to kāuri dieback therefore exemplifies calls in posthuman and multi-species scholarship for modes of attention capable of recognising multiple networks and entanglements. The human species is shifted from centre stage, which is now shared with other interrelating species, but again this is in keeping with an Indigenous epistemology, as it is specifically situated in the forests of the North Island. The Māori approach to dieback is a reminder that to fully consider the Anthropocene as invitation, we must be open to multiple ontologies, epistemologies and methodologies, especially those that, even whilst under threat, demand of us an attentiveness to relationality rooted in the places and beings with which we co-exist.

Between the ocean and the forest

As promised, I now want to return to the whale, and the ocean, without losing sight of the kāuri, and the forest. For posthuman scholars, attending deeply can involve being open to unexpected meetings: 'strange encounters are… key to this endeavor, a willingness to expose oneself to the unknown, to alienation' (Åsberg and Braidotti, 2018, p. 17). Strangeness here might emerge from what is considered capable of meaningfully relating to what and thus contributing to 'the social' (Adams, 2018); indeed, 'indigenous perceptions of whom and what contributes to a societal structure are quite different from traditional Euro-Western thought' (Watts, 2013, p. 21). This unsettling is arguably at the heart of endeavours to reconceptualise agency as involving more-than- and other-than-human entities (Bennett, 2005), the revival of geographical anthropological interest in animism (Harvey, 2006; 2013), and, as discussed above, is integral to many forms of Indigenous knowledge and scholarship. In what remains of this chapter, we explore what might appear as a strange encounter, at least to non-Māori – between the kāuri tree and the parāoa (sperm whale).

Māori worldviews vary according to one's *iwi*, but share many aspects of a cosmological whakapapa – the stories of the formation of the world and the origin of all forms of life, including the human psyche. The Māori creation story unites plants, rocks, wind, seas, animals and people in a shared genealogy, traceable back to the activities of various 'gods', foremost of which are Ranginui (sky father) and Papatuanuku (earth mother) and Tane Mahuta (god of the forest) (Henare, 2001). All things of the natural world are thus related by descent; humans, plants and animals are close kin (Hall, 2013). Included in these origin myths are tales of many species, including, as we have seen, the whale (Bradford, 2006), but whales and kāuri are explicitly and especially linked through *whakapapa* in various ways.[13]

They share a comparative status in their respective realms, acknowledging their physical size and presence: 'Imagine you'd stepped off a waka [large canoe] after crossing the Pacific, serenaded by singing whales, and were confronted with a six- or seven-metre-diameter kāuri trunk. What would come to mind?' (Warne, 2014). The whale – the largest sea creature – is the 'oceanic twin' of the kāuri – the largest native tree – and both are regarded as *rangatira* (chiefs), as respected *tupuna* (ancestors) of Māori and as *taonga* (treasured, sacred) species (Bradford, 2006; Warne, 2014). The enormous sperm whale, in particular, is the 'ocean twin' of the kāuri tree. In some versions of whale origins, they are the children of Tanagaroa, atua of the oceans, but in others, their forbearers are forest-dwelling ancients. According to

Rodgers, one tradition 'cites Te Hāpuku as the main ancestor of whales, dolphins and seals as well as tree ferns [including kāuri] which are often known as "ngā ika ō te ngahere" the fish of the forest' (Rodgers, 2017, p. 3). A particular origin story offered by Hori Parata, the kaumatua of the Kāuri Dieback Management Programme and the Ngati Wai Iwi, fascinatingly extends a whale-kāuri connection:

> The Legend of the Kāuri and the Sperm Whale: In times long past a sperm whale came ashore and spoke to the kāuri. 'Kāuri! Come with me to the sea, which is fresh and cool'. 'No!' said the kāuri. 'You may like the sea but I prefer to stand here with my feet in the soil'. 'All right said the whale. Then let us agree to exchange our skins'. So that is why the bark of the kāuri is thin and full of resinous oil... Moreover, their bark and skin show similarities of texture, while kāuri gum is like the ambergris found in the intestines of the sperm whale.
>
> *(cited in Shortland, 2011, p. 25; see also Bradford, 2006)*

The way this story – a strange encounter – frames the relationship between parāoa and kāuri, the apparent similarity of kāuri bark and whale skin, resin and oil, kāuri gum and ambergris, deepens the whakapapa connection and gives further meaning to kāuri as 'fish of the forest'. Parati and his iwi have recently suggested that the spread of dieback crisis and the increase in whale strandings might be interrelated – as connected responses to anthropogenic environmental impacts. Intriguingly, with western science failing to find an effective remedy for dieback to date, a Northland Māori collective, incorporating traditional knowledge experts and environmental scientists, wants to explore the role that whale oil and related derivatives might have in effective treatment (Roy, 2019). Such a possibility is built on the merits of the genealogical link between the whale and the kāuri tree, and involves experts in traditional medicine, historians and conservationists (Harrison, 2018). It is precisely the kind of claim that has been delegitimised in the past as mere superstition, 'a Māori hocus pocus kind of witchcraft type thing which is of no benefit [...] no use' (Mark-Shadbolt cited in Boynton, 2018).

As a non-Indigenous scholar, I am fast approaching the limits of my ability to flesh out the nature of a kāuri-whale connection from a Māori perspective, and there is very little, as yet, written about it by Indigenous scholars, though there are some fascinating glimpses. In a recent news report, specifically highlighting the possible role of whale oil in curing dieback, traditional medicines expert Tohe Ashby elliptically states 'that the ideology that land-based problems are only solved on land is obsolete, and [we need] to search further' (cited in Harrison, 2018). Perhaps inevitably, considering my own positioning, I briefly turn to recent developments in Western science to help make speculative sense of whale-tree interrelatedness, especially as it is defined by a shared precarity – 'the condition of being vulnerable to others' (Tsing, 2015, p. 20). I want to reiterate that this is done in a spirit of consilience, not an attempt to bestow 'scientific' legitimacy on 'traditional knowledge'

In earlier discussion of kāuri as a 'host species', we have a sense of the tree as being at the heart of a complex assemblage of companion species above ground. At the subterranean level, companionship is extended via mycorrhizal networks. A mycorrhiza is a symbiosis between a plant and fungus, a form of mutualism in which each flourish thanks to the activity of the other (Pringle, 2009). As Tsing describes it:

> The fungus extends its body into the host's roots to siphon off some of the plant's carbohydrates through specialized interface structures, made in the encounter. The fungus depends on this food, yet it is not entirely selfish. Fungi stimulate plant growth, first, by getting plants more water, and, second, by making the nutrients of extracellular digestion available to plants. Plants get calcium, nitrogen, potassium, phosphorus, and other minerals through mycorrhiza.
>
> *(Tsing, 2015, p. 138)*

Mycorrhizal networks are now considered ubiquitous and indispensable – involved in symbiotic association with almost all land plants (Van Der Heijden et al., 2015) – and 'fundamental agents' of the emerging properties of ecosystems in their own right (Simard et al., 2012, p. 39). Mycorrhiza can also connect plants and, specifically, link the roots between them, for example, transferring carbon, nitrogen or phosphorous (Simard et al., 1997; Simard, 2009; Teste et al., 2009). Mycorrhiza are also conduits for chemical compounds and electrical impulses, 'infochemicals' which traverse the soil to convey and detect warnings within and across species, help defend against threats, trade and 'lend' nutrients, help recognise kin and drive the 'community dynamics' of forest ecosystems (Barto et al., 2012). There is now more willingness to adopt behavioural, relational and communication terminology within a scientific framework, and explicit acknowledgement that 'underground "tree talk" is a foundational process in the complex adaptive nature of forest ecosystems' (Gorzelak et al., 2015, p. 1). Most recently, Simard has provided 'examples of neighboring tree behavioral, learning, and memory responses facilitated by communication through mycorrhizal networks' and tree behaviours that 'have cognitive qualities, including capabilities in perception, learning, and memory' (2018, p. 191). Simard has also helped identify larger 'mother trees' as important forest hubs apparently directing patterns of nutrient traffic, helping to nourish younger shaded saplings (Simard et al., 1997; Pollan, 2013; Toomey, 2016). In symbiosis with mycorrhizal networks, mother trees stabilise and significantly enhance the resilience and regenerative capacities of forest ecosystems (Beiler et al, 2010).[14]

These discoveries push established Western scientific paradigms to their limit. As Wohlleben summarises

> The wood wide web has been mapped, traced, monitored, and coaxed to reveal the beautiful structures and finely adapted languages of the forest network... These discoveries have transformed our understanding of trees from competitive crusaders of the self to members of a connected, relating, communicating system... there is a burst of careful scientific research occurring worldwide that is uncovering all manner of ways that trees communicate with each other above and below ground
>
> *(2016)*

Whilst Wohlleben speaks of 'discoveries' and 'uncoverings', scientific findings clearly resonate with established and in motion Māori understandings of *ngathe*, of the central and sacred significance of 'mother trees' and of the animated vitality of interspecies interdependency, as revealed in Māori knowledge frameworks and holistic approach to monitoring kāuri dieback. Clearly then there is potential here for greater consilience across cultural and knowledge frameworks, despite a history of divergent ontological epistemological and methodological approaches.

A final, intriguing step is to consider whether we might extend interspecies communicative capabilities to the kāuri and the whale. Radical developments in human understanding of interspecies communicative capacities paint a remarkably rich picture of 'tree cognition' and 'forest intelligence' (Simard, 2018), of connection and community through the air, across and under the earth. Might these capabilities extend to other species and even beyond the forest? Simard certainly thinks so, arguing for the existence of 'collective memory-based interactions among trees, fungi, salmon, bears, and people that enhance the health of the whole forest ecosystem' in making the case for a more holistic and empathic approach to forest health (2018, p. 191).

Let us briefly approach the issue from the other direction – the communicative capacities of whales, as far as our (human) methods can apprehend them. Marine mammals have combined an exceptional sense of hearing with adapted air passages in the body developed for breathing to develop remarkably effective forms of communicating through sound. Sound travels through water four times faster than through air and is less attenuated, and the sounds made by cetaceans, especially those at low frequency, many undetectable by human ear, can travel far – miles, even, underwater (Tyack and Miller, 2002; Whitehead and Rendell, 2014, p. 54). In this fluid, three-dimensional habitat, often lacking in light, 'sound is an essential component of a whale's perceptual system, their hearing to map their environment and their social world… giv[ing] the animals a detailed picture of their surroundings' (Whitehead and Rendell, 2014, p. 60). Beyond mapping and navigation, whales use elaborate, complex and dynamic vocalisations to communicate with other whales, epitomised in the song of the humpback whale, a phenomenon now firmly embedded in human culture (Ritts, 2017). Behavioural ecologists have made various claims about the function and purpose of these more complex forms of acoustic contact – expressions of association, belonging, courtship, group distinction, individuality, and even as contributing to interspecific co-operation, whereby a species of whale will engage in activities such as nursing, warning or protecting another species (Fox et al., 2017; Leung, Vergara and Barrett-Lennard, 2010; Pitman et al., 2017).

The size of these underwater acoustic communication networks varies enormously depending on species and location, but they can stretch for hundreds of miles (Janik, 2005, p. 393). Research in acoustical oceanography suggests the possibility that whales communicate over even longer distances by utilising the 'deep sound' or SOFAR channel, reflecting their ocean-spanning migratory patterns (Tsuchiya et al., 2004).[15] Together, whale communicative capacities are increasingly being stated as evidence of cetacean culture and personhood (Whitehead and Rendell, 2014). It follows that anthropogenic ocean noise pollution is considered highly disruptive and a significant source of cetacean stress. Evidence for a worldwide decline in whale vocalisation since the 1960s has amassed in recent years and is correlated with increases in noisy human activity in the oceans (Gavrilov et al., 2011, 2012; McDonald, Hildebrand and Mesnick, 2009).

In sum, both whales and trees are complex entities, revealing dynamic capacities for communication across multi-species networks. As branches of science develop better understandings of whale vocalisations that traverse miles of ocean, and root systems through which trees 'can hear and even hum', are they, really, as Harvey hopes, 'proving ancient conceptions of connectedness' (2019)? I agree that it will be profoundly interesting to see how 'far and deep' that understanding may go. Simone Vitale asserts that we should begin by asking ourselves the following kinds of questions more often:

> What if we lived in a world where the whales sing to the trees and the trees sing back to the whale as an important nourishing element of the ecosystem? What if the changing song of the sperm whale is no longer nourishing the Kāuri tree as it used to, depriving it of a strengthening nourishment that could possibly make it more resistant to its sickness?
>
> *(Vitale, 2017)*

Within a natural science framework, it would be an enormous, perhaps impossible, step to suggest that the networks of trees and whales somehow interspecifically cross, a mutualism evident in the distinct but interlinked anthropogenic impacts – kāuri trees affected by dieback and stranding whales affected by a polluted, including sonically, ocean environment. For a Western, rational, scientific psyche, this still might seem an implausible, inconceivable step, well beyond the limits of its epistemological and ontological frames. Whilst such a possibility has long been considered within Indigenous knowledge systems, the science and wider community has tended to disregard such knowledge as 'just myths, ancient legends, incredible stories and folklore… invalidat[ing] Māori ontological and epistemological constructs of the world' (Hikuroa, 2016, p. 2). A resurgent mātauranga Māori, as with other forms of Indigenous knowledge, might embody and extend an older, deeper and richer realisation of planetary connectivity and interspecies communication embodied in *whakapapa* that makes a culture, a science and a psyche more open to such a prospect. Meanwhile, pockets of

Western science are shifting distinctively towards models of species interdependency, in sylvian and soil science as we have seen, but more widely too (Bradshaw, 2010; Gilbert et al. 2012; Haraway, 2016; McFall-Ngai et al., 2013). Taking these strands together, we begin to discern a powerful evocation of a multi-species relational ontology, especially as it is defined by a shared Anthropocene precarity – 'the condition of being vulnerable to others' (Tsing, 2015, p. 20).

Finally: Anthropocene stories

Whale strandings and tree pathogens offer a glimpse of an alternative Anthropocene psychology, open to existing knowledge frameworks often at odds, inconceivable even, to established scientific frameworks underpinning the secularised Anthropocene narrative, but not wholly incommensurate. Contemporary whale strandings in Aotearoa New Zealand reveal a contemporary Māori/Ngatiwa framing of anthropogenic ecological devastation – an Anthropocene framing, but not as 'we' know it. It demands different affective engagements, affords alternative forms of intersubjectivity and multi-species network of relations, that stretch back up onto the shore, to the interior, underground, through root networks, out across the air and up into canopies. It is about loss, grief and mourning, but also about practical engagement – located in the body of the whale, of the kāuri, and their connections. This is not to suggest these are secure or fixed positions. There is no monolithic 'Māori worldview' that exists either in unity or in stasis, but only specific and situated instances of changing Indigenous knowledge, with increasing opportunities, in some quarters, for collaboration with, and representation in, academic departments and science. Neither is there an intention here to set an abstracted, romanticised indigene still in touch with nature against an alienated westerner.

My intention in this chapter has been to contribute to 'Anthropocene stories' which 'continuously highlight the multiple, interdependent relations within nature, within different forms of materiality, within technologies and within social systems, [and] the interconnections between these domains', and in doing so 'deepens our sense of the interrelatedness between nature and society' (Lidskog and Waterton, 2018, p. 39). I have attempted to approach the phenomena of mass whale strandings with curiosity and attentiveness, as a strange encounter, and in doing so picked up the threads of not one but multiple Anthropocene narratives (van Doreen & Rose, 2016). In particular, a Māori perspective has been approached as a specific and situated form of Indigenous thinking 'seen as not just a well of ideas to draw from but a body of thinking that is living and practiced by peoples with whom we all share reciprocal duties as citizens of shared territories (be they physical or the ephemeral)' (Todd, 2016a, p. 17). Anthropocene psychology is developed by hearing and telling stories of a landscape and its inhabitants, all active players in 'shifting assemblages of human and nonhumans: the very stuff of collaborative survival' (Tsing, 2015, p. 20). Whales emerge as much more than merely 'passive objects for humans to act upon or use as tools or resources' (Mullin, 2010, p. 148); they have meaningful lives and histories entangled with humans and others in animated multispecies worlds, 'woven through with co-forming patterns of responsiveness, attention, desire, and communication' (van Doreen & Rose, 2016, p. 81).

Where is the human here? *Anthropos* cannot, of course, be displaced from language, storytelling, technology, writing and reading that are making these words possible. But in opening up what it means to be human in a more-than-human world, we need not be restricted to tales in which we are the only or main players, but can freely, if carefully, incorporate whales, trees, pathogens, mycorrhizae and much more into our assemblages. As Anna Tsing asserts in following the trail of matsutake mushrooms:

> I am not limited to tracking human relations with their favored allies, as in most animal studies. Organisms don't have to show their human equivalence (as conscious agents, intentional communicators, or ethical subjects) to count. If we are interested in livability, impermanence, and emergence, we should be watching the action of landscape assemblages. Assemblages coalesce, change, and dissolve: this *is* the story
>
> *(2015, p. 158; emphasis in original)*

Whales strand and trees become diseased, human understandings of and responses to specific and situated challenges in nature retreat and advance. Amongst these dynamics of coalescence, change and dissolution, we can choose to 'turn towards the reciprocity and relatedness' addressed by Indigenous and non-Indigenous scholars in addressing specific and situated challenges of the Anthropocene (Todd, 2015, p. 252).

Papaschase Cree scholar Dwayne Donald's notion of 'ethical relationality' is perhaps a better conceptual frame for the potential that the Māori approach to dieback represents here (Donald, 2009; 2010). It involves 'paying attention to the webs of relationships that you are enmeshed in, depending on where you live... all the things that give us life, all the things that we depend on, as well as all the other entities that we relate to, including human beings' (cited in Todd, p. 250). Todd's reasoning for valuing Donald's framing specifically is revealing:

> his thinking serves as a powerful tool with which to examine underlying assumptions about, and responses to, human and non-human relationships in the Anthropocene... [and] a desire to acknowledge and honour the significance of the relationships we have with others, how our histories and experiences position us in relation to each other, and how our futures as people in the world are similarly tied together. It is an ethical imperative to see that despite our varied place-based cultures and knowledge systems, we live in the world together and must constantly think and act with reference to those relationships
>
> *(2014, p. 249)*

Following Todd's lead, I see in Donald's perspective a powerful statement of the political-ethical dimension of attentiveness – response-able practice comes to the fore (Haraway, 2008; Greenhough and Roe, 2010). In exploring a Māori perspective and practice as a specific and situated application of Indigenous knowledge in this chapter, we further scrutinise those assumptions, particularly as they are embedded in entrenched colonial histories and established Western conservation science perspectives. They help us 'stay with the trouble' (Haraway, 2016), attentive to multi-species co-becoming, but as it is embedded in the unwanted motility of pathogens, legacies of colonialism, contested scientific and cultural practices and much more. It is vital to enliven an Anthropocene psychology in this way, to reach out and in for worldviews that resonate with place and with which progressive science and humanities research can learn and collaborate; to highlight narratives which 'give life and dimension to the strategies—oppositional, affirmative, and yes, often desperate and fractured—that emerge from those who bear the brunt of the planet's ecological crises' (Nixon, 2011, p. 23). This is what it means to begin to 'decolonize', 'desecularize' and 'indigenize' the Anthropocene (Szerszynski, 2017; Todd, 2015).

Notes

1. Aotearoa is the Māori name for New Zealand. It is now common practice to refer to both names together. See https://sayit.co.nz/blog/aotearoa-new-zealand.

2. 'Although hundreds of locals participated in a mass civilian rescue effort, more than 300 whales died' https://www.theguardian.com/world/2017/feb/10/hundreds-whales-die-mass-stranding-new-zealand-beach. See also https://www.bbc.co.uk/news/av/world-43521353/over-100-whales-die-in-mass-stranding-in-australia.

3. Zoe Todd's response to a Bruno Latour lecture here is apposite:

> So, I waited. I waited through the whole talk, to hear the Great Latour credit Indigenous thinkers for their millennia of engagement with sentient environments, with cosmologies that enmesh people into complex relationships between themselves and all relations, and with climates and atmospheres as important points of organization and action... waited to hear a whisper of the lively and deep intellectual traditions... It never came... I was left wondering, when will I hear someone reference Indigenous thinkers in a direct, contemporary and meaningful way in European lecture halls?... As thinkers in their own right, not just disembodied representatives of an amorphous Indigeneity that serves European intellectual or political purposes.
>
> *(Todd, 2016a, p. 6)*

4. Though I find Konai Helu Thaman's poem *Thinking*, with which she closes her paper on 'decolonizing Pacific studies' (2003), extremely helpful:

> you say that you think
> therefore you are
> but thinking belongs
> in the depths of the earth
> we simply borrow
> what we need to know
> these islands the sky
> the surrounding sea
> the trees the birds
> and all that are free
> the misty rain
> the surging river
> pools by the blowholes
> a hidden flower
> have their own thinking
> they are different frames
> of mind that cannot fit
> in a small selfish world

5. There are obvious problems translating Māori terms into English and retaining their meaning outside of their original context. Where possible here, definitions and meanings are drawn from Māori scholarship.

6. Eleanor Ainge Roy (2019) A sign from the sea? Māori's fear greed of humans cause whale strandings. *The Guardian*, 5 January 2019.

7. After a protracted political struggle, the formal recognition of Māori harvesting rights over dead whales was granted in the 1990s (Te Karaka, 2014).

8. In 2015, a scientific observation flight over Patagonia, Chile, discovered the largest single mass beaching ever recorded – the bodies of 337 endangered sei whales; 2016 saw the largest stranding of sperm whales ever recorded in the North Sea (Seawatch Foundation, 2016). Besides Australia and New Zealand, there are numerous accounts across the globe of 80-plus mass beachings in the twenty-first century to date, for example, Madagascar in 2008; Japan in 2015; Florida, USA, 2017; Australia, 2018 (BBC, 2018b).

9. In the first of a number of strange parallel with whales, kāuri gum, a resin, like whale oil and ambergris, became an important export in the colonial and early industrial era (Lattimore, 2013). It was used in the manufacture of varnishes and many other resin-based products. According to the New Zealand Department of Conservation, 'the gum was obtained through digging, fossicking in treetops, or more drastically, by bleeding live trees' https://www.doc.govt.nz/nature/native-plants/kāuri/.

10. Human activities are centrally implicated in the spread and incidence of the disease, namely 'the transfer of contaminated soils between nurseries, recreational use of kāuri forests, and track building and maintenance practices, have been all correlated to the spread and incidence of the disease' (Bellgard et al., 2016, p. 115).

11. According to a recent news report, the pathogen 'can sense a kāuri tree's roots, and swim towards them to cause infection' (Smith, 2018), a point that seems to be supported by microbiologist Monica Gerth, who investigates how disease-causing microbes move, 'smell' and communicate: 'One key to the devastating spread of soil-borne Phytophthora are free-swimming cells, called zoospores. Zoospores swim through water-logged soils, and once a zoospore finds a host plant, it encysts on the root and initiates the infection. Our idea is that the spread of kāuri dieback can be mitigated by disrupting the ability of zoospores to "smell" and navigate towards their host plants' (Gerth, 2017; Lawrence et al., 2017).

12. Meyer captures this wonderfully (2014, p. 155) as follows: 'Here is the pivot of Indigenous epistemology... – the idea that spirituality is at the core of what knowledge is sounds more mythic than logical. Such is the contradiction of our times: to speak of an implicate order with an explicate lexicon. How, indeed, does one describe apples with an orange vocabulary?'

13. Tales of 'partnerships existing between creatures of the sea and "guardian" plants on the land', including whales and large trees (Cressey, 1998, p. 81–2), appear regularly in Indigenous legends and stories (Harvey, 2019).

14. In a 2016 TED talk, 'How trees talk to each other', Simard describes (at 13:52) their significance as follows: 'You can take out one or two hub trees, but there comes a tipping point. Hub trees are not unlike rivets in an aeroplane; you can take out one or two and the plane still flies, but you take out one too many, or maybe that one holding on the wings, and the whole system collapses' https://www.youtube.com/watch?v= Un2yBgIAxYs.
15. The deep channel is a layer 600–1,200 m below the surface 'in which sound is trapped and travels almost horizontally, with much less transmission loss' (Janik, 2005, p. 397).

References

Adams, M. 2018. Towards a critical psychology of human–animal relations. *Social & Personality Psychology Compass*, 12(4), 1–14.

Åsberg, C. 2018. Feminist Posthumanities in the Anthropocene: Forays into the Postnatural. *Journal of Posthuman Studies*, 1(2), 185–204.

Åsberg, C. and Braidotti, R. 2018. Feminist Posthumanities: An Introduction. In Åsberg, C. and Braidotti, R. (Eds.), *A Feminist Companion to the Posthumanities*. New York: Springer, pp. 1–22.

Awatere, S., Harmsworth, G. and Robb, M. 2017. Matauranga Māori: Māori knowledge. In Taura, Y., van Schravendijk-Goodman, C. and Clarkson, B. (Eds.) *Te reo o te repo – The Voice of the Wetland: Connections, Understandings and Learnings for the Restoration of Our Wetlands*. Lincoln, NZ: Manaaki Whenua – Landcare Research, pp. 151-155.

Barto, E. K., Weidenhamer, J. D., Cipollini, D. and Rillig, M. C. 2012. Fungal superhighways: Do common mycorrhizal networks enhance below ground communication? *Trends in Plant Science*, 17(11), 633–637.

BBC. 2018a. Whales stranded in New Zealand: Another 50 pilot whales die. BBC News Retrieved from 2019 https://www.bbc.co.uk/news/world-asia-46395410?intlink_from_url=https://www.bbc.co.uk/news/topics/cnyzy10vd01t/whale-strandings&link_location=live-reporting-story

BBC. 2018b. Hamelin Bay: Nearly 150 beached whales die in Australia. BBC News Retrieved from https://www.bbc.co.uk/news/world-australia-43519439

Beiler, K. J., Durall, D. M., Simard, S. W., Maxwell, S. A. and Kretzer, A. M. 2010. Architecture of the wood-wide web: *Rhizopogon* spp. genets link multiple Douglas-fir cohorts. *New Phytologist*, 185(2), 543–553.

Bellgard, S. E., Pennycook, S. R., Weir, B. S., Ho, W. and Waipara, N. W. 2016. Phytophthora agathidicida. *Forest Phytophthoras*, 6(1). https://doi.org/10.5399/osu/fp.5.1.3748.

Bennett, J. 2005. The agency of assemblages and the North American Blackout, *Public Culture*, 17(3), 445–465.

Bird-David, N. 2000. "Animism" revisited: Personhood, environment, and relational epistemology. *Current Anthropology*, 41(S1), 67–91.

Boynton, J. 2018. Boost in funding for Kāuri dieback, myrtle rust research, Radio New Zealand November 20 2018. Available at https://www.radionz.co.nz/news/national/376388/boost-in-funding-for-kāuri-dieback-myrtle-rust-research

Bradford, H. 2006. 'Te whānau puha – whales – Whales in Māori tradition', Te Ara. Encyclopedia of New Zealand. Retrieved from http://www.TeAra.govt.nz/en/te-whanau-puha-whales/page-1.

Bradshaw, G. A. (2010). You see me, but do you hear me? The science and sensibility of trans-species dialogue. *Feminism & Psychology*, 20(3), 407–419.

Chetham, J., & Shortland, T. 2013. Kāuri cultural health indicators: Monitoring framework. Report prepared by Repo Consultancy Ltd for the Kāuri Dieback Programme. Whangarei: New Zealand

Cloke, P., & Perkins, H. C.. 2005. Cetacean performance and tourism in Kaikoura, New Zealand. *Environment and Planning D: Society and Space*, 23(6), 903–924.

Coombes, B., Johnson, J. and Howitt, R. 2013. Indigenous geographies II: The aspirational spaces in postcolonial politics - reconciliation, belonging and social provision. *Progress in Human Geography* 37(5), 691–700.

Country, B., Wright, S., Suchet-Pearson, S., Lloyd, K., Burarrwanga, L., Ganambarr, R., Ganambarr-Stubbs, M., Ganambarr, B. and Maymuru, D., 2015. Working with and learning from Country: decentring human authority. *Cultural Geographies*, 22(2),269–283.

Country, B., Wright, S., Suchet-Pearson, S., Lloyd, K., Burarrwanga, L., Ganambarr, R., Ganambarr-Stubbs, M., Ganambarr, B., Maymuru, D. and Sweeney, J., 2016. Co-becoming Bawaka: Towards a relational understanding of place/space. *Progress in Human Geography*, 40(4), 455–475.

Cressey, J. 1998. Making a splash in the Pacific: Dolphin and whale myths and legends of Oceania. *Rapa Nui Journal*, 12, 75–84.

Dixon, J. 2014. Cultural Indicators. New Zealand Science Learning Hub Pokapū Akoranga Pūtaiao. Retrieved from https://www.sciencelearn.org.nz/videos/243-cultural-indicators

Donald, D. 2009. Forts, curriculum and Indigenous Métissage: Imagining decolonization of aboriginal-Canadian relations in educational contexts. *First Nations Perspectives*, 2(1).

Donald, D. 2010. On What Terms Can We Speak? Lecture at the University of Lethbridge. Retrieved from https://vimeo.com/15264558

Fox, K. C., Muthukrishna, M. and Shultz, S. 2017. The social and cultural roots of whale and dolphin brains. *Nature Ecology & Evolution*, 1(11), 1699.

Franklin, A. (1999). *Animals and Modern Cultures: A Sociology of Human-Animal Relations in Modernity*. London: Sage.

Gavrilov, A. N., McCauley, R. D. and Gedamke, J. 2012. Steady inter and intra-annual decrease in the vocalization of Antarctic blue whales. *Journal of the Acoustical Society of America*, 131, 4476–4480.

Gavrilov, A. N., McCauley, R. D., Salgado-Kent, C., Tripovich, J. and Burton, C. 2011. Vocal characteristics of pygmy blue whales and their change over time. *J. Acoust. Soc. Am.*, 130, 3651–3660.

Gerth, M. 2017. Preventing a fatal attraction: Disrupting the spread of kāuri dieback disease. *First National Meeting of The New Zealand's Biological Heritage Ng Koiora Tuku Iho National Science Challenge.*

Gilbert, S.F., Sapp, J. and Tauber, A.I., 2012. A symbiotic view of life: we have never been individuals. *The Quarterly Review of Biology*, 87(4), 325–341.

Giggs, R. 2015. Whale fall. *Granta*, 133 (18th November 2015). Available at https://granta.com/whale-fall/.

Gorzelak, M. A., Asay, A. K., Pickles, B. J. and Simard, S. W. 2015. Inter-plant communication through mycorrhizal networks mediates complex adaptive behaviour in plant communities. *AoB PLANTS*, 7 (plv050), 1–13.

Greenhough, B. and Roe, E., 2010. From ethical principles to response-able practice. *Environment and Planning D: Society and Space*, 28(1), 43–45.

Hall, M. 2013. Talk among the trees: Animist plant ontologies and ethics. In Harvey, G. (Ed.), *The Handbook of Contemporary Animism*. London: Routledge, pp. 385–394.

Haraway, D. (2016), *Staying with the Trouble: Making Kin in the Chthulucene.* Minneapolis, MN: University of Minnesota Press.

Harmsworth, G. R. and Awatere, S. 2013. Indigenous Māori knowledge and perspectives of ecosystems. In J. Dymond (Ed.) *Ecosystem Services in New Zealand—Conditions and Trends*. Lincoln, New Zealand: Manaaki Whenua Press, pp. 274–286.

Harmsworth, G., Awatere, S. and Robb, M. 2016. Indigenous Māori values and perspectives to inform freshwater management in Aotearoa-New Zealand. *Ecology and Society*, 21(4).

Harmsworth, G. and Jollands, N. 2007. Participation of indigenous groups in sustainable development monitoring: Rationale and examples from New Zealand, *Ecological Economics*, 62 (3–4), 716–26.

Harmsworth, G. R., Young, R. G., Walker, D., Clapcott, J. E. and James, T. 2011. Linkages between cultural and scientific indicators of river and stream health. *New Zealand Journal of Marine and Freshwater Research*, 45(3), 423–436.

Harrison, R. 2018. Potential whakapapa Māori solution for kāuri dieback outbreak. Te Ao Māori News. Tuesday 22 May 2018 https://www.Māori television.com/news/regional/potential-whakapapa-Māori-solution-kāuri-dieback-outbreak

Harrison-Smith, J. 1938. The kāuri as a host tree. *New Zealand Journal of Forestry*, 4(3), 173–177.

Harvey, B. 2019. Death of the gods: The woeful response to kāuri dieback disease. Noted. 21 February 2019. Retrieved from https://www.noted.co.nz/planet/kāuri-dieback-disease-auckland-woeful-response/

Harvey, G. 2006. *Animism: Respecting the Living World*. New York: Columbia University Press.

Harvey, G. 2013 (Ed.), *The Handbook of Contemporary Animism*. Durham: Acumen.

Head, L. 2016. *Hope and Grief in the Anthropocene: Re-conceptualising human–nature relations*. London: Routledge.

Henare, M. 2001. Tapu, mana, mauri, hau, wairua: A Māori philosophy of vitalism and cosmos. In J.A Grim (Ed.), *Indigenous Traditions and Ecology: The Interbeing of Cosmology and Community*. Cambridge, Mass: Harvard University Press, pp. 197–221.

Hikuroa, D. 2016. Mātauranga Māori—the ūkaipō of knowledge in New Zealand. *Journal of the Royal Society of New Zealand*, 47(1), 5–10.

Hindle, R. and Matthewman, S. 2017. Māori literacies: Ecological perspectives. *Set: Research Information for Teachers*, Issue 3, pp. 32–37.

Horner, I. J., Hough, E. G. and Zydenbos, S. M. 2014. Pathogenicity of four Phytophthora species on kāuri: *In vitro* and glasshouse trials. *New Zealand Plant Protection*, 67, 54–59.

Hurihanganui, T. A. 2017. Kāuri dieback fight: Scientist warns of 'Māori exclusion' Radio New Zealand, 7 September 2018 https://www.radionz.co.nz/news/te-manu-korihi/365776/kāuri-dieback-fight-scientist-warns-of-Māori-exclusion

Janik, V. M. 2005. Underwater acoustic communication networks in marine mammals. In McGregor, P. K. (Ed.), *Animal Communication Networks*. Cambridge University Press, pp. 390–415.

Jones, A. and Hoskins, T.K. 2016. A mark on paper: The matter of Indigenous-settler history. In Taylor, C. and Hughes, C. (Eds.) *Posthuman Research Practices in Education*. London, England: Palgrave Macmillan.

Kawagley, A. O. 1995. *A Yupiaq Worldview: A Pathway to Ecology and Spirit*. Prospect Heights: Waveland Press.

King, D. N. T., Skipper, A. and Tawhai, W. B. 2008. Māori environmental knowledge of local weather and climate change in Aotearoa–New Zealand. *Climatic Change*, 90(4), 385.

Kirksey, S.E. and Helmreich, S. 2010. The emergence of multispecies ethnography, *Cultural Anthropology*, 25(4), 545–576.

Kohn, E. 2013. *How Forests Think: Toward an Anthropology Beyond the Human*. University of California Press, Berkeley, CA.

Kuokkanan, R. 2007. *Reshaping the University: Responsibility, Indigenous Epistemes, and the Logic of the Gift*. Vancouver: University of British: Columbia.

Lambert S., Waipara N., Black A., Mark-Shadbolt M. and Wood W. 2018. Indigenous Biosecurity: Māori Responses to Kāuri Dieback and Myrtle Rust in Aotearoa New Zealand. In Urquhart J., Marzano M. and Potter C. (Eds.), *The Human Dimensions of Forest and Tree Health*. Cham: Palgrave, Macmillan. Pages 109–137.

Lattimore, R. 2013. *The New Zealand Economy: An Introduction*. Auckland: Auckland University Press.

Lawrence, S.A., Armstrong, C.B., Patrick, W.M. and Gerth, M.L. 2017. High-throughput chemical screening identifies compounds that inhibit different stages of the *Phytophthora agathidicida* and *Phytophthora cinnamomi* life cycles. *Frontiers in Microbiology*, (8), 1340–1340.

Leung, E. S., Vergara, V. and Barrett-Lennard, L. G. 2010. Allonursing in captive belugas (*Delphinapterus leucas*). *Zoo Biology*, 29(5), 633–637.

Lidskog, R. & Waterton, C. 2018. The Anthropocene: Its conceptual usage and sociological challenges. In Boström, M. and Davidson, D. (Eds.), *Environment and Society: Concepts and Challenges.* Basingstoke: Palgrave, pp. 25–46.

Lorimer, B. 2019. Worlds set adrift: Water, air and the more-then-human. 11 February 2019. Neue Kulturgeographie Keynote Lecture. Retrieved from https://kulturgeographie.org/2019/02/11/keynote-hayden-lorimer/

Mankiller, W. 2009. Being Indigenous in the 21st century. Cultural Survival Quarterly, 33-1 A Celebration of Pacific Culture. Retrieved from https://www.culturalsurvival.org/publications/cultural-survival-quarterly/being-Indigenous-21st-century

Mark-Shadbolt, M., Wood, W. and Ataria, J. 2018. Why aren't people listening? Māori scientists on why rāhui are important. The Spinoff February 2 2018 Retrievedfromhttps://thespinoff.co.nz/atea/02-02-2018/why-arent-people-listening-Māori -scientists-on-why-rahui-are-important/

Marris, E. 2018. This man has helped give 460 dead whales a second life—as art. National Geographic, April 9, 2018. Retrieved from https://news.nationalgeographic.com/2018/04/new-zealand-Māori-beached-whales-flensing/

Mcdonald, M. A., Hildebrand, J. A. and Mesnick, S. 2009. Worldwide decline in tonal frequencies of blue whale songs. *End Species Research*, 9, 13–21.

McFall-Ngai, M., Hadfield, M.G., Bosch, T.C., Carey, H.V., Domazet-Lošo, T., Douglas, A.E., Dubilier, N., Eberl, G., Fukami, T., Gilbert, S.F. and Hentschel, U., 2013. Animals in a bacterial world, a new imperative for the life sciences. *Proceedings of the National Academy of Sciences*, 110(9), 3229–3236.

McGregor, D. 2014. Traditional Knowledge and Water Governance: The Ethic of Responsibility. *AlterNative: An International Journal of Indigenous Peoples* 10(5), 493–507.

Meyer, M. A. 2014. Indigenous epistemology: Spirit revealed. In Black, T. (Ed.), *Mātauranga Māori and Indigenous Knowledge.* Wellington: New Zealand Qualification Authority.

Morgan K 2007. Translating values and concepts into a decision making framework: Application of the Mauri Model for Integrated Performance Indicator Assessment. National Workshop: 5–7 September 2007. *Roundtable on sustainable forests: A partnership for the future.* Madison, WI, Forest Products Laboratory. Retrieved from http://www.thesustainabilitysociety.org.nz/conference/2004/Session5/36%20Morgan.pdf

Mullin, M. 2010. Anthropology's animals. In DeMello, M. (Ed.), *Teaching the Animal: Human-Animal Studies across the Divide,* New York: Lantern Books, pp. 145–201.

Necefer, L., Wong-Parodi, G., Jaramillo, P. and Small, M. J. 2015. Energy development and Native Americans: Values and beliefs about energy from the Navajo Nation. *Energy Research & Social Science*, 7, 1–11.

Newton, J., Paci, C. and Ogden, A. 2005. Climate Change And Natural Hazards In Northern Canada: Integrating Indigenous Perspectives With Government Policy. *Mitigation and Adaptation Strategies for Global Change*, 10(3), 541–571.

Nixon, R. 2011. *Slow Violence and the Environmentalism of the Poor*. Cambridge, MA: Harvard University Press.

Ngakuru, W., Marsden, M. and Nutall, P. 2010. *Te Roroa effects assessment for kāuri dieback disease—(Phytophthora taxon Agathis—PTA)*. Te Roroa / Kāuri Die-back Joint Agency Response: New Zealand. Retrieved from https://www.kāuridieback.co.nz/media/1818/ngakuru-marsden-nuttall-2010-te-roroa-effectes-assessment-kāuri-dieback-_.pdf

Panelli, R. 2010. More-than-human social geographies: Posthuman and other possibilities. *Progress in Human Geography*, 34(1), 79–87.

Parsons, E. C. M. 2017. Impacts of Navy sonar on whales and dolphins: Now beyond a smoking gun? *Front. Mar. Sci.*, 4, 295. doi: 10.3389/fmars.2017.00295

Parsons, E. C. M., Baulch, S., Bechshoft, T., Bellazzi, G., Bouchet, P., Cosentino, A. M. 2015. Key research questions of global importance for cetacean conservation. *Endanger. Species Res.*, 27, 113–118. doi: 10.3354/esr00655

Pringle, A. 2009. Mycorrhizal networks. *Current Biology*, 19(18), R838–R839.

Project Jonah. (n.d.). Why whales strand. Retrieved from https://www.projectjonah.org.nz/Stranded+dolphins++whales/Why+Whales+Strand.html

Reed, M. S. 2008. Stakeholder participation for environmental management: a literature review. *Biological Conservation*, 141(10), 2417–2431.

Ritchie, J. 2013. Indigenous onto-epistemologies and pedagogies of care and affect in Aotearoa. *Global Studies of Childhood*, 3(4), 395–406.

Ritts, M. 2017. Amplifying environmental politics: Ocean noise. *Antipode*, 49(5), 1406–1426.

Rodgers, R.P. 2017. *The connection of Māori to whales*, unpublished Masters thesis, University of Canterbury, Christchurch. Retrieved from https://ir.canterbury.ac.nz/handle/10092/14087.

Roy, E.A. 2019. "What is the sea telling us?", Māori tribes fearful over whale strandings, *The Guardian*, 3 January, Retrieved from www.theguardian.com/environment/2019/jan/03/what-isthe-sea-telling-us-maori-tribes-fearful-over-whale-strandings

Royal, T. A. C. 2012. Politics and knowledge: Kaupapa Māori and matauranga Māori. *New Zealand Journal of Educational Studies*, 47(2), 30.

Seawatch Foundation. 2016. http://www.seawatchfoundation.org.uk/largest-sperm-whale-stranding-ever-recorded-in-the-north-sea/

Shortland, T. 2011. *Cultural indicators for Kāuri Ngahere*. A Report Prepared for the Tangata Whenua Roopu. Whangarei, New Zealand: Kāuri Dieback Joint Agency Response.

Simard, S. W. 2009. The foundational role of mycorrhizal networks in self-organization of interior Douglas-fir forests. *Forest Ecology and Management*, 258, S95–S107.

Simard, S.W. 2018. Mycorrhizal networks facilitate tree communication, learning, and memory. In Baluška, F., Gagliano, M. and Witzany, G. (Eds), *Memory and Learning in Plants*. New York: Springer, pp. 191–213.

Simard, S. W., Beiler, K. J., Bingham, M. A., Deslippe, J. R., Philip, L. J. and Teste, F. P. 2012. Mycorrhizal networks: Mechanisms, ecology and modelling. *Fungal Biology Reviews*, 26(1), 39–60.

Simard, S. W., Perry, D. A., Jones, M. D., Myrold, D. D., Durall, D. M. and Molina, R. 1997. Net transfer of carbon between ectomycorrhizal tree species in the field. *Nature*, 388(6642), 579.

Singh, R. K., Srivastava, R. C., Pandey, C. B. and Singh, A. 2015. Tribal institutions and conservation of the bioculturally valuable 'tasat' (*Arenga obtusifolia*) tree in the eastern Himalaya. *Journal of Environmental Planning and Management*, 58(1), 69–90. https://doi.org/10.1080/09640568.2013.847821.

Smart, A., & Smart, J. 2017. *Posthumanism: Anthropological Insights*. Toronto: University of Toronto Press.

Smith, L. T. 2015. Kaupapa Māori research: Some Kaupapa Māori principles. In Pihama, L., Tiakiwai, S. J. and Southey, K. (Eds.), *Kaupapa Rangahau: A Reader. A Collection of Readings from the Kaupapa Rangahau Workshops Series*. Te Kotahi Research Institute, pp. 47–53.

Souto, T., Deichmann, J. L., Nunez, C. and Alonso, A. 2014. Classifying conservation stranding of beaked whales (family ziphiidae) exposed to anthropogenic sonar signals. *Systems and the Natural World*, 26.

Sundberg, J. (2014). Decolonizing posthumanist geographies. *Cultural Geographies*, 21(1), 33–47.

Szerszynski, B. 2017. Gods of the anthropocene: geo-spiritual formations in the Earth's new epoch, *Theory, Culture & Society*, 34(2–3), 253–275.

TallBear, K. 2015. Why Interspecies Thinking Needs Indigenous Standpoints. Fieldsights,November18.https://culanth.org/fieldsights/why-interspecies-thinking-needs-Indigenous-standpoints

Taonui, R. (2011) Whakapapa – genealogy - What is whakapapa?' *Te Ara Encyclopedia of New Zealand*. Retrieved from http://www.TeAra.govt.nz/en/whakapapa-genealogy/page-1

Teste, F. P., Simard, S. W., Durall, D. M., Guy, R. D., Jones, M. D. and Schoonmaker, A. L. 2009. Access to mycorrhizal networks and roots of trees: Importance for seedling survival and resource transfer. *Ecology*, 90(10), 2808–2822.

Thaman, K. H. 2003. Decolonizing Pacific studies: Indigenous perspectives, knowledge, and wisdom in higher education. *The Contemporary Pacific*, 15(1), 1–17.

Tipa, G. and Tierney, L. D. 2006. *A Cultural Health Index for Streams and Waterways: A Tool for Nationwide Use*. Wellington, New Zealand: Ministry for the Environment. Retrieved from https://www.mfe.govt.nz/sites/default/files/cultural-health-index-for-streams-and-waterways-tech-report-apr06.pdf

Tipa, K. R. 2014. The science of strandings, Te Rūnanga o Ngāi Tahu, 21 December 2014. Retrieved https://ngaitahu.iwi.nz/our_stories/science-strandings/

Todd, Z. 2015. Indigenizing the Anthropocene. In Davis, H. and Turpin, E. (Eds.), *Art in the Anthropocene: Encounters among Aesthetics, Politics, Environments and Epistemologies.* London: Open Humanities Press, pp. 241–254.

Todd, Z. 2016a. An Indigenous feminist's take on the ontological turn: "Ontology" is just another word for colonialism. *Journal of Historical Sociology,* 29(1), 4–22. https://doi.org/10.1111/johs.12124

Todd, Z. 2016b. "Relationships." Theorizing the Contemporary. Retrieved April 1, 2018, from https://culanth.org/fieldsights/799-relationship

Toomey, D. 2016. Exploring How and Why Trees 'Talk' to Each Other. Yale Environment 360 September 1 2016 Retrieved from https://e360.yale.edu/features/exploring_how_and_why_trees_talk_to_each_other

Tsing, A. L. 2015. The mushroom at the end of the world: On the possibility of life in capitalist ruins. Princeton, NJ: Princeton University Press.

Tsuchiya, T., Naoi, J., Futa, K. and Kikuchi, T. 2004. Difference in simulated low-frequency sound propagation in the various species of baleen whale. *Japanese Journal Of Applied Physics,* 43(50), 3193.

Tyack, P.L. and Miller, E.H. 2002. Vocal anatomy, acoustic communication and echolocation, in Rus Hoelzel, A. (Ed.), *Marine Mammal Biology: An Evolutionary Approach,* Oxford: Blackwell, pp. 142–184.

van Der Heijden, M. G., Martin, F. M., Selosse, M. A. and Sanders, I. R. 2015. Mycorrhizal ecology and evolution: The past, the present, and the future. *New Phytologist,* 205(4), 1406–1423.

van Dooren, T. and Rose, D. B. 2016. Lively ethnography storying animist worlds. *Environmental Humanities,* 8(1), 77–94.

Vitale, S. 2017. Of whales & trees. http://thesoundhealer.org/of-whales-and-trees-sound-ecology/

Walker, S., Eketone, A. and Gibbs, A. 2006. An exploration of kaupapa Māori research, its principles, processes and applications. *International Journal of Social Research Methodology,* 9(4), 331–344.

Watts, V. 2013. "Indigenous place-thought & agency amongst humans and non-humans (First Woman and Sky Woman go on a European world tour!)", Decolonization: Indigeneity, *Education & Society,* 2(1), 20–34.

Warne, K. 2014. Talking with trees. New Zealand Geographic. Issue 128, July–August 2014. Retrieved from https://www.nzgeo.com/stories/talking-with-trees/

Weir, B.S., Paderes, E.P., Anand, N., Uchida, J.Y., Pennycook, S.R., Bellgard, S.E. and Beever, R.E. 2015. A taxonomic revision of Phytophthora Clade 5 including two new species, Phytophthora agathidicida and P. cocois, *Phytotaxa,* 205(1), 21–38.

Whitehead, H. and Rendell, L. 2014. *The Cultural Lives of Whales and Dolphins.* Chicago: University of Chicago Press.

Whitt, L.A., Roberts, M., Norman, W. and Grieves, V. 2001. Belonging to land: Indigenous knowledge systems and the natural world, *Oklahoma City Law Review*, 26, 701–722.

Wright, S. 2015. More-than-human, emergent belongings: A weak theory approach. *Progress in Human Geography*, 39(4), 391–411.

Wright, S., Lloyd, K., Suchet-Pearson, S., Burarrwanga, L., Tofa, M. and Country, B. 2012. Telling stories in, through and with Country: Engaging with Indigenous and more-than-human methodologies at Bawaka, NE Australia. *Journal of Cultural Geography*, 29(1), 39–60.

7
AFTERWORD

> *The Anthropocene is not only a period of manmade [sic] disruption. It is also*
> *a moment of blinking self-awareness, in which the human species is becoming*
> *conscious of itself as a planetary force. We're not only driving global warming*
> *and ecological destruction; we* know *that we are.*
>
> *Alex Blasdel*

What does it mean to know that we are 'a planetary force'? As discussed back in Chapter 1, it might encourage a kind of hubris or triumphalism, though only by proxy; after all, most of 'us' do not feel this ability to disrupt as a force – it is something we are aware of, conscious of, largely in the abstract – an aggregate accumulation of lifestyle. For those more concerned, more accepting of the scientific consensus, it is more like the burden of proof, an awareness that weighs us down with anxiety, grief, guilt or perhaps denial, or a sense of fatalism and powerlessness. Knowing might also engender anger, protest and rebellion, of course, collective responses that demand we face up to that knowledge, individually, culturally and politically, or that some of 'us' take responsibility and acknowledge the inherent injustices of Anthropocene impacts to date.

Whilst these are all viable elements of consciousness of ourselves as a planetary force, this book has elaborated on different, if related, elements of an Anthropocene psychology. Only as the impacts of human activity make their indelible impression upon the Earth are we beginning to realise how implicated, how much of an interrelational part, we are. Anthropocene psychology, for me, is about noticing the many aspects of that human and more-than-human interrelatedness. Across six chapters, pursuing the 'ordinary beings-in-encounter', we have taken in many of the 'human–animal' – and multi-species – worlds identified by Haraway: 'in the house, lab, field, zoo, park, truck, office, prison, ranch, arena, village, human hospital, slaughter house, vet clinic, stadium, barn, wildlife preserve, farm, city streets, factory, and more' (Potts and Haraway, 2010, p. 322). We have considered beings-in-encounter via geologists and deep time; human and canine laboratory workers in late nineteenth- and early twentieth-century St. Petersburg; broiler chickens, slaughterhouse workers and meat consumers in the global growth of industrial agriculture post-WWII; sheep, British wool merchants, colonial pastoralists and contemporary volunteer shepherds on English downland; Sheffield's street trees; open cast mining in New South Wales; Indigenous knowledge in and of Bawaka Country and rights of the Whanganui River, Māori, (beached) whales, mycorrhizal networks and kāuri trees. We have chased just a handful of the many human, multi-species and more-than-human entanglements at the heart of what it means to live in the Anthropocene.

An Anthropocene psychology is a way of approaching the world that readily extends agency to more-than-human others. It is a sensibility that acknowledges a profound interdependency and interconnection between human and more-than-human worlds. It prizes an ability to respond ethically and politically to the implications of that interrelatedness, and to acknowledge, learn from and engage with Indigenous knowledge in which such capacities have a history (and present) of articulation. Following Haraway's practice of 'staying with the trouble' (Haraway, 2008; 2016), it is committed to particularity, to attending deeply to the specific and situated contexts of encounter. When those encounters involve forms of suffering, as they so often do, attentiveness demands that we not simply renounce, moralise or idealise. It is not as simple as proclaiming that we 'go out in the street and start making any and as many kinds of political affiliations with as many kinds of beings, human or otherwise, that you possibly can, with a view to creating a more non-violent and just, for everybody, ecological world' (Morton, cited in Blasdel, 2017). Staying with the trouble entails 'continually questioning our responses and accountabilities and remaining curious about the ethical implications of certain acts... rather than taking them for granted' (Nxumalo and Pacini-Ketchabaw, 2017, p. 1416). Ongoing critical engagement with messy multi-species entanglements is not a recipe for easy remedies. Through these fragments – particular places, cases and voices – I have attempted to comprehend a fraught Earthly assemblage of countless networks of matter which we all, though with many asymmetries, have a hand in initiating, containing, embodying, diverting and disposing of, just as they exceed us.

References

Blasdel, A. 2017. 'A reckoning for our species': The philosopher prophet of the Anthropocene. *The Guardian*, June 15 2017. Accessed 24/08/19 https://www.theguardian.com/world/2017/jun/15/timothy-morton-anthropocene-philosopher

Haraway, D. 2008. *When Species Meet*. Minneapolis: University of Minnesota Press.

Haraway, D. J. 2016. *Staying with the Trouble: Making Kin in the Chthulucene*. Duke University Press.

Nxumalo, F., and Pacini-Ketchabaw, V. 2017. 'Staying with the trouble' in child-insect-educator common worlds. *Environmental Education Research*, 23(10), 1414–1426.

Potts, A. and Haraway, D. 2010. Kiwi chicken advocate talks with Californian dog companion. *Feminism & Psychology*, 20(3), 318–336.

INDEX

Note: Page numbers followed by "*n*" indicate notes.